Men's Health

Life Improvement Guides®

Sex Secrets

Ways to Satisfy
Your Partner
Every Time

by Brian Chichester, Kenton Robinson
and the Editors of Men'sHealth Books

Reviewed by Robert C. Kolodny, M.D., medical director,
Behavioral Medicine Institute, New Canaan, Connecticut,
and former associate director and director of training,
Masters and Johnson Institute, St. Louis, Missouri

Rodale Press, Inc.
Emmaus, Pennsylvania

Copyright © 1996 by Rodale Press, Inc.

Cover photograph copyright © l996 by Robert Whitman
Illustrations copyright © 1996 by Barbara Friedman; Mark Matcho; John A. Nyquist, M.S., CMI

Men's Health and *Men's Health Life Improvement Guides* are registered trademarks of Rodale Press, Inc.

Printed in the United States of America on acid-free ∞ , recycled paper ♻

Other titles in the *Men's Health Life Improvement Guides* series:

Fight Fat	*Stress Blasters*
Food Smart	*Stronger Faster*
Maximum Style	*Symptom Solver*
Powerfully Fit	*Vitamin Vitality*

Library of Congress Cataloging-in-Publication Data

Chichester, Brian.
    Sex secrets : ways to satisfy your partner every time / by Brian Chichester,
Kenton Robinson and the editors of Men's Health Books.
       p.   cm.—(Men's health life improvement guides)
    Includes index.
    ISBN 0–87596–338–2 paperback
    1. Sex instruction for men.   2. Sex.   I. Robinson, Kenton.
II. Men's Health Books.   III. Title.   IV. Series.
HQ36.C45   1996
613.9'6'081—dc20   96–13241

Distributed in the book trade by St. Martin's Press

  4 6 8 10 9 7 5   paperback

--- OUR PURPOSE ---

*"We inspire and enable people to improve
their lives and the world around them."*

Sex Secrets Editorial Staff

Senior Managing Editor: **Neil Wertheimer**

Senior Editors: **Jack Croft, Matthew Hoffman**

Writers: **Brian Chichester, Kenton Robinson, Perry Garfinkel, Stephen C. George, Guy Kettelhack**

Series Designer: **John Herr**

Book Designer: **David Q. Pryor**

Cover Designers: **Charles Beasley, John Herr**

Cover Photographer: **Robert Whitman**

Photo Editor: **Susan Pollack**

Illustrators: **Barbara Friedman, Mark Matcho, John A. Nyquist**

Associate Art Director: **Faith Hague**

Studio Manager: **Joe Golden**

Layout Artist: **Mary Brundage**

Technical Artist: **Thomas P. Aczel**

Researcher and Fact-Checker: **Sally A. Reith**

Copy Editors: **Amy K. Fisher, John D. Reeser, David R. Umla**

Production Manager: **Helen Clogston**

Manufacturing Coordinator: **Melinda B. Rizzo**

Office Staff: **Roberta Mulliner, Julie Kehs, Bernadette Sauerwine, Mary Lou Stephen**

Rodale Health and Fitness Books

Vice-President and Editorial Director: **Debora T. Yost**

Art Director: **Jane Colby Knutila**

Research Manager: **Ann Gossy Yermish**

Copy Manager: **Lisa D. Andruscavage**

Photo Credits

Page 144: **Matt Mendelson © 1994**

Page 146: **Courtesy of Samuel S. Janus**

Page 148: **Rossi Marco**

Page 150: **Katie Gray**

Back flap: **Photofest**

Contents

Introduction   vi

Part One
Becoming a Dream Lover

Sex in the 1990s   2
Sizing Yourself Up   4
Age and Sex   8
Fitness and Sex   10
Food and Sex   12
Stress and Sex   14
Sexual Chemistry   18
Sex on the Brain   22
Love Is in the Air   24
The Science of Attraction   26
Sex Myths   28
The Truth about Quantity   32
Surveying the Sexual Scene   34
Safe Sex   36
The Dream Lover   40

Part Two
The Enlightened Lover

What It Means to Be a Man   44
What Women Want   48
Communication: 54
The Key to Great Sex
Turn-Ons and Turn-Offs   58
Pleasure: 60
Ladies First
Overcoming Inhibitions   62
When to Go to Bed with a Woman   64
Keeping Love Fresh   66
Making Time for Sex   68

Part Three
The Skillful Lover

What Makes a Man   72
A Man's Guide to the   75
Female Genitals
Erogenous Zones   78
Masturbation   82
Foreplay   84
Becoming a Handy Man   86
His and Hers: 88
The Differences in Orgasms
Lasting Longer   90
Multiple Orgasms for Men   96
Positioning Yourself for Great Sex   98
Oral Sex   106

Anal Sex   **108**

After the Loving   **110**

Part Four
The Playful Lover

Make Loving Fun   **114**

Risky Business   **116**

Location   **119**

Welcome to Fantasy Island   **122**

Words of Love   **128**

Sex Toys   **130**

Cybersex   **132**

Sex on the Silver Screen   **136**

Books and Tapes   **140**

Part Five
Real Sex

Quest for the Best

John Gray, Ph.D.,   **144**
Best-Selling Author

Samuel S. Janus, Ph.D.,   **146**
Sex Researcher

Hoyt Richards,   **148**
Male Supermodel

Mitchel Gray,   **150**
Lingerie Photographer

You Can Do It!

An Open Mind—And Heart   **152**
Kent Arnold, Beaverton, Oregon

Affairs of the Heart   **153**
Bob Dunn, Portland, Maine

Online Lover   **154**
Hal Day, Colorado Springs,
Colorado

Sex from the Neck Up   **155**
Wellington Pendell,
Lansing, Michigan

Sex Menus

The Ultimate Quickie   **156**

A Night of Passion   **158**

A Weekend of Great Sex   **160**

Index   **163**

Introduction

The Dream Team

Every guy's an expert on sex. Just ask him—especially when his buddies are around.

The reply is likely to be along the lines of, "Sex? I could write the book." But get that same guy alone, and odds are there are some things he'd really like to know. About what makes women tick. About what turns women off. About how to give—and receive—more sexual pleasure.

That's why we wrote this volume for the *Men's Health* Life Improvement Guides series. Because even though we live in a society saturated by sex, there is a dearth of honest, straightforward, practical information for men who want to become better lovers—in every sense of the word.

Now, like most of you, we always thought we knew everything we needed to know about our real national pastime. But it's one thing to brag about writing the book. It's quite another to actually *do* it.

So we turned to the leading experts in the field to help us figure out what it takes to be a dream lover in today's world.

Here's the starting lineup for our dream team.

• John Gray, Ph.D., author of two of the best-selling books of our time—*Men Are from Mars, Women Are from Venus* and *Mars and Venus in the Bedroom: A Guide to Lasting Romance and Passion.* Through his books and frequent public appearances, Dr. Gray has helped men and women gain a greater understanding of one another.

• Samuel S. Janus, Ph.D., co-author, along with his wife, Cynthia, of *The Janus Report on Sexual Behavior.* A Diplomate of the American Board of Sexology, Dr. Janus's groundbreaking work helped break down misconceptions and stereotypes about sex and foster an atmosphere of greater openness.

• Barbara Keesling, Ph.D., a sex therapist in private practice and author of *How to Make Love All Night (And Drive a Woman Wild).* Dr. Keesling formerly was a sex surrogate for 12 years and is perhaps the leading expert on male multiple orgasms.

• Judy Kuriansky, Ph.D., sex educator and clinical psychologist who hosts the popular *Love-Phones* call-in radio show in New York City. Dr. Kuriansky is the author of *Generation Sex* and *How to Love a Nice Guy.*

• Robert T. Michael, Ph.D., head of the *Sex in America* study, a large-scale, scientific survey of what really goes on behind closed doors. Dr. Michael is dean of the Graduate School of Public Policy Studies at the University of Chicago.

• Bernie Zilbergeld, Ph.D., a sex therapist in Oakland, California, and author of *The New Male Sexuality.* Dr. Zilbergeld is a pioneer in redefining men's roles and sexuality.

• Betty Dodson, Ph.D., a New York City sex educator known as the mother of masturbation for her outspoken advocacy of self-pleasuring. Dr. Dodson is the author of *Sex for One: The Joy of Selfloving.*

• Cathy Winks and Anne Semans, the friendly folks behind Good Vibrations, an adult store in San Francisco, and co-authors of *The Good Vibrations Guide to Sex: How to Have Safe, Fun Sex in the Nineties,* a comprehensive and practical sex manual.

We thank them all—and everyone else who shared their wisdom and insights for this book. And we're confident you—and your partner—will thank them, too.

Neil Wertheimer
Senior Managing Editor, *Men's Health* Books

Part One

Becoming a Dream Lover

Sex in the 1990s

An Era of New Possibilities

Surveying the sexual landscape in America, sex therapist Barbara Keesling, Ph.D., quips: "Are people still having sex these days?"

Well, yes, they are, although there are times when you have to wonder. Lack of time, growing work pressures, changing definitions of manhood, new models of attractiveness—when it comes to sex, all the rules seem to be changing at once. And the stakes—with AIDS and other sexually transmitted diseases (STDs) on the rise—couldn't be higher.

"Sex in the 1990s is as fast-paced as MTV, as complicated as American politics, as unstable as the corporate work environment and as troublesome as any individual problem these days," says sex educator Judy Kuriansky, Ph.D., host of the popular *LovePhones* radio show in New York City and author of *Generation Sex* and *How to Love a Nice Guy.* "Now add to all this the medical problems and the demand for instant gratification, and sex can really end up causing more pain and confusion than ever before."

Are we really talking our favorite, oldest, simplest pastime?

Well, yes. But what is crucial to understand is that within all these changes there are some very big positives. For the open-minded, these are particularly exciting times on the sexual frontier—times of exploration, self-expression and intimacy that once seemed unthinkable to most Americans. If you are willing to go along for the ride, your opportunities for stellar sex have never been greater.

Opening the Doors

Change is rarely comfortable, as many men have discovered in recent years. The whole idea of what it means to be a man has shifted radically, from the workplace to the bedroom. And that has opened new realms of opportunity if men would just embrace the possibilities, experts say.

"Sex roles are being diffused, which, to me, is bliss," exclaims Betty Dodson, Ph.D., a New York City sex educator, therapist and author of *Sex for One: The Joy of Selfloving.* "What this means is that there's not as rigid a notion of what's sexually in a woman's realm and what's in a man's.

Another prominent—and encouraging—change in the sexual topography is in the way we approach sex, adds Dr. Keesling, of Orange, California, who is the author of the best-selling *How to Make Love All Night (And Drive a Woman Wild)* and *Sexual Pleasure.*

"Forty or fifty years ago, men just weren't concerned about pleasing women. Some people didn't even believe women were orgasmic or that they got anything out of sex," Dr. Keesling says. "Now the social pressure is better. Now a woman can choose her sex partners without being considered promiscuous."

Perhaps the most important change in this vein, Dr. Keesling adds, is what happens once our sex partners are chosen and we're quivering in anticipation behind closed bedroom doors.

"These days, everybody's responsible for their own enjoyment. If you're a woman and you're not having orgasms, then you need to—and can—assert yourself," she says. "If you're a man, the pressure has now lifted when it comes to being the ultimate authority in the sexual domain."

Robert T. Michael, Ph.D., dean of the Graduate School of

Public Policy Studies at the University of Chicago and one of the lead researchers of the large-scale *Sex in America* study, says that, after polling 3,432 Americans on their sex lives, he's concluded that "people are most definitely willing to talk to scientists about their sex lives, and that's one indication of a healthy attitude about sex."

Dr. Michael says his study's findings indicate there isn't as much wild sex out there as you'd be led to believe by advertising and other media. But, he adds, "we seem to be doing normal, ordinary things most of the time and, ostensibly, are very happy about it."

Knowing the Risks

The most prominent change on the sexual horizon is the frightening frequency of AIDS cases and other STDs. Despite advancements in medicine and technology and despite bringing the issues to light in countless public forums, we still have a "disquietingly high rate of STDs" for one of the leading industrialized nations in the world, Dr. Michael says.

An estimated 40 million Americans have a sexual disease, with another 12 million added to the rolls each year. In fact, by age 35, every other person you know will have had an STD at one time or another. AIDS, by far, is the worst of the lot. It's claimed more than 300,000 American lives and is the number one killer of people between the ages of 25 and 44. But AIDS isn't the only health concern. In 1990 the number of new syphilis cases in the United States rose to its highest level in 40 years.

Obviously, the prevalence of disease has affected the way we view sex in the 1990s, and it will continue to affect us in years to come.

"People are not having one-night stands as much as they used to," Dr. Kuriansky says. "Because of this, many of today's younger generation are envious of the Baby Boomers. Today's twentysomethings just can't go out and have wild sex like you used to in the 1970s, and

there's some bitterness about this."

Dr. Keesling says cutting down on the number of sexual partners leads to increased intimacy in relationships.

"Back in the 1970s I never would have pictured myself being satisfied with just one person, but by today's standards, that looks better and better," Dr. Keesling says.

"The upshot is that I think there's a social trend to start looking inside a relationship for satisfaction. We realize a little better now that we've been taking our partners for granted," Dr. Keesling adds. "We didn't realize all that a good partnership was capable of. It may have taken the threat of disease to trigger this."

Where Are We Going?

What do all these changes mean, and where will we find ourselves as we head into a new millennium?

Dr. Dodson says changing roles in the workplace will continue to have an impact in other areas of life, including the bedroom. "The idea that the little lady stays at home to manage the house and kids is long gone, but it's placed a lot of stress on women who want to do it all," she says.

"I think in the future we'll see a backlash of some sort," she adds.

Richard A. Carroll, Ph.D., director of the Sex and Marital Therapy Program at Northwestern Medical Center in Chicago, reminds us that one major change in future American sexuality will come from the Baby Boomers and the graying of America.

"We see many people now who expect to perform the way they did in their twenties, and that only makes you feel inadequate when you can't," Dr. Carroll says. "There are a number of changes age brings to sex, but they're perfectly normal. Just because you don't have the same sexual responses you did at age 20 doesn't mean you can't have, and shouldn't have, a normal, happy sex life as you age."

Sizing Yourself Up

Are You Man Enough? Probably

Dr. Nicolas Venette, a royal professor of surgery in seventeenth-century France, wrote a popular sex manual for married couples that addressed the delicate subject of penis size. The optimal erect penis, he wrote, should not exceed six to eight inches in length and three to four inches in circumference.

"That's just the right size which Nature has maintained in forming this organ," Venette opined. "Penises that are too long or too fat are not the best, either for recreation or procreation."

His measurements were just a tad generous by today's standards. But it doesn't matter. The basic message—that most men have nothing to worry about—has been ignored for more than 300 years.

"Concern about penis size is something that's been around forever. It has just never been talked about in the mainstream so much until recently," says urologist Melvyn Rosenstein, M.D., of the Rosenstein Medical Group in Culver City, California, and one of the world's foremost surgeons for thickening and lengthening penises. "I think talk about penis size in 20 or 30 years is going to be as common as talking about the shape of your nose."

Doctors Know Best

Whether the subject of penis size ever becomes commonplace or not, the big concern for men now is whether they're "normal." What is normal? According to experts,

normal penises measure about 2½ to 4 inches long flaccid, and 5 to 7 inches erect.

One study, conducted by Tom Lue, M.D., and his colleagues at the University of California–San Francisco, concluded that 98 percent of all men measure up just fine in the penis department. Dr. Lue's study of 60 men, chosen at random, found that the average flaccid penis measured 3.5 inches long and 3.9 inches in circumference. Erect, the average penis measured 5.1 inches long, 4.9 inches in circumference.

"Even in terms of the guys coming to me for penile augmentation surgery, the overwhelming majority are normal," Dr. Rosenstein says.

Perhaps the main reason men shouldn't worry about penis length is simple female anatomy. Her vagina simply isn't as sensitive in the deeper regions as it is in the first inch or so. Experiments by the late, pioneering sex researcher Dr. Alfred C. Kinsey found that fewer than 14 percent of women could tell when the deep walls of their vagina were probed by cotton-tipped swabs. But 97 percent of the women that Dr. Kinsey tested could easily tell when their vulva and vaginal openings were probed.

So thickness, rather than length, is probably a more important consideration when it comes to sizing yourself up. Indeed, a *Psychology Today* survey of more than 950 women found that women cared more about penis girth than length. Why? A thick penis was "more satisfying during intercourse," they said.

The only time length truly is an issue is in a rare condition called micropenis. As the name implies, this is where a penis is perfectly formed, but extremely small, say about 3½ inches or less erect for a man in his twenties. The condition has been attributed to testosterone deficiency and is usually treated at an early age with hormone supplements.

The Root of the Problem

The big to-do over penis size is almost as old as history itself. In ancient Egyptian mythology, the god Osiris is killed and his body dismembered. When his companion, the goddess Isis, fetches his body, she cannot find his penis, so she makes a huge replica of it and orders all Egyptians to revere it like the original. Ancient Romans, ever the promiscuous pagans, had this proverb, according to the satirist and poet Juvenal: "If you've run out of luck, it doesn't matter how long your penis is."

Although shrouded in legend and lore, the mystique of the penis is probably attributable to the fact that it's so visible compared to female genitalia. "The big problem with penis size is that the penis is on the outside of the body, so it's easily seen and measured," says Marilyn K. Volker, Ph.D., a sex therapist in private practice in Coral Gables, Florida. "Clitorides and vulvas come in different sizes, too, but we don't go around measuring them. Different shapes and sizes are what make the human body beautiful."

Dr. Volker should know. She spent eight years of her early counseling days as a sex surrogate, helping many men overcome anxiety about their size and performance. During those years she discovered what most men are already keenly aware of: "When it comes to emasculating a man, a derogatory comment on penis size is a razor—it's one thing that can bring the strongest man to his knees," she says.

Hang-ups over size usually stem from the past, experts say. Maybe as a boy you looked up at dad in a public restroom one day and marveled at his manly member, only to ponder the puniness of your own. "Or sometimes someone way back made an adverse comment about your size, maybe a relative,

Tale of the Tape

Doctors have a scientific name for the condition that causes men to measure their male members: I-N-S-E-C-U-R-I-T-Y.

Okay, maybe it's not so scientific. But odds are you're overreacting if you feel compelled to set tape to penis. Statistics indicate that 98 percent of men fall within the normal range when it comes to penis size, so the chances are excellent that your machinery meets specs. If you insist on seeing how you measure up, here's how to do it.

1. Measure yourself while fully erect by holding a ruler over your penis, which you might need to straighten out along the ruler.

2. Measure from the tip of your penis head to the pubic skin at the end of the shaft. Don't push the ruler into the skin on the pubic bone; you have a fatty pad there called the mons pubis. Pushing the ruler into it gives you an inaccurate reading.

friend or past partner," Dr. Rosenstein adds. "It probably wasn't malicious, but it may have caused you to focus on your size. Once you do that, it can do a job on your self-esteem."

Measuring Up

Dr. Rosenstein and other experts offer this advice when it comes to penis size: If it ain't broke, don't fix it. In all likelihood, you're perfectly normal, and if you need convincing, consider seeing a sex therapist, urologist or psychologist.

If you're still unsure how you're measuring up, here are some things to keep in mind.

Add by subtracting. Before you consider expensive surgery to add an inch to your penis, consider shedding a few pounds first. Reducing your body fat can make your penis look larger. A loss of 35 pounds of fat translates into an inch gain for your penis.

Don't worry, be Mr. Happy. Don't confuse penis size with the ability to be a great lover. "Just having a large penis does not make you a great lover or more of a man," Dr. Rosenstein says. "Being a great lover involves so many different factors. Penis size isn't necessarily one of them."

Don't dare to compare. Some guys sneak surreptitious glances around the locker room to see how they measure up. Don't. The viewing angle with which you see your own penis makes it appear shorter, note William H. Masters, M.D., Virginia E. Johnson and Robert C. Kolodny, M.D., in *Masters and Johnson on Sex and Human Loving.* The view you get of the other guy is more flattering to him size-wise.

In the same vein, don't compare yourself to adult movie stars, either. These guys are chosen for the length of their equipment, not the depth of their acting ability. Plus camera angles and close-ups make even average penises look larger than life.

Beware penis permutations. Depending on whether you're standing or sitting, aroused or not, your penis will appear longer or shorter throughout the day. Just compare yourself after a warm bath and cold shower.

Living Large

For the squeamish, the best way to increase penis size is anything that doesn't involve a sharp knife. So it may be worth considering trying a penis pump. This is a vacuum device that one-ups what Mother Nature

---

Why Mr. Happy Has a Name

With apologies to the Bard, a hose by any other name would still be a penis. Yet many of us insist on bestowing a moniker on our member.

Robin Williams wisecracks about Mr. Happy in his stand-up routines. And while Johnson is one of the more popular penis pseudonyms, the late Lyndon Johnson dubbed his Jumbo. (Everything's bigger in Texas, you know.)

In September 1995, Brazilian officials discontinued an AIDS awareness commercial that showed a man arguing with his penis, which he called Braulio—a popular penis nickname in Brazil. The ad was pulled because mothers complained their children named Braulio were being mercilessly teased by schoolmates.

Why this penis personification? No one names his fingers or toes or coos lovingly about his spleen.

Martha Cornog is a Philadelphia librarian with a master's degree in linguistics who made genital nicknames

---

already does by gorging your penis with extra blood. Whenever you're aroused, blood rushes to your penis—that's what makes it erect. By slipping a tubular penis pump over your erection and pumping out the air, gravity causes more blood to flow into the erectile tissue, producing a bigger, firmer erection. A penis ring, a small circular ring placed around the base of the penis, holds all this blood in place.

Penis pumps generally work well, but some have drawbacks. First, many magazines sell cheap imitations that can break easily or not generate enough suction power to work well. Second, pumps can be overused, resulting in chronic swelling and damage to your penis's natural hydraulics. Moreover, penis rings can damage your urethra, the tube through which you urinate, or they can become stuck, requiring a decidedly unromantic trip to the her specialty after marrying a sex researcher. In an article in the literary journal *Maledicta*, she says that nicknamed genitalia is an old tradition, as witnessed by the fictional character Mellors in *Lady Chatterly's Lover*, who calls his penis John Thomas.

"The names can serve as a private language between lovers . . . such a language permits discussion of sexual matters in front of unknowing friends and parents," Cornog writes. "The pet name can also serve as a method of facilitating communication about sex."

The question has always interested Dr. Melvyn Rosenstein, a urologist and surgeon in Culver City, California. "I really don't know why some guys do this, but I think they're trying to objectify their penis.

"If they're not happy with their penis, they're trying to dissociate themselves from it," Dr. Rosenstein adds. "If they are happy, they give it a life of its own, so to speak."

emergency room. What to do? Talk to your doctor about penis pumps first. He can tell you how to order yours through a reputable company.

If circumcision and Lorena Bobbitt weren't enough to scare you off knives forever, you might consider penile augmentation surgery. But be forewarned: It gets mixed reviews from the medical world. One type of augmentative surgery thickens the penis, another lengthens it. Since penile augmentation is considered cosmetic, most insurance companies won't cover it unless you're officially underendowed. And at up to $6,000 a pop, augmentation isn't something you undertake lightly. Here are the details.

Penile thickening. Most thickening surgeries are done by removing fat from one part of your body and squeezing it under the skin of the penis shaft. The most common procedure is penile fat injection. In this operation, doctors liposuction fat, usually from your stomach area, process it, then inject it under the penis skin.

Another thickening operation, called dermal fat grafting, takes slabs of fat from another body part, such as the buttocks, and places them under the skin of the shaft.

The problem with thickening operations is that the fat doesn't always take, meaning it either clumps up in unsightly bulges or is reabsorbed by the body, requiring yet more surgery later.

"Ninety percent of plastic surgeons disapprove of fat injections under any circumstances, and 95 percent feel that fat will redeposit over time," says Charles Horton, M.D., director of the Horton Genitourinary Reconstruction Center in Norfolk, Virginia.

Penile lengthening. This procedure has been around for 20 years. Called ligament transection, the operation involves cutting the fan-shaped ligaments that anchor the penis to the pubic bone.

"What we do is cut the ligaments to bring the penis downward to some degree and away from the pubic bone," Dr. Rosenstein says. "Then we bring some skin in front of the pubic bone to cover the newly exposed portion of the body."

The major drawbacks of the surgery are loss of penis control and appearance. Since the roots of the penis are no longer holding it in place, things may get unstable.

Another big drawback is unsightly hair. When doctors graft skin onto the newly exposed shaft, they use pubic skin, which means your new-and-improved penis may sprout pubic hair around the base and look like it's wearing a boa.

Age and Sex

The Heat Goes On

Okay, it's quiz time. Which group had the *least* amount of sex during the past year?

a) men ages 18 to 24
b) men ages 40 to 49
c) men ages 50 to 59

Time's up. If you guessed *b* or *c*, you've been watching entirely too much TV. The answer, according to the University of Chicago researchers who conducted the 1994 *Sex in America* survey, is *a*—the young studs.

Surprised? Don't be. Despite the images Madison Avenue rams down our throats, the truth is that sex isn't just a young man's game. It may not be played as fast or furious as when you were younger, but it's still great fun.

"There are plenty of men and women in their seventies who are very sexual—you don't necessarily burn out after retirement," says the Northwestern Medical Center's Dr. Richard A. Carroll.

Sex educator, author and radio talk-show host Dr. Judy Kuriansky says she has seen society's attitude toward seniors and sex change in recent years: "Fifteen years ago, when I was studying this, people were lax to admit they wanted to be sexual in old age. Society wasn't as permissive as it is today."

Knowing about the sexuality of aging isn't just important for wrinkled, old guys lusting after the Golden Girls. Guys of all ages should take a peek at what the future holds. Why? Because we're living longer.

- Over the last 90 years, we've gained 28 years of average life expectancy.

- Each day, 6,000 Americans turn 60.
- Forty-two million people—one out of every six of us—are 60 or older.
- In colonial times, half the population was under 16. In 1990, half was 33 or older. By 2050, half will be 39 or older.

The Aging Man

As men, we have an unusually heavy burden to bear as we age. Society bombards us with the message that our masculinity and sexual prowess are inextricably bound. If we can't perform, or at least perform as well as we could in our twenties, we're not the men we used to be. The popular perception is that erections fail, desires wane, and age becomes the ultimate emasculation.

There is only one problem: The perception is wrong. "We need to get over that image. Sex does not make the man," Dr. Carroll says.

Of course there are changes in our bodies as we age. Changes we must accept. Changes like:

- It takes more stimulation and more time to get erect.
- Our erections won't always be as strong as they used to be, and often they won't last as long.
- The time between erections, our refractory period, increases, meaning we might become erect once a day rather than once an hour.

What does it all mean? The *Sex in America* survey gives us an idea. True, the number of guys having sex four or more times a week plunges with age. But let's get real: Only about one in ten young guys is ever that lucky to begin with. That means about 90 percent of you have always had a lower frequency rate. Gradually, you go from having sex two or three times a week to a few times a month. So as you age, you don't stop having sex. You just have it slightly less often. The survey found that 43 percent of guys between the ages of 50 and 59 enjoy sex a few times a month, and 20 percent are still active two or three times a week.

"Many of these changes are because the levels of what's called bioavailable testosterone decline as we age," Dr. Carroll explains.

But remember this: How you live today will have a major influence on how much you enjoy sex in your golden years. Too many cheeseburgers will clog blood flow in your arteries, including the ones in your penis, and a lack of exercise can leave you aerobically inadequate.

The Aging Woman

One of the most telltale signs of aging in a woman is her vagina's inability to produce as much lubrication as it used to. This is the counterpart to a man's erection problems, and the resulting dryness can make intercourse painful for her. She—or her partner—might also mistakenly equate dryness as a lack of desire.

A woman's vagina also loses much of its elasticity as she ages, so her orgasms take longer to come, are less intense and don't last as long. But unlike that of a man, a woman's refractory period remains the same, so a 60-year-old woman is capable of having as many orgasms in a row as a 20-year-old woman. Also, a woman's sex drive, unlike a man's, remains relatively stable through her golden years.

Going the Distance

There's no reason any of us should fear sex as we age. Here are tips culled from the experts on how to keep sex sparkling in the golden years.

Use it or lose it. The most important thing you can do to preserve your sex drive as you age is to make the most of it now, says the Northwestern Medical Center's Dr. Richard A. Carroll.

"This is, in part, because having sex and orgasms stimulates testosterone production," he says. "There's a feedback cycle here. If you're sexually active, you'll keep producing testosterone. There's also a psychological factor. If you're happy and are enjoying your sex life, you'll keep at it."

Scrutinize medications. Many people take medications as they age, and sometimes side effects surface in the bedroom. "Some of these changes can be very distressing," says sex educator, author and radio talk-show host Dr. Judy Kuriansky. Ask your doctor about any sexual side effects for every medication you're on.

Invest more in foreplay. Older men and women need more stimulation for a full sexual response. Spend more time caressing each other, hugging and enjoying tender moments. Don't rush.

Try variations. Intercourse isn't the only dish on the sex menu. Many couples find a renewed appreciation for oral sex or mutual masturbation as they age.

"Then there are the physical changes: Many women are concerned about the way their body looks aesthetically, especially if they've had a mastectomy or similar operation," says Dr. Kuriansky. "All these things affect the way people feel about sex as they age."

Fitness and Sex

Get Exercised about Lovemaking

Everyone has at least one personal Sexual Olympics story to tell. A story of gold-medal lovemaking so phenomenal you wouldn't believe it yourself if you weren't there. Maybe you were 17 and you'd ride your bike five miles across town to sneak into your girlfriend's room and make love until dawn. Or maybe you were in college and you'd steal away from the dorm to a motel, where you'd rock the bed so hard you'd knock those cheesy paintings off the wall. Those are memories of a lifetime. But those days are gone—they're only for horny teens and carnal collegians.

Or are they?

After all, you're older now. Wiser. World-lier. Wealthier. What's keeping you and your partner from going for the gold now? Could it be you have no energy from a 9-to-5 job that runs 8-to-7, a house where kids are running amok and a spare tire in need of deflating? If you shed that tire, you might find yourself with energy to spare—enough to make it through the day, keep up with the kids until bedtime and still have the gusto for Olympic sex at night. That's because, of all the natural aphrodisiacs in the world, fitness is one of the most potent around.

Maybe a little more. Consider these facts.

• One study of 78 sedentary men at the University of California, San Diego, found that after a nine-month exercise regimen, the men's sex lives soared. Their frequency of intercourse jumped 30 percent, orgasm 26 percent and masturbation 50 percent.

• Exercise keeps your sperm healthier. That's really good news, considering the average 1990s guy produces little more than half the amount of whip-tail warriors his dad did 50 years ago.

• Exercise improves self-esteem. If you look better, you feel better about yourself. In an opinion poll of 2,500 readers of *Men's Health* magazine we found that 66 percent of the men who said their health was excellent ranked their sex lives as good to excellent. Of those who rated their health as fair, only 22 percent thought their sex lives were something to shout about.

• Exercise seems to enhance free-floating levels of testosterone, the hormone responsible for sex drive in men and women.

"A lot of guys expect to have sex like athletes, but they're not athletes—they're couch potatoes," says sex therapist and author Dr. Barbara Keesling.

"There's nothing wrong with being a couch potato and wanting to enjoy sex, but if you want to last a long time and make love in a strenuous way, you need some level of conditioning," Dr. Keesling says. "Sex, in many ways, is like any other aerobic exercise."

Fit for Sex

The basic benefits of fitness in the bedroom are clear: The fitter you are, the longer you live. The longer you live, the more sex you can have. Class dismissed. Thank you very much. Need we say more?

Get Worked Up

Here's how to supercharge your sex life by starting down that road to fitness.

Arouse with a workout. A study of women at Chicago State University found that nearly one in four had been aroused—some even climaxed—while exercising. How's that for incentive to work out together?

Warm up. If it's been a while since you could see your toes, let alone touch them, then it's not a bad idea to warm up a bit before marathon lovemaking. There's nothing more un-romantic than a pulled hamstring halfway through your best bedtime performance. Try some calisthenics and light stretching. "If you're exercising, you need a warm-up period. You can't just build to a pitch right away," says sex educator, author and radio talk-show host Dr. Judy Kuriansky. "I used to run in high school—you can't just jump into exercise. Athletic sex is the same thing. It's a physical activity."

Run for it. Aerobic conditioning should be high on your list of priorities. It gives you the stamina you need to last all night. Try low-impact aerobics at least three days a week for 20 to 30 minutes. Good choices include running, swimming, stair climbing and rowing.

Have trouble getting through that two-mile run? Don't think about it. Researchers at the University of Alabama found that runners whose minds wandered felt more invigorated than those who concentrated on the running itself.

Don't crimp your style. During orgasm, guys tend to overflex their calf muscles, resulting in painful cramps. Maybe they're pushing off with their toes as they thrust, or perhaps they're curling their toes under too tightly in the midst of passion. Here's how to avoid such a crimp on your evening. It's called the runner's stretch: Stand about four steps from a wall, facing it with one leg forward about eight inches and bent at

Too Much of a Good Thing

Exercise can be the cheapest, most effective libido pick-me-up this side of an all-you-can-eat oyster bar. But as with most things in life, there's always the risk of having too much of a good thing.

Overdoing exercise kills your sex drive. For starters, knocking yourself out for hours on end in the gym might mean you'll be so sore and stiff the next day you won't be able to move, let alone groove. But there's a more compelling, chemical reason to avoid excessive exercise: Too much exercise drives down your testosterone levels and, thus, your sex drive.

How much is too much? It's safe to assume that unless you're an ultramarathoner, you're probably okay. One researcher estimated that you'd have to run somewhere around 200 miles a week to seriously impair testosterone production. Nevertheless, keep your training down to the equivalent of running 30 miles a week or less, just to stay on the safe side.

And don't neglect the psychological traps some people fall into by working out too much.

"How you feel about your own body is certainly important, and you do want your body to function properly," says Ted McIlvenna, Ph.D., president of the Institute for Advanced Study of Human Sexuality in San Francisco. "But don't kid yourself into thinking that you'll automatically be getting it more often and be a superstud."

the knee. Your back leg should be straight. Now reach out and touch the wall at chest level and lean into it, keeping your heels on the floor. You should feel the stretch from your heel to the knee of your straight leg. Hold for 20 seconds, switch legs and repeat.

Food and Sex

Erotic Recipes for Sex-cess

The 1992 film *Like Water for Chocolate* is a delicious blend of romance, folk magic and desire that highlights a sex secret lovers have known for years: the eroticizing power of food. In one scene the main character, the youngest daughter of a Mexican family, bakes a wedding cake that mysteriously makes all who eat it long for their lost loves. In another scene the bewitched baker cooks a steamy quail in rose petal sauce that literally turns the dinner table into an unbridled passion pit.

In ancient times the food-mood connection enjoyed a colorful, albeit simplistic, history of sensuality, says George Armelagos, Ph.D., professor of anthropology at Emory University in Atlanta. This connection boiled down to what was called the Doctrine of Signatures, where people felt that the shape of things indicated their inherent preternatural powers. For example, the phallic form and size of a rhinoceros horn obviously meant it possessed the power of potency.

"Overall, though, the relationship between food and sex was that if you were well-fed and healthy, you were more likely to think about sex," Dr. Armelagos says. "Even today, that's why nutrition and sex go together."

Food and Mood

Food continues to play a crucial role in love and lovemaking—and we're not only talking about the creative ways to use whipped cream.

Although we don't care much about the shape of our

food these days, the link between the bedroom and the kitchen remains strong. Something as simple as making dinner, washing the dishes or using the right fork at her annual office party can be all the impetus your mate needs to make her simmer in bed. Ditto for more overtly sensual things, like playfully feeding her grapes or hors d'oeuvres.

"Everything's a prelude to a sexual encounter—we need not define sex as the minute we take our clothes off and are in bed," says Doreen Virtue, Ph.D., a relationship expert and psychologist in Anaheim, California, and author of *In the Mood.* "Even what we do at the dinner table helps warm us up toward each other."

Finally, there's the chemical connection. The chemicals in food affect our moods and the way our bodies work, too. Researchers even think they've cracked that age-old sex/chocolate connection. It seems there's plenty of phenylalanine in chocolate, a type of amino acid that increases the body's level of endorphins, our natural painkillers and antidepressants.

Food for Two

Here's how to use the erotic power of food to supplement your romantic interludes. We don't promise it will have the same effect the quail and rose petal sauce did in *Like Water for Chocolate*, but it will point you, your stomach and your libido in the right direction.

Think erotically. Any meal can be erotic. It's all attitude. Sometimes, just taking the initiative to prepare dinner or help in the kitchen is all that's needed to arouse your partner.

"The mind—and your imagination—is the greatest aphrodisiac around," says John Renner, M.D., president of the Consumer Health Information Research Institute in Independence, Montana.

The Revlon company surveyed more than 1,000 American adults on all things sensual. They found the following to be the most sensual foods around; add them to your menu of arousing vittles.

- Champagne or wine (34 percent)
- Strawberries (29 percent)
- Chocolate (23 percent)
- Whipped cream (19 percent)

Surprisingly, the least sensual foods were liquor, caviar and beer.

Add these to your list. As we mentioned before, chocolate is rich in phenylalanine, a chemical found in food that researchers suspect causes a libido-lifting natural high. Here are other foods that make that list, too: Almonds, apples, avocados, baked beans, beef, beets, carrots, chicken, cottage cheese, eggs, herring, milk, parsley, peanuts, pineapples, soybeans, spinach and tomatoes.

Make all foods erotic. "Some people find the art of eating oysters erotic or sensuous, but eating almost any food with the right frame of mind can be just as erotic," says sex therapist Dr. Marilyn K. Volker. "Try having your partner eat a hot dog or banana and then show her what you can do with your tongue and some ice cream.

"You'll be surprised at the results," Dr. Volker says, "because you're adding this sensual, visual element to eating."

Keep up with the Joneses. Remember that sumptuous and sensuous feast in the movie *Tom Jones*? (If not, run down to your local video store and check it out. We'll wait.) Here's how to create your own, using some tips offered by sex therapist and author Dr. Barbara Keesling.

Prepare a dinner for two, adhering to the following rules.

Cheers to Your Sexual Health

A keen porter in Shakespeare's *Macbeth* has the definitive last word on alcohol and sex when he says that drinking "provokes the desire, but it takes away from the performance."

"Alcohol, which is a drug, can turn up the hypothalamus, the brain's sex center, and that's why many people find they're uninhibited and aroused when they're drinking," says sex therapist Dr. Marilyn K. Volker. "But alcohol is also a depressant, and too much will have a real depressing effect on your sex drive and performance."

More than, say, two drinks in an hour is enough to send your libido packing. In one study researchers found that men who had a blood alcohol level of .06 took significantly longer to ejaculate. Many men whose level was .09—nearly the level of impairment in many states—were unable to ejaculate at all. (For comparison's sake, to raise the blood alcohol level to .05, a 150-pound man would have to drink roughly three mixed drinks in one to two hours.)

- No feeding yourself, no utensils and no talking. Enjoy the strictly sensual facet of feeding time.
- Serve only finger foods. Good choices are sliced fruit, cheese and crackers and meat that can be pulled from the bone.
- Dine naked on the floor. Cover the carpet with a sheet, if need be.
- Feed and be fed. Feed each other creatively. Eat off each others' bodies. Use your tongues instead of napkins.

Finish by toweling each other off with warm bath towels—or, better yet, take a warm bath together.

Stress and Sex

Keep the Big Picture in Mind

The nighttime is the right time for sex. The sun heads for the hills. The moon works the night shift and things grow quiet, calm and still. You're in bed—how convenient—and only inches from your loved one. The kids are sleeping, the TV's off and the hurly-burliness of the day is finally on hold.

Unfortunately, the nighttime's also prime time to grumble about the boss, fret about next month's mortgage payment and ponder life's mysteries, like why yogurt has an expiration date if it's already spoiled milk.

As a result, many of us squander potentially precious moments between the sheets. By the time the Sandman throws a handful our way, we've already dwelt on the day's mishaps, brooded about the future, tossed, turned and tumbled our way to sleep instead of opting for life's most potent sleeping pill: satisfying sex.

Killing the Mood

The reason we toss and turn and clutter our evenings with worry is not because we're deep thinkers or masochists who like sleep deprivation. Many of us can't help thinking about these things. It's stress, and—short of your kids strolling in while you're in the heat of passion—it's the fastest way to kill the mood.

"Stress more and more is becoming one of our biggest barriers to sexual desire today," says Northwestern Medical Center's Dr. Richard A. Carroll. "People who are preoccupied with finances or with what's happening at work make it

almost impossible for themselves to relax and enjoy sex."

According to a sensuality survey of more than 1,000 American adults by the Revlon company, 45 percent of those responding said stress was the biggest wet blanket under the blankets. Women, more often than men, were more likely to say so.

But, of course, stress doesn't all happen at night. In today's era of longer work hours, two-income families and an increasingly technical line of electronic leashes—beepers, e-mail and cellular phones—we're up to our ears in stress from the moment the alarm clock buzzes. Unremedied, it's a stake through the heart of even the best sex life.

"Nowadays, there's such a strong correlation between stress and sex," says sex therapist Dr. Marilyn K. Volker. "People are so stressed that it affects their desire, their function, their orgasms. It truly can be devastating."

Sources of Stress

Stress can strike from external or internal sources, Dr. Carroll and Dr. Volker say. Outside sources could include deadlines at work, the mortgage or the kid's college tuition.

"Internal sexual stress is the stress you put on yourself," Dr. Carroll says. "It can be performance anxiety—the way you feel about how well you're doing in bed. Or it could be trying to live up to the belief that you have to be a certain sexual ideal to please your mate."

Sex therapist and author Dr. Barbara Keesling says this kind of self-inflicted stress is especially debilitating to men, because we're expected to be the Big Kahuna in the bedroom. When we fail to live up to that ideal—say we can't get or keep an erection—we feel tremendous stress, making matters worse.

"There's such an emphasis on men to be in a performance-oriented mode of sex," Dr. Keesling notes. "Men seem so much more intent on watching the clock to see how long they're lasting—or not lasting—than they are about enjoying the experience."

Finally, any type of stress—external or internal—can be aggravated by psychological and even genetic components, either of which could compound problems in the bedroom.

For example, guys who suffer from low self-esteem might be more prone to stress in bed. And roughly 25 percent of all men seem "genetically predisposed" to abnormally high stress responses, meaning they were dealt a lower stress threshold than everyone else.

"Overall, stress is probably something that, at one time or another, affects all of us. Regardless of its source, it demands attention because it can be so deleterious to our sexual health," Dr. Carroll says.

Fight or Flight

Stress affects our lives in many ways. It's been linked to nearly every modern malady: Acne. High blood pressure. Jaw troubles. Sperm problems. Even the common cold. You name it, stress has probably been fingered as a contributing factor somewhere along the line. Moreover, it's so pervasive that up to 90 percent of all visits to primary-care physicians stem from stress-related complaints.

Physiologically, damage from stress comes from the fact that it sends our bodies into the fight-or-flight mode: our muscles tense, our heart rates and breathing rates rocket and our blood vessels constrict, reducing circulation to our extremities. Biologically, this prepares us to fight someone or beat a hasty retreat. While good from an evolutionary standpoint in terms of self-survival, it's hardly conducive to love-making.

Hormonally, we're headed for even more trouble. Stress touches off a cascade of changes in our bodies, the most important of which is what it does to testosterone.

"Chronic stress can decrease testosterone levels, and testosterone is the hormone responsible for sex drive in men and women," Dr. Carroll says.

In studies on military recruits stressed by a variety of activities, like parachuting or enduring boot camp, scientists found that the young soldiers' sex drives plummeted because their testosterone levels dropped. Again, biologically this makes sense: When you're facing imminent danger, the last thing you need are thoughts about sex rolling around your head. But it's of no use when you bring these feelings to an amorous outing.

De-stressing Your Life

With all our schooling in life—our certificates, diplomas and all the lessons we learned in the School of Hard Knocks—few of us are ever formally taught to handle stress. In fact, experts say men tend to have the worst coping skills around. When you throw in the self-imposed sexual performance anxiety, it paints an even grimmer picture.

Nonetheless, there's hope. With the right training—by learning effective coping techniques—you can drastically diminish the stress in your life. That means more energy at night—and during the day—and more opportunity to get the most out of your sex life. It sure beats worrying about the mortgage or yogurt.

Here's how to get started.

Keep your perspective. When an important deadline's bearing down on you at work, it's easy to focus your entire life around it. But—in the cosmic scheme of things—is it really *that* important? On your deathbed will you be thinking, "Gee, I wish I had spent more time at the office," or "Gee, I wish I worked harder on that project"?

Of course not, experts say. Realize that stress seems worse than it really is. Remember how nervous you were before the first time you ever gave a speech? You thought you'd die—but you didn't, even if it went over poorly. Cast stress in the big picture to see that it's often not as bad as it seems.

Relax. Another way to control stress so it doesn't control your sex life is to identify exactly what activities relax you. Essentially, there are two types of such activities, Dr. Volker says: those that speed you up and those that slow you down.

"These are the two extremes to relieving stress," she says. "Some people like to keep moving, say, by running or exercising. Others like to really slow down with a hot bath or by meditating."

Identify the activities that bring you such pleasure, whether it is reading Clive Cussler novels or training for a marathon. You'll know what your relaxing niche is when you "lose yourself" in it. When you're so absorbed in doing it, you'll forget to worry about whatever it was that seemed so damn important.

Surrender. "I've had many clients who, during the day, have had to stomp around like big, tough men—state troopers, business executives, New York City cops—and this can be very stressful. So one of the ways high-powered men can take the pressure off themselves is by fantasizing about being in passive roles," says Patrick Suraci, Ph.D., a psychologist in New York City and author of *Male Sexual Armor.* This might mean that you like her to be on top or you like to be bound up and at her mercy or you fantasize about being her servant or slave.

Exercise. Even if it's not something you look forward to, there are compelling physiological reasons to exercise. Besides keeping your heart healthy and burning fat, exercise flushes stress hormones from your body. It also releases endorphins, chemicals that make you naturally feel good.

So exercise, preferably three or four sessions of at least 30 minutes a week, can be your

Not Tonight, Dear

Feigning a headache to avoid sex is almost a laughable cliché, but an honest-to-goodness throbbing head in the height of passion dampens a sexual appetite faster than you can say migraine. Not only does it hurt, you're left wondering if you worked yourself up so much you blew a gasket.

Relax. Ninety percent of Americans suffer headaches each year, sometimes during sex. The phenomenon of sex headaches dates back to ancient Greece. The most common sufferer is a middle-age man who is slightly overweight and has high blood pressure. Happily, less than 10 percent of all sex headaches are serious. Often they're harmless, attributable to stress or some other cause. And they can be treated medically.

According to John R. Ostergaard, M.D., Ph.D., a researcher at the University Hospital of Arhus in Denmark, sex headaches typically come in three varieties: a dull throb that begins early in sex; an explosive, painful headache at or near climax; and an explosive, painful

most reliable stress reliever, whether it's brisk walking, weight lifting or cycling around the block a few times.

Forget sex. That's right, one of the best ways to keep stress out of the bedroom is to forget sex for a while. After all, it's okay if you don't feel up to it now and then—it doesn't mean you're any less of a man. Rather, Dr. Keesling says, it's proof that you're human. Instead of intercourse, concentrate on building intimacy. Give each other an invigorating massage, or simply lounge in each others' arms. Sometimes this is enough to relax you into feeling frisky.

Focus with sensate exercises. Dr. Keesling says "sensate focus" exercises are an excellent way to relax and build intimacy. They headache that starts after sex as soon as you stand up.

The first type, Dr. Ostergaard says, is usually a tension headache from spasms in your facial muscles and back muscles. The second, which accounts for 70 percent of all cases, has been theorized to stem from soaring blood pressure, which comes about during arousal and orgasm. The last headache could come from some type of tear in the membrane of your spinal column, perhaps from overly vigorous sex, and is exacerbated by certain sexual positions.

If your sex headaches are infrequent, they're probably nothing to worry about. Some doctors have successfully treated them with the drug propranolol. Exercise is another good suggestion, since vigorous exercise has proven to reduce headaches and increase endorphins, our body's natural painkillers.

Don't be shy, however, about telling your doctor if you suffer from regular, intensely painful headaches during sex. There could be something wrong, and your chances for recovery are excellent.

bored with your caressing, slow down. Chances are, you aren't letting yourself really be in the moment."

Take matters in hand. Dr. Betty Dodson, a New York City sex educator, therapist and author, says masturbation is an excellent hands-on way to relax. The key, she says, is to break lifelong habits of rushing through masturbation and feeling guilty about it.

"Masturbation is a fun thing to do, it's a healthy thing to do, it's a sexual thing to do," Dr. Dodson says. "And if you're stressed, it can be the most enjoyable way to relax and connect with your body."

Dr. Volker suggests treating yourself to quickie masturbation if you're really stressed and don't have the time to make your self-gratification session a long, leisurely one.

Suppose you're working at home and are on a tight deadline, she says. Escape for 15 minutes to relieve sexual tension. "For many people, releasing stress like this can indeed be re-energizing, even if it's an intense, quick session. Orgasm can be a great release," she says.

Beware of sex-stress traps. True, orgasm is a great release and re-energizer. Sex is even better. But don't find yourself having sex just to relieve stress, Dr. Volker cautions. This depersonalizes the intimacy of lovemaking and reduces its ability to leave you and your partner feeling deeply fulfilled.

"Sex is a shared experience. You should be focusing on yourself sometimes but also on the other person. If it's just a way to relieve stress, it's no longer a shared experience," she says.

"But if you strike an agreement with your partner, you could make some sex sessions strictly for release," she adds. "I call it 'This one's for you, kid.' And if you're both in agreement, it's a convenient way to relax each other."

ground you in the present moment, so you can really appreciate touching and feeling. Here's how to do a sensate focus exercise.

Ask your partner to lie down and relax. Then, ever so slowly, begin to caress her genitals. Not fondle. Caress. Your goal is to explore them as if it were the first time. Enjoy the touching yourself—you're not doing it to arouse her. You're not doing it to bring about orgasm or wind her up to have sex. You're touching slowly and gently simply for touching's sake.

"This is a wonderful technique for learning to relax and connect to your feelings," Dr. Keesling says in her book *How to Make Love All Night (And Drive a Woman Wild)*. "If you find yourself getting mechanical or getting

Sexual Chemistry

Testosterone's the Key, but Other Hormones Unlock Passion

The human body is Mother Nature's version of a deluxe Mr. Wizard chemistry set. From the calcium in our bones to the iron in our blood, the average person's body has enough raw materials to make a three-inch iron nail, 900 carbon pencils and seven bars of pure fat soap. It also has enough sulfur to kill all the fleas on your family dog and enough water to fill a ten-gallon fish tank.

But when it comes to sex, the chemicals our bodies use are somewhat more specialized. Aside from the obvious—extra oxygen for deeper breathing, for example—sex chemicals are by and large unique hormones, some of which literally make you the man you are. And of all the sex-related substances coursing through your veins, the one that carries the most import, for men and for women, is testosterone.

"The human sex drive, from a hormonal point of view, is neither male nor female but rather an undifferentiated urge created by a single hormone, testosterone," writes Sherman J. Silber, M.D., in his book *The Male.*

And while it's true that a man's body has about ten times more testosterone than a woman's, testosterone and some other chemicals are the crucial players behind the hormonal curtain in, and even out of, the bedroom.

"Good sex has far more to do with available testosterone levels than you may think," says Dr. Ted McIlvenna of the Institute for Advanced Study of Human Sexuality.

Priming the Puberty Pump

Most guys equate testosterone with puberty, but this virile substance makes its debut much, much earlier in life. Like shortly after conception. As a fetus is developing, testosterone provides the protean blueprint for the clump of dividing cells that's soon to be a person. Whether you're male or female is determined by your chromosomes at conception. Males develop testes, which provide the surge of testosterone that helps form male physical attributes.

After birth, and throughout life, these tiny amounts of testosterone set the tone for some of our decidedly male attributes: more muscle mass, larger body frames, more aggressiveness and competitiveness and—in the case of animals—brighter plumage, larger antlers, flowing manes and nicer tail feathers.

The next time testosterone rears its head in such a dramatic way is in puberty, that magical time of life that turns young boys into young men, seemingly overnight. As one boy told Dr. William H. Masters, Virginia E. Johnson and Dr. Robert C. Kolodny, of the former Masters and Johnson Institute in St. Louis, in their seminal work, *Masters and Johnson on Sex and Human Loving*, it's as if "one morning you wake up with pimples."

Puberty may seem to happen overnight, but it actually begins much earlier. The process starts slowly around the age of eight or ten, when the biologically pre-programmed hypothalamus and pituitary glands begin releasing chemicals to enlarge the gonads. Shortly thereafter, the production of testosterone and a flood of other hormones kick into high gear. So much so that adolescent boys have as much as 20 times more testosterone than girls. In boys this testosterone comes from the testicles; in girls the adrenal gland.

"Testosterone is the driving force behind all the changes that are going on during that awkward time of life," says the Northwestern Medical Center's Dr. Richard A. Carroll.

The momentum of puberty's testosterone spurt doesn't end after adolescence, Dr. Carroll says. Even today as an adult, a large degree of what makes you a man depends on how much testosterone is running through your body. The average man has about 500 nanograms of testosterone per deciliter of blood, though a range of 300 to 1,100 nanograms is considered healthy. The impact of all this testosterone is so pronounced that a good hormone doctor can tell a lot about your hormone levels just by looking at your body hair, particularly your pubic hair distribution.

Fuel for Our Sex Drive

Body hair aside, the most sterling example of the lifelong importance of testosterone is its effect on sex drive. Yours and hers. Testosterone, more than anything else, creates the urge to merge in both sexes. In the Wild Kingdom this urge can surge, which is why many animals go into "heat." These hormonal tidal waves are most prominent in cold-climate animals, such as deer and moose, for example, who produce less testosterone in the winter months than in the warm spring. (Which precisely explains, among other things, why you'd never want to meet an 800-pound, love-starved moose in a lonely stretch of woods.)

In humans, however, testosterone levels and sex drive remain fairly constant year-round, though our individual levels vary somewhat throughout the day and our total levels vary from man to man, woman to woman. The important thing about testosterone in determining our sex drive isn't necessarily the total amount our testicles are churning out but how much is available for our bodies to use— what scientists call bioavailable testosterone.

"It's this stuff—bioavailable testos-

terone—that has to do with our sex lives, in many ways more than what we look like or how we feel about our bodies," Dr. McIlvenna says. "Bioavailable testosterone is what turns us on. We don't have a lot to say about that."

The Good, the Bad and the Ugly

It's become somewhat fashionable to make testosterone a scapegoat for all the evils men do. Magazine articles and even books have been written blaming society's ills—war, rape, violence—on too much testosterone. While it's true that some studies have found that men guilty of violent crimes, on average, have higher testosterone levels than other men, it's nothing short of a scapegoat to lay all the world's short-comings on the shoulders of this vital hormone, Dr. Carroll says.

"Testosterone is responsible for a lot of good things, too," he says. To wit: Studies in which men with low testosterone levels were given extra doses show that they dropped their guts and increased their total lean muscle. Another study found that men with higher levels of testosterone had lower levels of heart blockage, theoretically because testosterone may boost the body's level of good cholesterol. Other studies show that testosterone helps increase bone density and preserve bone tissue, a prime consideration for men facing osteoporosis.

Perhaps the two ugliest faces of testosterone are what it does when you get too much or far too little. The most notorious examples of too much testosterone are seen in athletes who take anabolic steroids. Anabolic steroids, a form of weakly androgenic hormones—sort of a distant cousin to testosterone—are taken to increase muscle strength and size. Side effects include uncontrollable bouts of aggression known as 'roid rages. Steroids also trigger the body to shut down its own natural production of testosterone. The result? A hampered—or nonexistent—sex drive and shrunken testicles.

The other extreme, too little testosterone, is far more common. Bioavailable testosterone naturally declines as we age, Dr. Carroll says, especially if we avoid testosterone-producing activities such as having regular sex and exercise. But an estimated four million to five million men—as many as 20 percent over age 50—get a condition called hypogonadism, which means they have abnormally low levels of testosterone (that is, below the 300 nanograms threshold).

Men diagnosed with hypogonadism are treated with testosterone supplement therapy to make up for what's lacking. Supplements commonly take the form of an injection or a skin patch attached to the scrotum. A new patch approved by the Food and Drug Administration in the fall of 1995 was found to be more than 90 percent effective in normalizing testosterone levels in hypogonadal men ages 15 to 65. Unlike many of the first patches, which had to be adhered to the scrotum, the new patches can be worn on the stomach, back, thigh or upper arm. Their biggest drawback is that they sometimes irritate the skin. Future testosterone supplements may also include tablets or testosterone-laced pellets inserted under the skin.

Despite all the good things testosterone can do for you sexually, there's little chance you'll be taking these hormones regularly, unless you have a bona fide deficiency. Unlike women, who can take estrogen after the onset of menopause, men aren't prescribed testosterone to make up for the natural deficiency that occurs with aging. One intriguing possible future use, however, is for birth control. Researchers at the University of California in Los Angeles found that men who

Sex, Drugs and . . . What You Need to Know

Many guys have sexual skeletons in the closet that involve experiments with sex, drugs and rock 'n' roll. While there's nothing wrong with a backdrop of Jethro Tull or Rolling Stones in the bedroom, drugs and sex make poor bedfellows and, like drinking and driving, shouldn't be mixed.

"Many illicit drugs, even when used recreationally, have serious negative side effects on sex," says Dr. Ted McIlvenna of the Institute for Advanced Study of Human Sexuality. Here's a rundown of some commonly used drugs—including cigarettes—and how they can drive a wedge between you and super sex.

- **Nicotine.** Yet another reason to quit smoking, or even more reason not to start. Several studies show that cigarette smoking is more prevalent among impotent men. Other studies have shown that animals exposed to nicotine were unable to get or keep erections. Why? Nicotine constricts blood vessels. Smoking reduces the size of the arterial blood vessels, which means there's less blood on hand to fill an erection.

- **Marijuana.** Although many people report feeling more relaxed when they smoke pot—and, indeed, this relaxation might make for better sex initially—long-term smoking packs a powerful punch, and it's your virility that takes it on the chin. For starters, pot smoke contains some of the same tars as tobacco smoke, as well as the cancer-causing benzopyrene. It can also interfere with fertility in both

took a weekly 200 milligram dose of testosterone enanthate for 18 weeks had a protection rate better than condoms.

The Supporting Chemical Cast

Testosterone may play the starring role in sex, but like any great actor, it needs a strong men and women and can lower your testosterone and sperm count. While the euphoric effect of pot may increase ejaculatory control for some men, particularly younger men who have a problem with it, one New York City pharmacist found that 10 percent of young men who had smoked pot at least four days a week for six months were completely impotent.

- Cocaine. At first, cocaine seems like a real aphrodisiac: It gives you a surge of excitement, a tidal wave of euphoria and a rush of sexual energy. Even Sigmund Freud, an early user, considered it a lovemaking enhancer. But cocaine's boost to your libido is illusory, and it can ultimately leave you void of all sexual desire. The rush you get from cocaine comes from its ability to make the brain dump large amounts of dopamine into the system. Dopamine is a natural hormone that produces feelings of euphoria and well-being. But the body can't make enough dopamine to keep that rush going, and when it peters out, all those good feelings plummet. Moreover, the initial rush of cocaine sends your heart and blood pressure soaring—add to this the excitment of sex, which also sends your system racing, and you have a potentially deadly combination.

- Amphetamines. Also called speed, amphetamines speed up your body's functions—but kill your libido. Dudley Seth Danoff, M.D., in his book *Superpotency* says that speed's long-term effect "is devastating . . . Unquestionably, these recreational drugs produce the antithesis of penis power."

supporting cast to truly shine. Stay with us as we roll the credits.

- Phenylethylamine (PEA) is a small molecule that's one of the body's natural feel-good drugs. Perched on the ends of nerve receptors in the brain, PEA molecules are largely responsible for feelings of elation, exhilaration and euphoria—all of which are no stranger to us in sex. Ditto for dopamine and norepinephrine, other amphetamine-like chemicals that put our big heads in happy moods while our little heads are off enjoying themselves elsewhere.

- Oxytocin is a small peptide molecule secreted by the pituitary gland and by certain neurons in the brain. Scientists think oxytocin is the chemical "glue" that keeps couples together. Researchers have long known that oxytocin was responsible for milk production in nursing mothers, but they've only recently learned that it's also coursing through the veins of lovers during sex, and it seems to have a direct impact on sexual function. Especially in creating those warm, fuzzy feelings of "afterglow" after sex.

Helen Singer Kaplan, M.D., Ph.D., wrote in her book *The Sexual Desire Disorders*: "It does not take a great leap of imagination to speculate that . . . oxytocin, the same basic hormonal-behavior mechanism that produces maternal/infant bonding, is also involved in the pair-bonding of sexual partners." What that means is, if oxytocin is so vital in establishing mother/child bonds, it might be just as vital in bonding the love of a man and woman. Moreover, Dr. Kaplan added, investigators found that female animals are likely to choose mates based on oxytocin levels.

- Vasopressin is another peptide that works hand in glove with oxytocin. It's been dubbed the monogamy hormone because it's seemingly responsible for monogamy in animals that mate for life, like the prairie vole and—despite the way it sometimes seems—humans.

Coincidentally, animal studies indicate that vasopressin may also be responsible for a father's paternal feelings.

Sex on the Brain

Doing What Comes Naturally

While you've been busy looking for her G-spot, you probably would have spent your time more productively looking for her P spots—small molecules known as phenylethylamine, or PEA.

The PEA molecule, which perches on the ends of nerve cells in the brain, is a natural amphetamine. Along with other naturally occurring chemicals in the body, it's responsible for revving feelings of elation, exhilaration and euphoria. Whatever attraction you happen to be experiencing—call it infatuation, sexual attraction or love—can ultimately be explained by chemistry.

There is some comfort in knowing that the chemistry of attraction—that click, that tingle, that buzz you feel around certain people—has been scientifically analyzed, codified and corroborated. It takes the pressure off. Yeah, your cologne, lean physique and Gucci shoes may get the process started. But ultimately it's an avalanche of chemicals—not just PEA, but also such things as dopamine and norepinephrine—that fuel the fire of love.

Basically, neuroscientists are telling us that we're creatures of habit, albeit a 70-million-year-old habit. They have identified a small nodule deep in the brain of birds and mammals that has evolved very little in all those years. Sometimes called the hub of emotions, this tiny gland (the hypothalamus) plays a major role in directing sexual behavior.

In other words, research is substantiating what *some*

women have been saying about *some* men for *some* time: We're all just a half-step down the evolutionary road from *Australopithecus afarensis*, early men whose entire strategy for impressing women was more or less limited to standing upright. When it comes to love, sex, attraction, emotional involvement and relationships—whether long-term or one-night stands—we're doing, quite literally, what comes naturally.

"Our primal motivations remain survival and procreation," says anthropologist Helen Fisher, Ph.D., research associate at Rutgers University in New Brunswick, New Jersey, and author of *Anatomy of Love*. "Our cravings come from our evolutionary past."

It's All in Your Head

That three-pound mass of gray matter the size of a grapefruit sitting in your cranium is the horniest organ in your body. You may think your erogenous zone begins farther south, but without input from the brain box, your sex life would be about as exciting as solitaire.

Ultimately, most of our emotional and sexual desires—both at ebb and flow—can be traced to hormonal changes in the brain. It's natural, for example, for that first flush of infatuation to fade over time. In part this occurs because PEA levels gradually decline or because nerve endings simply become less responsive.

In other words, in the interval between that first opening line and your silver anniversary, the brain gradually builds up resistance to your natural love drugs.

Conversely, there are chemicals that help keep us together. Feelings of love and commitment may be attributed to brain chemicals called endorphins (short for "endogenous morphines"). Endorphins calm the mind, relieve pain and reduce anxiety, enabling us to "experience a sense of safety, stability and tranquillity," says Dr. Fisher. In other words, we really do get addicted to love.

It's hardly news that having an orgasm can create powerful feelings of attachment. Chemistry is behind this, too. A chemical called oxytocin, which is secreted by the pituitary gland in the brain, is three to five times more abundant during an orgasm than at other times. Oxytocin may play a role in stimulating the sex drive and feelings of pleasure and satisfaction during body contact, sexual arousal and fulfillment. These emotions, in turn, can produce chemical changes that increase feelings of attachment.

Not surprisingly, the more orgasms you have, the more you want to have. "The more you have intercourse, the more frequent and more powerful your orgasms will become," explains neurosurgeon Richard Bergland, M.D., author of *The Fabric of Mind.*

It's not only spousal attachments that have a molecular basis. The guilt you'll feel about having an affair is centered in the brain as well. Dr. Fisher points to research done by anthropologist Robin Fox that suggests the seat of the conscience—the very epicenter of our moral sense—is a tiny structure in the brain called the amygdala. The amygdala is connected to areas of the brain that control memory and thinking.

When you sit up at night wringing your hands, anguishing about whether to confess your sexual indiscretions, it's thanks (or no thanks) to the amygdala. It helps keep us honest—which isn't always the most comfortable feeling.

Head Games

That rocket in your pocket probably gets its firepower from your brain. But what exactly happens is still something of a mystery to the folks in white lab coats.

"These are the big, big questions of neuroscience," confides Lucy Brown, Ph.D., professor of neurology and neuroscience at Albert Einstein College of Medicine in New York City.

A man's arousal begins with testosterone, the hormone that makes it possible for us to get aroused by images, smells or fond memories. "That's the missing link—exactly why and how some stimuli trigger sexual response," says Dr. Brown.

Nonetheless, the hormone makes its way to your brain, specifically to the hypothalamus, the brain region that controls our sex drive. "But it's not just one pulse of testosterone and you're hard," explains Dr. Brown. "Your body's been sending doses of testosterone for days, weeks, maybe months. Then, once your brain has been 'prepared,' the next dose triggers your arousal through circuits in the hypothalamus. Suddenly, that girl you never noticed looks cute," he adds.

Once testosterone hits the hypothalamus, it sends an erection alert from the brain through the autonomic nervous system, along the spinal cord and into nerves that "feed" the smooth muscles and blood vessels of the penis.

In response to these urgent signals, blood vessels expand and blood rushes into the erectile tissues surrounding the penis, causing it to become firm and erect. What happens after that, of course, is entirely up to you.

Love Is in the Air

Secrets to Scent-sational Sex

It has been repeated often enough now that it no longer matters whether the story is apocryphal. Someone once asked Sigmund Freud, the cigar-chomping father of psycho-analysis, if his sizable stogies were phallic symbols.

"Sometimes," Freud purportedly replied, "a cigar is just a cigar."

A more telling question, perhaps, would have been whether Freud was just blowing smoke. After all, it was the good doctor who theorized that odors conjure up such powerful sexual urges that we spend half our lives repressing smells to avoid becoming oversexed savages. What better to quash amorous aromas than the pervasive, pungent puffs of a hand-rolled Cuban?

The relationship between the nose, the sense of smell and sex predates Freud by a long shot. But Freud was onto something because the part of the brain that interprets smell, the olfactory lobe, is in the same area that processes emotion, the limbic system. It's also the same area that manages sexual thoughts and desires.

The nose itself is an amazing creation. The olfactory cleft at the top of the nose contains six million smell cells, which allow you to detect some 10,000 different odors. As for its importance in sex and romance, smell gets a gold star by most Americans, who ranked it the third most sensual sense in The Revlon Fire and Ice Survey on Sensuality and the Self in the 90s, conducted in the fall of 1994.

Alan R. Hirsch, M.D., of the Smell and Taste Treatment

and Research Foundation in Chicago, has found that certain smells increase penile blood flow. In one study of 31 men, ages 18 to 64, Dr. Hirsch found that a combination of pumpkin pie and lavender elicited a whopping 40 percent increase in penile blood flow, more than any other smell he tested. Second place went to a cross between black licorice and doughnuts. Kind of makes you wonder what Homer Simpson is really thinking about when he closes his eyes and drools, "Mmmmmm, doughnuts."

"Does this mean that the way to a man's heart is through his nose, or just that men are always hungry?" Dr. Hirsch asks. "We're not sure." It may be that nostalgic smells relax us enough to increase penile blood flow. But it appears there is something deeper and more embedded in our nature at work here, Dr. Hirsch says.

"We think this is an instinctual reaction that dates back to our ancestors, who would gather around food kills," he explains. "What better way to find a mate than when you're mingling with the opposite sex at dinner?"

Love at First Smell

We can't guarantee pheromones and food smells will liven your libido any time soon. But you might be able to use this knowledge to improve your sex life. Just get a whiff of these tips.

Share an aroma memory. Because the emotion and smell centers occupy the same part of the brain, smells can elicit powerful nostalgic memories. Homemade chicken soup, for example, might remind you of your childhood.

Use this effect to power-pack a romantic evening by recalling the scent of a particularly fond experience for you and your partner and recreating it. Say you spent a blissful weekend camping in an evergreen forest. Fill your living

room with the aroma of pine, perhaps by hanging fresh-cut pine boughs or by hiding dozens of pine-scented deodorizers. Then pitch a tent on the rug and enjoy your romantic getaway. (Bugs are optional.)

Get incensed. Scented smoke might fire up your sex life, suggests Dr. Betty Dodson, a New York City sex educator, therapist and author. Incense as a mood-setter has a long and colorful history, and it can heighten any amorous adventure by providing more sensuous stimulation. "It's always nicer to try to please all your senses in a sexual experience," Dr. Dodson says.

Incense is available at novelty shops, smoke shops and even some supermarkets. It's inexpensive and comes in punk-like sticks and cones. Sensual scent-sations include:

- Orange: Can increase penile blood flow by 20 percent.
- Strawberry: The favorite of those who reported the highest level of sexual satisfaction in Dr. Hirsch's studies.
- Oriental spice: A favorite of Dr. Hirsch's subjects who reported having the most sex.

Go natural. Unless you have been digging ditches for 12 hours or are boycotting bathwater for political purposes, there's no reason to shower before *every* romantic interlude. The French call the body's natural odor *cassolette*, or perfume box. Of course, they also call Jerry Lewis a genius. But in this case, they're right. The cassolette can be a titanic turn-on for men and women. In his best-selling book, *The Joy of Sex*, Alex Comfort, M.D., calls the cassolette—particularly a woman's—the single greatest sexual asset after beauty.

But don't ban the bath. Even the cassolette is no excuse for poor hygiene. If natural

---

My, What a Big Nose You Have

The link between sex and smell extends through the ages, and it's a coupling both colorful and comical. In the ruins of Pompeii, for example, archaeologists have found special perfume jars in rooms explicitly reserved for sex. Ancient Sumerians used perfumes to entice women, and the Chinese have long maintained that there's a relationship between affection and smell. Moreover, nearly every culture in the world uses some type of perfume or incense in its marriage rituals.

The nose itself is an archetypal phallic symbol. Just look at the appeal of Rostand's *Cyrano de Bergerac*, the classic character with the large nose and silver tongue, or consider the true-life story of Queen Johanna I of Naples. In 1343 Johanna chose Hungarian Prince Andrew to be her hubby because she thought his sizable schnoz spoke well of his manhood. Much to his misfortune, the prince was a pauper in the penis department, so the crestfallen queen lamented, "Oh nose, how horribly you have deceived me."

Johanna then had her lackluster groom garroted. He was, you might say, a loser by a nose.

---

body odors get unnaturally strong, hit the shower. Showering in tandem can be the perfect prelude to magnificent—and malodorless—lovemaking.

Use common scents. Finally, since the link between smell and sex is so strong, create your own odoriferous calling cards by "imprinting" your favorite smells on each other. If you let her choose your cologne, and you wear it consistently, rest assured she'll think of you every time she passes the men's fragrance counter. Or, even better, when she passes another handsome guy wearing your scent.

The Science of Attraction

Sing the Body Symmetric

Admit it. Have you ever caught yourself wondering: "What *does* she see in me?"

Poets and artists would say it's indescribable. It's the mystery of love. But science, with its cold, hard analytical nature, doesn't care much for things it can't describe. You may not be able to dissect love to see what makes it tick, but you can make observations and look for patterns. And a growing number of scientists believe that symmetry—the body's balanced proportions—may be one of the keys to sexual attraction.

Turns out beauty may be more in the brain of the beholder than in the eye.

The Shape of Things to Come

While studying the sexual shenanigans of Japanese scorpion flies in the early 1990s, Randy Thornhill, Ph.D., a behavioral ecologist at the University of New Mexico, Albuquerque, found that the male flies with the most symmetrical wings got the most female flies. Other studies throughout the world were turning up similar results: Anders Moller, of the University of Copenhagen in Denmark, found he could foil a male swallow's chance of attracting a mate by making his tail less symmetrical. Soon, like the biblical story of Noah's Ark, animals from all around stepped forward to show their preference for symmetry, thanks to controlled laboratory studies.

"This asymmetry stuff is so far out of the mainstream it's hard to get funding for it," Dr. Thornhill told *New Scientist* magazine. "Looks really matter. We're trying to find out what these looks are and how they evolved."

Although many symmetry studies have been on animals and insects, some researchers have put humans under the microscope. They speculate that we, too, are suckers for symmetry. According to them, our penchant for symmetry may be pure Darwinian drive. In other words, survival of the fittest: Symmetrical bodies suggest healthier genes, stronger immune systems, better diets and—most important—the best chances for procreation.

In one study of 72 student volunteers Dr. Thornhill and his colleague Steven Gangestad found that students with the most symmetrical bodies were consistently perceived to be the most attractive. They discovered this by measuring the length and width of the students' ears and the width of their feet, ankles, hands, wrists and elbows. Those whose left and right sides differed by just 1 or 2 percent were judged most attractive, while the most unattractive had differences of 5 to 7 percent.

Symmetrical preferences apparently extend beyond the physical. Jared Diamond, M.D., a physiology professor at the University of California, Los Angeles, School of Medicine, writes in his book *The Third Chimpanzee* that, whether we know it or not, we develop a "search image" of what we consider to be the ideal mate. That is, we create a mental picture of what we want, to which we compare every potential partner. What comprises these ideals? Researchers found the most important factors were religion, ethnic background, race, socioeconomic status, age and political views. The next most important were intelligence, personality and living habits, such as neatness or sloppiness.

"In short, likes tend to marry likes," Dr. Diamond writes.

Mind over Matter

Although a great deal of our attraction may indeed be physically based, there are mental factors to consider, too. For example, some men might have a psychological need to be mothered, so they'll seek mothering-type women above all others. Other similar mental rules of attraction:

• Many men seek coy women because coyness implies sexual reservation, which might mean there's a better chance she'll be faithful.

• Youth is another contributing factor, because young women have a higher reproductive value. Studies suggest that men in their thirties prefer women roughly five years younger. Men in their fifties prefer women 20 years younger.

• Your mood might affect your choice, too. In one study, guys in a good mood from watching funny movies were more attracted to glamorous women, while guys in a down mood from watching depressing movies went for women who appeared friendlier. Moreover, being in a heightened emotional state seems to affect us: In one study, people who were expecting to get an electric shock were more attracted to people they met than people not expecting a shock. Another study found that men who ran for ten minutes were more attracted to women they met than men who didn't run. (Reason number 1,253 in favor of working out.)

"Perhaps the most important thing to know is that men often underestimate what women want," says Dr. Ted McIlvenna of the Institute for Advanced Study of Human Sexuality. "Many men are concerned with how they perform and look when it comes to sex

Shaping Up

Having trouble stomaching the notion that body symmetry actually might affect who we're attracted to? That may only be part of the equation, according to the University of New Mexico's Dr. Randy Thornhill.

Thornhill looked at the sexual histories of 122 students. On average, students with the most perfect body symmetry—as defined by measurements of their hands, wrists, feet, ankles, ears and elbows—reported two to three times as many sex partners in their lifetime as students with the most asymmetrical measurements. Thornhill's studies have also found that most symmetrical men started having sex three to four years before their less symmetrical counterparts.

The most astonishing finding, however, came when Thornhill looked deeper into the relationship between symmetry and sex. After surveying and measuring 86 couples in their early twenties, he found that the women who were with the most symmetrical men claimed, on average, to orgasm 75 percent of the time, compared to 30 percent of the time for women who were with the most lopsided men. Moreover, couples were more likely to climax simultaneously if the man's body was symmetrical.

and attraction, but to many women the most important thing, overall, is how they're treated, how they're valued."

But not always, Dr. McIlvenna adds.

"I was with a group of athletes once. They were all very beautiful people, and there was a famous football quarterback there. I looked to the woman he was with and asked her what it was about him that turned her on the most," Dr. McIlvenna recalls.

"She turned to me and said, 'His American Express card.' "

Sex Myths

Don't Believe What You Think You Know

Albert the Great was a medieval doctor and an inquiring mind who wanted to know. In the name of unwavering scientific curiosity, he delved deep into the mysteries of human sexuality and answered two of the most probing questions of the time: How do women become pregnant, and what makes a man's penis erect?

On pregnancy: Women emit their own sperm during orgasm, which mingles with a man's to cause pregnancy, Albert said. Women *had* to climax to procreate.

On erections: When a man thinks of a woman, it conjures up heat in his body. This heat accumulates in the lower abdomen until it vaporizes in the penis, causing it to expand and swell.

These findings represented Albert the Great's crowning achievements. Yet clearly, Albert's findings were far from great. Today, thanks to advanced research and technology, we know what really makes a penis erect and a woman pregnant. But many people still are confused about sex.

Not so many years ago, for example, teenagers feared you could get pregnant by kissing in a bikini. Even today, people you would think would know better believe you can avoid sexually transmitted diseases by peeing after sex. We even know one guy whose seventh-grade teacher offered this enigmatic lesson in sex education: "You can't catch anything from doorknobs." The poor bloke wondered for years what perverse things people did with doorknobs.

Here's a compilation of today's most pervasive sex myths, gleaned from experts who deal with them every day.

The Facts and Fiction of Sex

Myth: ***Women don't like sex.*** Hardly. Women enjoy sex as much as the next guy. Or gal. The problem is, society tells us that "good girls" should be indifferent to sex, or at least not too eager for it. Truth is, a woman's sex drive is as great as your own, and she loves it just as much as you do.

Myth: ***Penis size matters, and you're stuck with what you have.*** For the millionth time, penis length doesn't matter. Remember, a woman's vagina is only so long—and vaginas come in different shapes and sizes, too. The only penis size that *does* matter, albeit to a small degree, is girth. Studies show women prefer a thicker penis over a longer one. As for being stuck with the cards Nature dealt you, that's not true, either. You have many options, including surgery, to lengthen or thicken your manhood. Just be warned that these procedures carry a good deal of cons in exchange for the few purported pros.

Myth: ***Men must settle for one orgasm per sex session.*** Reach orgasm, then go limp—bedroom scientists thought this for a long time. So did the scientists in white lab coats. But now experts say we can have more than one orgasm without downtime if we're patient enough to practice. Although multi-orgasmic men are still something of a rarity, this phenomenon shouldn't be as startling in the future as it sounds today. Any man can do it. All it takes is some conditioning of your pelvic muscles and a few tips on keeping the right mind-set.

Myth: *Single, young guys are having sex all the time.* According to the *Sex in America* study, our era's most comprehensive, scientifically valid sex study, it's the *married* guys who are getting it more often. But that's only half the story. The study also showed that while married men have sex more frequently, the duration of each sex act was significantly shorter than the single guys' escapades. So while single guys might be having sex twice a month, it could be for two hours at a clip, whereas the married men might be having sex twice a week at 15 minutes a session. As for which is better, you decide: There's good news here for married and single guys alike.

Myth: *Sex with your partner will never be as exciting as it was in the beginning of your relationship.* Mundane sex with a longtime partner is an example of the Coolidge Effect, a phenomenon described best by paraphrasing Mark Twain: Familiarity breeds boredom. It's normal to fall into a dull routine after you've explored the same body hundreds of times. But that doesn't mean you're sentenced to a lifetime of sexual ennui: Variety is the spice of your sex life, too. Keep things fresh by experimenting with different positions or locations, taking private vacations, using sex toys, watching adult movies—whatever brings back the fireworks.

Myth: *Big feet, big hands and big noses are signs of big penises.* About the only thing you can say for sure about guys with big feet is that they have big shoes. Despite locker-room lore, there appears to be no correlation between body-part size and penis size.

Myth: *You must be a freak if you're turned on by kinky things.* Many of us are turned on by what some would consider kinky. This doesn't mean we're freaks. It's a way of learning about and enjoying our sexuality, and it's perfectly healthy. (Not to mention it keeps sex from becoming routine.) Unorthodox sex behavior becomes problematic, experts say, when it turns into a way of escaping from or coping with problems, hurts yourself or others or becomes an obsession or addiction.

Myth: *Masturbation has no place in a good sex life.* Many experts believe masturbation enhances sex. For example, masturbation can teach you ejaculatory control. Watching your partner masturbate can also tell you what kind of touching turns her on. Masturbation is also convenient when you want to feel good fast, without a big buildup or without waking your partner.

Myth: *Sex is natural—no one really needs help.* Sex isn't as innate as you think. Sure, we have procreative proclivities. We can put tab A in slot B to make babies. But sex is more than that in a healthy, loving relationship. Sex is the ultimate expression of intimacy. It's physical and metaphysical bonding.

Most of us approach it from a rigid framework of values and notions that come from our upbringing, life experience and social influences. To enhance sex, we can explore these boundaries by learning more about our bodies and our partner's body. By finding what works and doesn't work for us in the bedroom. By experimenting with books, movies or toys, or by talking to sex therapists. Sex is a cosmos of exploration. You don't have to stay on your home planet unless you're both perfectly happy there.

Myth: *Good sex means rip-roaring, sheet-splitting, mattress-melting sex.* This myth is perpetuated by the media, especially movies. But every encounter needn't end with fireworks. Maybe this time she wants a spark of compassion, not a firestorm of lust. In fact, the single most important intimacy builder for many women is how they're treated, how they're seen and how they're valued. Not how they're ravaged. Realize that truly enlightened sex is something you do with your big head, not just your little one.

Myth: *Simultaneous orgasms are best.* Although pervasive, this myth isn't what it's cracked up to be. Yes, simultaneous orgasms are nice, and they can build intimacy.

But the logistics—properly timing the moment for both of you—can put undue pressure on a couple. Plus, you won't get the joy of watching your partner revel in her ecstasy if you're in the midst of your own. Try climaxing together and separately, just to experience each. Then concentrate more on simply enjoying sex without hanging a predetermined outcome over your heads.

Myth: *If life is good, you won't have sex problems.* Life's too complex for such wishful thinking. In addition to intangibles like stress, there are physical factors, like impotence, that can adversely affect one's sex life. That said, a solid, loving relationship based on trust, honesty and good communication is perhaps the best foundation for excellent sex. And that goes for dealing with whatever curveballs life throws you along the way.

Myth: *Women cannot ejaculate.* Although traditional thinking confines ejaculation to men, many researchers now believe that women do it as well. Proponents say female ejaculation comes in the midst of climax for women experiencing deep vaginal stimulation, particularly of the G-spot, a sensitive bundle of nerves on the upper, front wall of a woman's vagina.

Myth: *Women hate quickies.* There's a mistaken belief that quickies are passé—that they're the quintessence of sexual selfishness for men and the ultimate form of sexual neglect for women. On the contrary, quickies can be passion's payload for both of you. The obvious prerequisite is that you both enjoy them and that you don't favor quickies at the expense of prolonged loving—especially if that's what your partner wants or needs.

Myth: *Men can't fake orgasms.* They can. Despite the popular belief that orgasm equals ejaculation—which, indeed, is pretty hard to fake—sex therapists say there's a difference between the euphoric feelings of orgasm and the actual process of ejaculation. Some multi-orgasmic men, for example, have trained themselves to enjoy several "dry" orgasms before ejaculating on the last climax. These non-ejaculatory orgasms are said to be just as pleasurable as the "traditional" ones and, in some cases, more so.

Myth: *An experienced man can tell when a woman climaxes.* A man who claims he knows when a woman has climaxed is deluded. Most women, if they so choose, can fake an orgasm so convincingly they'd win an Oscar. Remember that deli scene in *When Harry Met Sally?* The one where Meg Ryan reenacts an earth-shattering orgasm to show a smug Billy Crystal that men can never be sure if a woman's faking it? The only real way to tell if your partner climaxed, especially in the beginning of your relationship when you're still learning about each other, is to ask—to make good communication a cornerstone of your sex life.

There are also a few classic, though far from foolproof, signs to look for. As a woman's arousal rises, her lips become pink, her pupils dilate, her breasts swell, her skin flushes and her nipples perk up erect. As she enters climax, her body acts like yours: Her muscles tense, her face may grimace, she may moan or scream and thrust her pelvis.

Myth: *It's unhealthy to have sex with a woman who is menstruating.* Some couples prefer having sex during a woman's period because they claim the woman's at her randiest then. Medically, there's no reason not to enjoy sex before, during and after menstruation. However, if a woman is suffering a vaginal infection—marked by unpleasant odor, itching, burning or discharge—she should abstain from sex; menstrual blood lowers the vagina's natural acidity, making it more hospitable to pathogens and increasing your chance of catching something.

Myth: *You can't have sex during pregnancy.* A healthy woman can enjoy sex up to labor, though you both may need to alter your technique and positioning. Many women report immensely satisfying sex during pregnancy, because their bodies are raging with libido-lifting hormones. Just hold off on the athletic, vigorous sex, and go easy on her breasts, which can become tender. Prime sex positions for pregnancy: rear entry, side-by-side and seated positions.

Myth: *A real man pleases his partner every time.* It once was a man's job to satisfy his partner all the time, every time. If he didn't, he wasn't considered a real man. Perhaps this came about because medieval scientists thought female orgasm was necessary for procreation. Perhaps it's just another lofty ideal dictated to men by society. Regardless, sex therapists today say the whole notion is poppycock: Everyone is responsible for his or her own orgasm, they insist. Putting the onus on men increases our anxiety, making us more likely to suffer performance problems if our partners don't climax. A woman should talk openly with you about what works best for her—and don't take her suggestions as criticism. Likewise, you should tell her what works best for you.

Myth: *Black men have longer penises.* On average, an erect penis for most men falls within the five- to seven-inch range. Black men, however, *on average*, appear to be slightly longer than White men, and White men, *on average*, appear to be slightly longer than Asian men. Despite this, it's difficult, if not impossible, to draw accurate conclusions for individuals based on race alone.

Myth: *Women don't like porn movies.* Some studies suggest men are more visually oriented than women, but, on the whole, women enjoy erotic movies, too. They're just not as overtly stimulated by them as we are, and many are downright turned off by the hard-core variety.

Myth: *Good sex must include intercourse, and a sexually responsive woman should climax from intercourse alone.* While sex generally connotes intercourse, it's not essential for satisfying lovemaking. Some couples enjoy extended petting sessions, perhaps with a relaxing massage, just

as much as they enjoy intercourse. And although some women can climax from deep vaginal penetration, many find it difficult to climax from that alone. Most require some kind of direct, prolonged clitoral stimulation to achieve orgasm.

Myth: *Having sexual fantasies is a sure sign something's wrong with your relationship.* Quite the contrary: Sexual fantasies improve the quality of your sex life. Men who indulge their fantasies have fewer sexual problems and enjoy more sexual satisfaction than their inhibited brethren. And studies show that men with a greater variety of sexual fantasies tend to have a greater variety of sexual experiences. So dream on.

Myth: *Fantasizing about sex with a woman other than your partner must mean there's something lacking in your relationship.* Once again, the opposite is true. You can be exquisitely happy with your current partner and still fantasize about the beautiful redhead you see every morning at the coffee shop. Don't worry—it keeps you from actually following through with something you might thoroughly enjoy, only to regret later on.

Our experts: Richard A. Carroll, Ph.D., Northwestern Medical Center, Chicago; Betty Dodson, Ph.D., private practice, New York City; Erica M. Goodstone, Ph.D., private practice, New York City; Barbara Keesling, Ph.D., private practice, Orange, California; Judy Kuriansky, Ph.D., private practice, New York City; Ted McIlvenna, Ph.D., Institute for Advanced Study of Human Sexuality, San Francisco; Robert T. Michael, Ph.D., Graduate School of Public Policy Studies, University of Chicago; Galdino Pranzarone, Ph.D., Roanoke College, Salem, Virginia; Melvyn Rosenstein, M.D., private practice, Culver City, California; Anne Semans and Cathy Winks, co-authors of The Good Vibrations Guide to Sex, *San Francisco; Ralph R. Stevens, private practice, Iowa City, Iowa; Marilyn K. Volker, Ph.D., private practice, Coral Gables, Florida.*

The Truth about Quantity

Loving Happily Ever After

Sit around any barroom when the talk turns to sex and you'd think married guys are the only people in the world who aren't getting enough.

But talk to any single guy—honestly and candidly and not when he's trying to impress a barful of married guys—and you'll find that he's not getting enough either.

Our sex lives are rife with misunderstanding when it comes to quantity. Most guys seem to think everyone else is getting more than they are.

So it's a good thing those intrepid researchers in the *Sex in America* survey settled the matter once and for all.

After interviewing 3,432 Americans on the details of their sex lives, University of Chicago researchers developed a scientifically accurate snapshot of American sexuality. They not only discovered what is done in the bedroom; they found out how much and with whom.

"When we did the *Sex in America* study, we stressed that we needed to know these facts for public policy health information," says lead researcher Dr. Robert T. Michael. "We stressed that this was a time for honesty, not bragging. At $450 a case, you don't spend that kind of money for rough estimates."

According to Dr. Michael and the statistics from the study itself, here's the whole truth—and more—about who's getting what and when.

How Much Sex Are We Having?

Pick up any magazine. Odds are you'll see a waif model peddling expensive cologne, or a busty beauty wearing skintight jeans—and not much else. Or a half-dressed hunk hawking underwear. And that's just the ads. Judging from the barrage of media we endure every day—and judging, apparently, from how well sex sells—you might think Americans have time for nothing else but sex.

Most of us know better. And the experts bear out the bare facts: Only a third of us ages 18 to 59 are having sex as often as twice a week. Another third are doing it a few times a month and the rest, a few times a year, if at all.

Specifically, 8 percent of all men in the survey said they had sex four times or more a week over the last year, 26 percent had it two or three times a week, 37 percent a few times a month, 16 percent a few times a year and 14 percent hadn't had any sex at all in the last 12 months.

Not surprisingly, there isn't much, if any, overall difference between men and women when it comes to how much sex we're having. The numbers were nearly identical.

Race and Religion

Along the racial divide, things shape up pretty evenly, too, despite society's pervasive myths about sex drive and skin color. Overall, Blacks had sex about as often as Whites. Hispanics, however, reported slightly higher rates. Thirty-eight percent of White men, for example, said they had sex two or more times a week; 37 percent of Black men and 43 percent of Hispanic men said the same.

"Our prejudices and envies may say that Blacks and Jews are more sexual and that the highly religious are less sexual. But these assumptions are wrong, because there is nothing about being a member of these groups that translates into more sexual desire or more sexual opportunity," the researchers concluded.

Another stereotype that can't stand the light of scientific study is that religious folks don't like sex. The truth is that Catholic and conservative Protestant men reported slightly higher rates of having sex at least twice a week than guys who identified themselves as mainline Protestants or as having no religion.

In fact, those without religion also were most likely to go with little or no sex—by a substantial margin. According to the survey, 38 percent of the men who claimed "none" under religion reported having sex a few times a year or not at all, compared to 27 percent of main-line Protestant men, 26 percent of conservative Protestant men and 25 percent of Catholic men.

Married Life versus Single Life

This isn't exactly rocket science here, but the most critical factor in how much sex people have is determined by whether there's anyone around to accommodate them. Not surprisingly, married couples and people living together enjoy the most frequent sex—after all, it's harder to enjoy a roll in the hay if you're by yourself most of the time.

"It's not too surprising when you consider you're sleeping in the same room and in the same bed as your partner every night," Dr. Michael says. "Having sex under these circumstances is a lot less hassle than when you're single and have to make arrangements. Sexually speaking, partnerships are more convenient."

Of course, frequency and volume aren't

the same thing, Dr. Michael points out. "It's the younger and unmarried who report having sex for more extended periods of time," he says. "Married couples don't tend to have sex for an hour or more very often."

The reasons for this are unclear. It might be definitional. "That is, unmarried couples might include foreplay in their definition of sex, while married people may just be referring to intercourse itself," Dr. Michael says.

Or, Dr. Michael adds, it may just be "human supply and demand."

"Unmarried people don't have a steady supply of sexual outlets, so they might make the most of them when they come along," he speculates.

Bottom line? There's good news here for married and single guys alike.

The Quality of Our Quantity

Overall, our sex lives are astoundingly, well, normal. No swinging from chandeliers. No Roman orgies. For the most part, it's good old-fashioned sex.

"It seems men and women are reasonably pleased with their sex lives, even though we found there isn't as much wild, erotic sex as we'd be led to believe," Dr. Michael says. "Americans aren't Pollyannas about their sex, but they're reasonably happy."

Ninety-five percent of all respondents had vaginal sex the last time they had sex; 80 percent said they had vaginal sex *every* time they had sex.

And despite the fact that just 29 percent of all women climax with each sexual encounter, compared to 75 percent of men, the overwhelming majority said they were happy, if not thrilled, with their sex lives.

"Despite the popular notion that frequent orgasms are essential to a happy sex life, there was not a strong relationship between having orgasms and having a satisfying sex life," researchers said.

Surveying the Sexual Scene

Real Answers from Real Men

If truth is the first casualty of war, then honesty is the first casualty of sex. At least when men gather together to talk about it. The air is usually filled with braggadocio, wild embellishment and coarse humor. It's like swapping old war stories, with tales of conquest and feats of amazing daring, skill and strength. But what do men *really* think about sex?

We decided to ask. Not in a locker room or at a bar, but in the privacy of guys' own homes, through a written survey. We asked 776 men questions you've probably asked yourself but have never discussed with other guys. Questions that expose vulnerability, doubts and raw emotions. The results are enlightening. And best of all, they're honest. So if you want to know what guys really think about sex, read on.

	Under 25	25 to 34	35 to 44	45 to 54	55 and Over
How would you characterize your sex life?					
Excellent	12.3	20.3	17.1	20.6	13.9
Good	46.2	39.6	38.6	41.9	37.7
Fair	23.1	22.8	24.8	19.4	17.2
Poor	10.8	9.1	14.3	14.4	16.4
Nonexistent	4.6	7.1	3.3	2.5	12.3
In general, how important is good sex to a happy long-term marriage or relationship?					
Absolutely critical	23.1	22.8	18.6	18.8	13.9
Very important	60.0	52.8	53.3	53.1	63.9
Moderately important	12.3	22.8	26.7	24.4	19.7
Not very important	1.5	1.0	1.0	1.3	0.8
Have you ever used any of the following erotic items?					
Videos	46.2	58.4	63.3	54.4	43.4
Lingerie	70.8	58.4	50.5	40.6	16.4
Fantasy	30.8	33.5	26.7	29.4	13.1
Toys	30.8	27.9	31.4	31.3	13.9
Games	18.5	14.7	11.4	7.5	4.9
Never used any	10.8	14.2	16.7	26.3	46.7
Do you feel men are naturally monogamous?					
Yes	23.1	25.9	24.8	27.5	27.9
No	67.7	65.5	68.6	63.1	61.5

	Under 25	25 to 34	35 to 44	45 to 54	55 and Over
Do you feel women are naturally monogamous?					
Yes	58.5	59.9	56.7	56.3	45.1
No	32.3	27.4	34.8	33.1	42.6
Do you ever feel guilty or ashamed about sex?					
Yes	32.3	25.4	27.6	19.4	12.3
No	61.5	72.6	69.5	75.0	85.2
Do you ever get angry about sex?					
Yes	20.0	26.9	31.4	28.1	20.5
No	29.2	43.7	45.2	50.0	49.2
In your own life, what do you feel is the biggest barrier to great sex?					
Fatigue	49.2	54.3	59.5	55.0	47.5
Lack of time	46.2	50.3	46.7	33.1	32.0
Partner not interested	27.7	37.6	39.0	39.4	34.4
Presence of children	4.6	18.8	39.0	21.9	18.9
Lack of personal interest	15.4	14.7	16.2	24.4	11.5
What is the one thing about male sexuality you feel women don't understand?					
Intensity of sexual drives	36.9	44.2	39.0	38.8	41.0
It's more emotional than they think	36.9	31.5	33.8	33.8	33.6
It's more physical than emotion	26.2	25.9	25.7	28.8	18.0
What is your greatest sexual fear?					
Impotence	15.4	20.3	29.5	36.9	54.1
Contracting AIDS	41.5	34.0	28.6	18.8	13.1
Losing interest with age	9.2	16.8	24.8	26.3	27.0
Losing your partner	13.8	17.8	14.8	14.4	13.9
Getting a sexually transmitted disease	16.9	11.7	5.2	8.8	4.9
What was your most terrifying sexual experience?					
Getting my partner pregnant	18.5	20.8	15.2	14.4	11.5
Fearing I had an STD	9.2	16.8	16.7	14.4	12.3
Impotence	3.1	6.1	8.1	22.5	27.0
Getting caught in the act	3.1	13.2	13.8	16.3	9.0
First sexual encounter	13.8	11.7	12.4	6.3	4.9

Safe Sex

Your Life Depends on It

You have a kitschy, mini Eiffel Tower from Paris, an "I Love N.Y." mug from the Big Apple and an autographed Cubs ball from Chicago. Now, after an unexpected one-night stand in your own hometown, you have a leaky penis and an itchy rash. Souvenirs are great. *Except* when they come from sexual travels.

Yet lots of guys bring home unwanted remembrances by having unprotected sex. And you don't have to be bedding someone new every weekend: Even a new partner every year or two can be dangerous. Of course, the first thing that probably springs to mind is AIDS, as well it should. But AIDS isn't the only thing you have to fear. Despite years of medical advances and intense public education, other sexual diseases—many of which have been around for centuries—are still running rampant. Some, like syphilis, are soaring to their highest levels in decades.

"Sex these days is not just a series of individual events, but a continuum," says Cathy Winks, co-owner of Good Vibrations, a retail and mail-order adult store in San Francisco, and co-author of *The Good Vibrations Guide to Sex.* "Nowadays, you need to look at sex in terms of risk management. Practicing safer sex is a necessity of the 1990s."

The Facts of Life

More than 20 sexually transmitted diseases, or STDs, exist today, and experts say one out of every 20 Americans will catch one this year. Also consider that:

- Younger and middle-age people are more at risk. Half the U.S. population will acquire an STD by age 35.
- Eighty-six percent of all STD cases occur between ages 15 and 29.
- Forty million people are infected with an STD right now. Another 12 million will be in a year.

The frustrating thing about all this is that STDs are so easily avoided.

"We're able to take care of almost anything if we use protection," says Dr. Ted McIlvenna of the Institute for Advanced Study of Human Sexuality. "The problem is that most people, kids especially, think they won't catch anything.

"I remember one time we did a study to see who had a greater prevalence of disease: swingers or regular young people," recalls Dr. McIlvenna. "Surprisingly, not one of the swingers had an infection, but about 10 percent of the regular folks tested positive. The difference was that the swingers knew they were at risk and they knew how to prevent infection."

For men, contracting STDs is especially galling because the male anatomy is more resistant to sexual diseases than the female's. Her vagina is warm, dark and moist—conditions that make bacteria and viruses feel right at home. We, on the other hand, urinate away many nasties before they set up camp deep inside us.

That said, there are still plenty of reasons to be on guard. For starters, men claim to have more sex partners on average than women. It doesn't take an actuary to figure out that the more sex partners you have, the greater your risk. And while no one can say definitively that men get more STDs than women, it's safe to assume that unless you abstain from sex or are in a healthy, monogamous relationship, you're always at risk.

A Primer

Here's a roster of the most common STDs and what you must know to avoid and treat them.

AIDS

AIDS is the sexual scourge of our era. There's no cure, and there's no way we can underscore its severity more effectively than by stating the facts.

- As of 1993, AIDS was the number one killer of people ages 25 to 44.
- In the 27-to-39 age group, HIV—the virus that causes AIDS—infects one out of every 139 White men, one of every 33 Black men and one of every 60 Hispanic men.
- Eighty percent of all AIDS victims are men, and the disease has claimed more than 300,000 American lives.

AIDS attacks the body's immune system. Although white blood cells, the body's disease fighters, create antibodies to counter the virus, the virus sneakily enters the protection of neighboring cells, where it remains impervious to antibody attack. In time, HIV-infected cells gather in the lymph nodes, where they produce more HIV cells. And although many HIV-infected men don't progress to AIDS or develop other serious illnesses for years, the disease eventually renews its attack on the immune system until it becomes full-blown AIDS. That crushes your immune power and leads to opportunistic diseases, like pneumonia, tuberculosis or Karposi's sarcoma, a rare form of cancer.

For the record, you can't catch AIDS from casual, nonsexual contact, like holding hands. Or from mosquitoes, toilet seats, swimming pools or hot tubs. You can't even catch it from repeated contact with an AIDS patient or by sharing utensils. You catch AIDS from sharing needles, from transfusions of infected blood and from high-risk sex, the most common medium for transmission.

High-risk sex includes unprotected sex with strangers, sex with many partners, unprotected oral sex and just about any other activity where you swap bodily fluids.

Chlamydia

Chlamydia is the most common STD in America. It's a bacterial infection that's responsible for three to five million infections a year. Chlamydia spreads through sexual contact only, not by kissing, sharing toilets or hot tubs. Yet, despite its frequency, many guys don't have a clue what it is. That's because chlamydia is hard to detect in men. Studies show that about 25 percent of all infected men never develop symptoms.

When they do develop, symptoms make their appearance in about two weeks. They consist of penile discharge (usually whitish and runny), a burning sensation during urination and, occasionally, swelling of the testicles. Untreated, this can lead to epididymitis, an inflammation in the scrotum that may leave you sterile. Treatment for chlamydia consists of antibiotics, usually doxycycline (Doryx) or tetracycline (Achromycin V).

Crabs

Crabs are pubic lice, and about one million people each year get them, mostly from skin-to-skin contact, such as during sex. You can also catch crabs from personal belongings: towels, clothing, even by sharing the same toilet seat. Symptoms, which surface in about five days, include itching in the pubic areas. You also might see small blue bite marks, or the crabs themselves, which look like tiny scabs to the naked eye.

Treatment consists of over-the-counter medications or shampoos, such as A-200, that you apply directly to the infected area. Personal belongings can be stored in sealed plastic bags for a couple of weeks to starve the lice. Large items, like couches or mattresses, should be cleaned with bug sprays containing disinfectants.

Genital Warts

Genital warts are the most common STD in men, having an incident rate even higher than herpes. But because warts are tiny and painless, many guys are walking around oblivious to the fact that they're infected. When the warts grow and become obvious, they look like raised or flat bumps and are usually located along the penis or anal region. Then they're hard to ignore.

Although genital warts sometimes disappear without treatment, they often require a trip to the doctor, since they're so contagious and can spread through sex, sharing towels and even touching. Treatment consists of medication or cryotherapy, where a doctor freezes the warts off with liquid nitrogen. (Never use an over-the-counter wart-remover; they're far too potent for penile skin.)

Another reason to see a professional: What appears to be a wart might be the symptom of another STD or, in rare cases, a malignant tumor. Plus, since warts are so contagious, you might pass them to your partner, and genital warts are far more serious in women, playing a role in cervical cancer.

Gonorrhea

Gonorrhea, commonly called the clap, spreads easily, accounting for some 700,000 new cases a year. Symptoms appear 3 to 5 days after exposure, though they may appear in as little as 1 day or in as many as 30. (Approximately 10 percent of infected men will show no symptoms at all.) Symptoms include greenish or yellowish penile discharge, painful urination and sometimes swelling of the penis head. As a rule, the disease spreads only through sexual contact, though cases have been reported involving people catching it from infected objects, such as sex toys. Treatment consists of the antibiotic shot ceftriaxone (Rocephin) or ofloxacin tablets (Floxin).

Herpes

The herpes virus is very common: It's the same virus that causes cold sores, and as many as 40 percent of all American adults have been exposed to it. But, surprisingly, catching the virus on your genitals isn't as easy as it sounds.

An Ounce of Prevention

Here are the most effective ways to avoid STDs.

Put yourself to the test. If you're enjoying an active—or even infrequent—sex life with a partner, put your mind at ease and get tested for STDs. Some diseases, like chlamydia, aren't obvious in men, so it won't hurt to make sure you're safe. Without testing, you might suffer long-term consequences, like sterility, or you might infect others. Testing can be done by your doctor or at most health clinics.

Don't go for broke. In the days of sex, drugs and rock 'n' roll, promiscuous sex was a badge of honor in some circles. But today, a record number of partners is nothing to brag about. The more partners you have, the greater your chances of contracting a disease.

Consider the *Sex in America* survey that found people with two to four sex partners had a 3 percent chance of contracting a bacterial disease, such as chlamydia or gonorrhea. Add one more partner, and the chance of infection jumps to 11 percent.

Abstain from disease. Abstaining from sex is the only surefire way to avoid an STD. This doesn't mean you'll lack intimate moments—you'll always have sensual massages and mutual masturbation—but, until you're in a healthy, disease-free, monogamous relationship, any type of sex puts you at risk.

Practice protection. Thanks to modern science, public service announcements and subsidized clinics that dispense free condoms, there's no reason to have unprotected sex. Next to abstinence, religiously practiced protected sex is the best way to prevent disease. Use only latex condoms, preferably those laced with a spermicide, like nonoxynol-9, which has been shown to help kill the AIDS virus in laboratory studies.

Another option is for her to wear a condom. Female condoms are like traditional condoms, only bigger and with two flexible rings around each end. The female condom lines the inside of a woman's vagina, which protects you both from swapping bodily fluids. It's made of polyurethane, which is 40 percent stronger than latex and appears to be better at preventing STD transmission when used properly.

Watch your mouth. Oral sex can be just as dangerous as intercourse when it comes to catching an STD. You might like being on the receiving end of oral gratification, but you'll get more than you bargained for if she has a cold sore or a syphilitic chancre on her mouth. Also, deep French kissing theoretically may pose a low risk for HIV transmission, especially if there's a little bit of infected blood in your partner's mouth that can be absorbed by the mucous membranes in your mouth.

causing more sores. Subsequent outbreaks usually aren't as bad as the first.

About a third of the people who contract herpes have no reoccurrences to speak of. Another third have only about three a year, and the remaining third have more. Although it can't be cured, herpes can be treated successfully with acyclovir (Zovirax), a drug that reduces the number of occurrences and lessens their severity.

Syphilis

Syphilis is an age-old bacterial infection that strikes some 100,000 people every year. In 1990, syphilis cases reached their highest point in 40 years. Syphilis spreads by direct contact with a syphilitic sore or rash. It's commonly passed in sex but can be caught from kissing, if there's a sore on the inside of the mouth, or from touching, if your fingers stumble across an open sore.

Symptoms progress in three stages: The first stage occurs between 10 and 90 days after infection. It's marked by the appearance of a small, painless sore, called a chancre (pronounced SHANK-er), which pops up where the bacteria entered your body. The second stage features a rash that appears when the chancre fades. In textbook cases, the rash covers the palms of the hands and soles of the feet, but it can appear anywhere. It rarely itches.

Other stage-two symptoms include fever, swollen lymph glands, sore throat, patchy hair loss and weight loss. Stage-three symptoms, which may occur years after infection, include paralysis, blindness, heart problems, nerve damage, insanity and, ultimately, death. Syphilis is treated with injections of penicillin (Pen-Vee K), but catch it early, because the drug won't reverse damage already done.

A man who has sex for a year with an infected woman has less than a 5 percent chance of catching the disease.

Symptoms are hard to miss: After initial exposure, you'll feel tingling and itching at the site of infection. That area soon erupts into a painful ulcerated sore that crusts over and heals in three to four weeks. You might run a fever. When the sore heals, the disease isn't gone—it's just dormant, and it may recur at any time,

The Dream Lover

Making Great Sex a Reality

We live in a society saturated by sex. Turn on the tube in prime time and chances are some handsome young stud with rippling muscles is having his way with a buxom, scantily-clad young lass. And it's not just TV. It's almost everywhere you turn. Billboards. Magazines. Movies. Advertisements—for beer or perfume or whatever, it makes no difference.

We've known for years that sex sells. But the time has come to ask the question: *What* are we being sold? In most cases, a bill of goods.

If you're like most of us, you look at all of those sexy images, shake your head sadly and say to yourself, "That's not me."

Well, join the club. And quit hanging your head. Because being a fabulous lover has nothing whatsoever to do with looking like Fabio. You say your center of gravity has shifted downward in recent years, while your hairline is in full retreat? We've got news for you, buddy. You can have the sex of your dreams. And while you're at it, you can have the sex of her dreams, too.

What does it take to be a dream lover? All of you—body, mind and soul. Hey, we never said it would be easy, but the payoff is beyond your imagination. Sex is full of wonder and mystery and awe. It's also a lot of fun. As the old Irish saying goes, "When sex is bad, it's still pretty good." That's certainly true. So think of the sublime ecstasy that comes from truly great sex. Or better yet, stop

thinking about it and start *experiencing* it.

What does it take to be a dream lover? An enlightened outlook. Skillful technique. And a playful mind.

The Enlightened Lover

Buddhist monks call spiritual enlightenment *satori*, and it's a state that takes quite a bit of effort to achieve. You have to answer questions like, what is the sound of one hand clapping? And you have to sit mute and motionless for hours on end. (In Buddhism this is called meditating. In America it's called watching TV.) Reaching sexual satori—a higher plane of sexuality—is much the same: It takes a lot of time and hard work.

At first, you fumble, fret and stumble your way through the infancy of your sex life. But through a lifetime average of five or so sexual relationships, you learn bits and pieces of the finer points of love and sex. You learn how to (usually) avoid corny opening lines. How to surprise your beloved with tokens of your appreciation. How to sweet talk her when you want your way. And it's the same in bed: As your experience grows, you learn the power of rhythm, timing and teasing.

Then, like most guys, you probably fall into a routine, taking your lover for granted and forgetting about the white-hot sparks that flew when you first met. Avoiding these common pitfalls and concentrating on the simple-but-effective finer points you already know is what being an enlightened lover is all about. There's no secret. Most of it is common sense. Enlightened love is knowing that your brain is your most important sex organ. It's knowing what she means when she doesn't say it and what she wants when she doesn't ask. It's about shedding inhibitions, it's about keeping love alive, it's about making time for love and not falling prey to routine. Enlightened love is, quite simply, knowing what your partner wants and knowing how to give it to her.

The foundation of enlightened love boils down to communication, honesty and openness, and we cover this in great detail in Part Two. Without communication, love is impossible to keep fresh and exciting. Just ask the pioneering sex researchers Masters and Johnson, who, after conducting their famous sex surveys, lamented: "One of the most amazing things to us about sexual behavior is how reticent most people are to talk with their lovers."

The Skillful Lover

Picture a locker room where two men are talking about sex, says sex therapist and author Dr. Barbara Keesling. "But instead of one guy saying, 'Oh, man, I was, like, banging her for hours last night,' pretend he's saying, 'Oh, man, she touched my penis, and it felt so good.'"

Say what?

"It'd be pretty shocking, wouldn't it?" Dr. Keesling says. "That's because it's a socialized phenomena: It's okay for men to talk about sex from a performance level, but not okay from a personal level."

One of the most common mistakes men make is to confuse skill with performance, Dr. Keesling says. They deemphasize their own feelings to uphold some ideal performance-oriented expectation, like being a stoic superstud. In doing so, they create a huge source of angst for themselves. It's then that they're most open to sexual dysfunction, like performance anxiety or psychological-induced impotence. It's also then that they're

Dream Weaver

Would your partner describe you as the man of her dreams? You'll never know unless you ask, says Gayle Delaney, Ph.D., author of *Sexual Dreams: Why We Have Them, What They Mean.* "By paying attention to his partner's dreams, a smart lover can get a clearer idea of how his partner really experiences him in bed."

Here's Dr. Delaney's recipe for a "dream interview":

- Designate a quiet time with no interruptions to talk about your dreams.
- Ask your partner to describe her most sensual, arousing dream experiences.
- Ask simple questions to encourage her to provide very detailed descriptions, but don't impose interpretations.
- Ask questions to help her form a connection between her dream experiences and her sexual life with you.

In the 22 years that Dr. Delaney has been listening to women's dreams as a therapist, she's found that most women dream of a lover who takes his time, enjoys foreplay and expresses his emotions during sex. But the only way to tailor your efforts specifically to your partner is to ask.

Says Dr. Delaney, "A man who studies women's sexual dreams in general, and his partner's in particular, can become the kind of emotionally and physically tuned-in lover most women would kill for."

most likely to be closed to their partner's needs and to miss the important cues that make good love great.

True sexual skillfulness comes in reveling in sex, not worrying about how long you'll last or what you look like. Skillfulness also comes in learning the basic techniques, and never being afraid to practice and improve. Remember the first time you rode a bike without training wheels? You thrilled in knowing you were on the brink of a major life accomplishment. But to succeed you had to go back to basics: balance, eyes forward, hands steady and—voilà!—before you knew it, you were cruising down the sidewalk on two wheels.

"One of the biggest sex complaints I hear stems from the myth that good sex isn't a skill," says sex therapist Dr. Marilyn K. Volker. "A person might know the basics of what to do, but that certainly doesn't qualify him as skillful. Good sex—and good love—is something a couple must work on.

"Sex responses change in a relationship," Dr. Volker adds. "Just because you love your partner, doesn't mean there aren't things you'll need to build on."

In Part Three you'll learn the basics of skillful loving. You'll get a lesson in anatomy—hers and yours. You'll hear from experts on massage and other types of touching. You'll learn the intricacies of foreplay, lasting longer and having multiple orgasms. Positioning. Oral sex. Anal sex. And—last but certainly not least—what to do after the loving.

The Playful Lover

One of the most amazing things about children—besides the fact that they have a seemingly endless supply of energy—is that they're so adept at amusing themselves. Give a child a few seashells and a cardboard box, and you have an afternoon of imaginative aquatic adventures. Give the same thing to an adult and you have tomorrow's trash. Imagination and creativity—in the form of playfulness—are the final ingredients in being a dream lover.

"We definitely come down on the side of the playful lover," say Anne Semans and Cathy Winks, co-owners of Good Vibrations, an adult sex store in San Francisco, and co-authors of *The Good Vibrations Guide to Sex.* "Playfulness is something that keeps love alive. It keeps sex interesting and keeps you from taking things

too seriously so you can enjoy the moment without worrying about anything else."

Of course, you don't want to commit yourself to just one label, Semans and Winks caution. "Just because you're a playful lover doesn't mean you can't be a skillful lover or an enlightened lover," they say.

The elements of a playful lover are limited only by your imagination, but the basic tenet is to embrace your own personal creativity and your individual adventurous spirit. We're not talking about becoming a sexual contortionist or an exhibitionist. We're talking about having the sex of *your* dreams. And *hers*, too.

In Part Four, experts will discuss some variations to spice up your love life and keep things interesting. Your options include experimenting with sex in different locations, using fantasy or sexy talk to enhance lovemaking, exploring the benefits of sex toys, watching skin flicks or engaging in online cybersex. Try one or try them all—it's up to you.

Putting It All Together

Being the perfect dream lover is something none of us will ever likely be—except in our dreams. After all, we are human, and we'll probably never be perfect at anything—especially since we're forced to juggle so many things in our daily lives in addition to our sex lives. But the thousand-mile journey to perfection begins with one step, and simply knowing how to improve your sex and love lives—and working at it in good faith a little every day—is the only way you'll ever have a shot at perfection. And at becoming a dream lover. Besides, even if you never attain perfection, the journey is guaranteed to be a helluva lot of fun.

You may never be mistaken for Brad Pitt or Antonio Banderas. And there's absolutely nothing you can do about that. But you do have direct control over the two factors that matter most to women: communication and consideration.

Part Two

The Enlightened Lover

What It Means to Be a Man

Dealing with Shifting Roles and Expectations

Used to be you wanted to buy a basketball, you went out and bought a basketball. You didn't worry about what your new basketball would look like. There was only one way for a basketball to look. Immutable as some Platonic idea, basketballs were invariably pumpkin orange, agreeably knobby on your palms and smelled as sweet as a box of new sneakers.

Nowadays you go out to buy a basketball, you have to choose from a hundred hues of different size and rubber. In fact, there are now whole new species of basketballs that didn't exist 40 years ago.

Used to be if you were a guy, you pretty much knew what was expected of you: Guys were tough, indifferent to pain, in control. Guys were the breadwinners. They hacked their way through the treacherous jungles of the office or factory while their women stayed home and raised their babies. Guys didn't talk much; they did stuff. And when they did talk, most of their talk was about doing stuff. (All of these clichés, by the way, got to be clichés because a lot of guys *were* these clichés.)

Now you have your hard guys, your sensitive guys, your guys spilling their lusts on Oprah, your guys beating drums in the woods, your nearly naked guys modeling underpants in *The New York Times Sunday Magazine*: whole new species of guys that didn't exist 40 years ago.

This is, of course, pure nostalgia. There never was any golden age of guydom when men were men and women were women and basketballs were basketballs.

From the first day the first guy started trying to figure out how to deal with his ex-rib, being a man has been a confusing business. If you study history (and prehistory), you'll see that every time we men got comfortable with a certain definition of manhood, various social trends and upheavals forced us to redefine ourselves, says social historian Peter N. Stearns, Ph.D., dean of the College of Humanities and Social Sciences at Carnegie Mellon University in Pittsburgh and author of *Be a Man! Males in Modern Society*.

Decoding the Mixed Signals

But perhaps no time has been more confusing than now, when all the roles and prerogatives of our sex seem to be shifting.

"One of the complexities of the last decade," says Dr. Stearns, "has been the really mixed signals we're getting about sexuality." While we are bombarded daily with messages in movies and television that say we should be rutting sex machines, we also are warned that rutting sex machines are likely to end up rotting in jail or the hospital.

"We're in the business now of telling men to be sexy. We still think that part of the  definition of manhood is sexual prowess and sexual performance," Dr. Stearns says. "But we're also very, very busy telling them not to be sexy in inappropriate places, to be very careful about the attitudes of partners as well as the possibility of disease."

There are whole new categories of behavior—date rape and sexual harassment, for example—that simply didn't "exist" before because our culture had not defined them.

In addition to that, the male role of sole provider has been diminished, making it harder for a man to define himself by his work (though this still remains the main way most of us define ourselves). And there are new pressures on men to be more involved in the business of maintaining a household and raising a family.

Changing Roles

But the real difficulty is in the new emotional agenda our society has outlined for us, says Samuel Osherson, Ph.D., a practicing psychotherapist and research psychologist at the Harvard University Health Services and the author of *Wrestling with Love: How Men Struggle with Intimacy.*

"It isn't as if we've shifted toward a kind of changed expectation; it's rather that we've added on a new set of expectations and retained the old ones," Dr. Osherson says. "So I think that many men feel pressured to do both."

In addition to being strong and in control, we are now expected to be sensitive, gentle and responsive to our lover's (and our own) emotions. No surprise, then, that a lot of us are feeling a bit schizophrenic.

"There is a greater expectation in relationships that men will be more emotionally responsive and available," Dr. Osherson says. "There is pressure on men both to live up traditionally and to be emotionally available and responsive. And it's a difficult agenda for men to live up to both sides of that."

Particularly in the bedroom.

"Men have a lot of trouble in letting go and just being there and not trying to be the

The Real Thing? Not Hardly

Remember the Diet Coke ad where a horde of attractive female office workers ran to the window to stare at the same shirtless construction worker at the same time every morning?

It bought Lucky Vanos his 15 minutes of fame but left some guys wondering, "Is that what women really want in a man?"

Not really, says Dr. Bonnie Jacobson, author of *Love Triangles* and *If Only You Would Listen.* "That Coke commercial about the construction worker and his female admirers is mostly a male fantasy," she says. "Men are projecting being adored by a group of women, then they get nervous about not being 'hot' enough to be adored. It's part of an inbred hierarchical structure where the whole point is to one-up the next guy."

Men have a tendency to project their own expectations onto women, Dr. Jacobson says. It's as if at some level we say to ourselves, "If I were a woman, I'd go for the guy who has abs like a cobblestone street."

Then we actually start believing that, assuming that what we think we'd want if we were women is what women actually want. Next thing we do is say to ourselves, "Omigosh, if that's what women want, where does that leave *me*?"

Right where you started, Dr. Jacobson says. Looking for the real thing—not some projected male fantasy.

phallic, potent male all the time. So sexuality often focuses just on intercourse, and men don't understand the softer parts of sexuality that really build a base for a good sexual relationship," Dr. Osherson says.

Hunk-o-rama

At the same time that there is a deepening of the definition of manhood, beefcake has become almost as common as cheesecake in the world of advertising, and men are getting more than a taste of something women have known for generations: what it's like to be viewed as a sex object.

The pressure of this increased attention on the male body has had some powerful effects on the average man's self-view, says Bonnie Maslin, Ph.D., author of *The Angry Marriage*.

Breathes there a man who feels his abs are flat enough? Not likely. Then again, says Dr. Maslin, that may not be all bad. "The new focus on men as sex objects has given women permission to look at men sexually," she says. "This greater willingness to admire the male body has helped both men and women to loosen up, to be more playful about sex."

Perhaps.

But it also tells men that anyone over 25 is over the hill.

This male image is "very youth-oriented," says certified social worker Reuven Closter, an analyst also licensed as a marriage, family and child counselor in New York City. "Older men are starting to feel invisible. Something I hear from a lot of men over 40—sometimes over 30—is, 'How relevant am I?' "

Under Pressure

How this will all shake down in the long run is a matter of debate. "Both men and women are moving to a more experimental, egalitarian state," says Bonnie Jacobson, Ph.D., the author of *Love Triangles* and *If Only You Would Listen*. "The twentysomething generation is already there. I see more and more young men and women playing with gender roles, ex-

Why Can't a Woman Be More Like a Man?

With all the talk about how men should change their ways, you may feel under the gun these days.

Why, you well may ask, don't *women* have to change?

You'll be happy to know that some of the people who make it their business to study cultural trends believe the tide may be turning.

Social historian Dr. Peter N. Stearns of Carnegie Mellon University says he thinks the "feminization" of men is meeting some cultural "kickback." Consider, he says, "the assumption that since men and women have different reactions to emotion, men should change. That's not necessarily true. Maybe women should change. Or maybe the

perimenting much more freely with sexual assumptions and expectations."

Dr. Stearns disagrees that the changes are as sweeping as all that. "Men continue to be much less willing to talk about emotional issues than women are," he says. "And I think that informally continues to build into the definition of what it is to be an appropriate male."

However it turns out, manhood will continue to be, as Dr. Stearns has put it, "a solemn thing."

So how do you deal with it?

Do a reality check. "It's difficult in any relationship for the partner to not live up to the kind of idealized goals and fantasies of the other partner, and I think women have certain yearnings and fantasies about what men will be like. Just putting it crudely, women yearn for a strong male," Dr. Osherson says. "I think it's important to understand that there's also some disappointment as well as gain in seeing the other partner for who they are."

"Men need to relax more," says Dr.

two genders should simply admit that this is a congenital area of difficulty and both parties need to be alert to the different styles of the other without pretending that they're going to reach some sort of perfect harmony."

For example, says Nijole V. Benokraitis, Ph.D., a sociologist at the University of Baltimore who studies the differences between men and women, "When a man changes the oil in a woman's car or fixes something or works hard to make sure that the bills are being paid, that's to him a show of affection, love and understanding.

"I would like to see women try a little harder to understand what men think they are communicating when they change our oil," says Dr. Benokraitis.

Jacobson. "My best advice is, when the pressures start to interfere with sex, stay out of the bedroom for a while. Talk to each other. Learn to listen to each other. What you fear your partner is thinking may be very far from the truth. Your partner probably isn't requiring you to be as perfect as you think you have to be."

Expand your horizons. Dr. Maslin says men need to worry less about what's expected of them and avail themselves more of the many options they are now free to pursue. "Chill out and enjoy yourself," she counsels. "Think about the opportunities that being a man offers you today, not the burdens.

"You can be interested in activities now that you weren't allowed to explore earlier. A boy can now cook, for example; home ec isn't the purely female province it used to be. Enjoy the greater latitude, the opportunity to do more things without social stigma. Men no longer have to be brutes conquering the world."

Talk with women. The strong, silent model of manhood is no longer an option, says clinical psychologist Bernie Zilbergeld, Ph.D., author of *The New Male Sexuality*.

"Being silent doesn't work. The guy doesn't get what he wants," says Dr. Zilbergeld. "Women don't like silent men. They've made that abundantly clear. In fact, they can't stand them. And women are basically not willing to put up with guys like that."

Closter adds, "Now that women are more insistent that men talk, men should try to increase their willingness to talk. Be more cooperative. You don't have to pull the whole cart yourself anymore."

Talk with men. "It's much more permissible now for men to look for a men's group where they can discuss these issues," Dr. Osherson says. "These are very hard things to try to solve on your own. Of course, the traditional male strategy is to get isolated and try to fix things, but you really can't. It's often very helpful to talk to a men's group, attend a weekend workshop or even speak to a counselor. There are a lot of counselors now who specialize in sexuality and sexual issues."

Be brave. If there is one trait of manhood that goes back to the caves, it is courage. Our forebears needed it then to face the beast as it charged them. We need it now to face the boss as she charges us. And while we may not need raw physical courage as much or as often as our forebears did, we still need intellectual and emotional courage: the strength of character to break free of traditional definitions of gender roles.

What then does "manliness" mean today?

Dr. Jacobson offers this definition: "Manliness means having the courage to go where you're afraid to go."

In other words, if you have the courage to redefine yourself, you're a twenty-first century man.

What Women Want

The Link between Love and Sex

What do women want?

There are a million bad punchlines to that question, but the plain truth is almost ridiculously simple: Women want foreplay.

We're not talking neck-nibbles and nipple-twists here. We're talking you getting up from the dinner table and saying, "Sit tight, honey, and tell me more about your day while I take care of these pesky dishes."

We're talking when she got up the day before, you said, "I love the way you look so sleepy-eyed and sultry in the morning."

We're talking how for no particular reason you stopped off on your way home from work last week and picked up a pint of pistachio, her favorite ice cream.

You see, the great secret of womankind is this: *Everything* is foreplay.

That's because women are not only wired (and plumbed) a lot differently than men, but they also come with different software. For men, sex is not a lot more complex than Pong. For women, it's as labyrinthine as Myst, and what you do when you're *out* of the bedroom can have a lot to do with what you're allowed to do when you're in it.

"It may be putting it crudely," says the University of Baltimore's Dr. Nijole V. Benokraitis, a sociologist who studies the differences between men and women and who wrote the textbook *Marriages and Families: Changes, Choices and Constraints*. "But one of the major differences in

everything that I've seen in all of the scholarly research is that men's orgasms are between their legs and women's are between their ears.

"If you could get that point across, and if men, first of all, believed it, and second, remembered it for longer than three seconds, the relationships between men and women would be much less warlike."

What She Needs

Right about now, you may be saying to yourself, "What on Earth does all *that* mean?"

Another way of putting it is this: For men, sex isn't necessarily connected to anything. It doesn't take a 12-course meal with wine and candlelight to make Mr. Happy happy; sometimes all he needs is a snack at halftime.

For women, on the other hand, sex is very much woven into the web of your relationship. And the first thing that women want is a relationship to weave it into.

"Sex opens a man's heart, whereas a woman's heart needs to be opened and then she can enjoy sex," says therapist John Gray, Ph.D., the author of the best-selling *Men Are from Mars, Women Are from Venus* and *Mars and Venus in the Bedroom: A Guide to Lasting Romance and Passion*.

And what opens a woman's heart is communication. "Communication leads a woman to her feelings, and from her feelings she can feel love and be loving and then she wants sex," says Dr. Gray.

Yes, we're talking the L-word here. Women need to feel loved. This is not to say women aren't capable of pure, slavering lust with a virtual stranger (otherwise there would be no one-night stands). But in general they're more likely to feel that lust when they feel close to the object of that lust: that is, you.

A woman needs to feel, says Dr. Benokraitis, "that she's not taken for granted, that she's important, that there is affection, that she's not just sort of a great big thing with a vagina."

This link between the ability to connect emotionally and to get rowdy has been documented by several studies conducted by Barbara L. Andersen, Ph.D., professor of psychology at Ohio State University in Columbus.

"A big dose of what constitutes women's view of their sexuality is this self-view that they are romantic, loving persons as well as sexually arousable people," she says. "A woman who has a positive view of herself as a sexual person has both of those pieces of herself."

So it's not surprising that a woman needs to feel good about the rest of her relationship with you before she's going to feel like having sex with you. She needs to feel that the two of you are connected emotionally before she's going to want to connect with you physically.

The tighter she feels with you emotionally, the looser she's going to be in the bedroom. And the looser she is in the bedroom, the more fun both of you are going to have. Or as marriage and family therapist Patricia Love, Ed.D., author of the book *Hot Monogamy*, puts it: "Intimacy begets sexuality."

The Art of Scoring

One of the hardest things for men to understand is the calculus of commitment, says Dr. John Gray, author of *Men Are from Mars, Women Are from Venus* and *Mars and Venus in the Bedroom: A Guide to Lasting Romance and Passion*.

This is because women keep score differently than men.

"Men think, 'Okay, if I take her on a big vacation, that's a thousand points.' Or 'I went out and did the yard. It took me five hours. That should keep her happy for a week, and that's at least worth 300 points.'"

Dr. Gray pauses.

"That's *one* point. Everything you do for a woman scores equally with everything else you do. A woman gives you one point for everything, and men don't realize that."

A man who is savvy to the ways of women's bookkeeping, Dr. Gray says, doesn't go out and buy her two dozen flowers thinking he'll get 24 points. Instead, he buys her 24 flowers one at a time, because that will earn him 24 points.

If all this seems unfair somehow, there are some small consolations.

"Anything you do for a woman, if you do it without her having to ask, you get a bonus point," Dr. Gray says. "And if you offer to do something, even if she doesn't want you to do it, you get a point for offering."

Satisfaction

Consider what researchers at the University of Chicago found when they conducted a survey of sexual practices in the United States: Marriage is more fun.

Those who reported having the most physically pleasing and emotionally satisfying sex were those persons who were married or in long-term relationships with one partner.

While the scope of the study did not include the cause of all this satisfaction, the researchers did speculate that "the longer the partnership is likely to last, and the more commitment one has to that partnership, the greater is the incentive to learn what pleases that partner, what excites, what frustrates, what angers—in short, what works sexually and what does not."

If you sometimes find yourself wailing "I can't get no satisfaction" along with Mick Jagger, here are some tips to help deepen your sexual relationships—satisfaction guaranteed.

Be a romantic athlete.
Women look for and respond better to men who are "not just sexual athletes, but romantic athletes, too," Dr. Andersen says. They want men "who can form attachments and are romantic, loving and warm and are open to emotional expressions of feeling, not just sexual expressions of feeling."

Now the term "romantic athlete" may have you thinking you have to be some kind of Romeo who is constantly showering her with roses, chocolates and puerile poetry. That stuff is okay as far as it goes, but that's not what we mean. We're talking the simple day-to-day business of sharing her life and being her friend.

Get to know her. Well, okay, it's not that simple. In fact, it can be damnably difficult because, in our culture, men aren't trained to tune in to other people the way that women are, Dr. Benokraitis says.

"We really are interested in what makes a man tick," she says. "Why is he sad? What does he really want to do in life? What is his favorite kind of pie? And all kinds of things, because we're very interested. And men, for the most part, are not.

"If you asked my husband what my

What Is Foreplay? (An Annotated Fantasy)

Pay attention to women's fantasies! You can learn a lot from them.

Consider, for example, this (annotated) excerpt from a story by Marilyn Harris Kriegel in *Erotic Interludes: Tales Told by Women*, a collection of erotic fiction edited by Lonnie Barbach, Ph.D., assistant clinical professor of medical psychology at the University of California at San Francisco Medical School.

Read it. Study it. Commit it to memory.

Dear L.,
I have been thinking about foreplay. I have wondered if reading these letters might not be the foreplay for some yet to be discovered joy, the exact, right gesture to open us up to love that might have otherwise remained hidden and unrecognized.
Foreplay.
Our hike to Steep Ravine. The hot day, the arduous walk up the coastal trail and then the descent into the cool lushness of the creek, the ferns, the redwoods. Walking slowly for hours we become one in spirit. . . .[1] *It is our bodies' longing for the same closeness as our souls that catapults us into each other's arms at the end of the day, even when our legs ache for rest.*
Foreplay.
Breaking for lunch. Hearing about your morning's work.[2] *Sharing our doubts and fears as we indulge ourselves in your latest pasta creation. . . .*[3] *Laughing about how miraculous it is that we are able to live and do the work that turns us on. Turns us on. Our work becoming a source for our lovemaking.*
Foreplay.

favorite color is, he'd look at you blankly. If you asked him any number of questions, he wouldn't know. But if you asked me similar

Sitting down to make the schedule for the week. The grocery list, Little League games, who will cook and who will clean and who will get the mail and take the car in to be fixed. **4** *And oh, yes, I'll do the laundry, and in the middle of the mundane events of our life, folding your yellowed T-shirts and pairing up your socks, my juices flow, my heart beats more rapidly and I know we are likely to make love again soon.*

Foreplay.

1 Okay, class, notice how something as simple as walking together (and sharing the experience of a walk alone in the woods) can be foreplay? It is implicit that, in those hours alone, L. established a real feeling of connectedness with the writer through words and touch. So lesson number one is that just spending time really being with your lover is foreplay.

2 It doesn't matter that what L. is sharing with her here are the mundane details of his work; the point is that L. is sharing, and that, too, is foreplay.

3 Even more important, each of them shares their feelings—doubts and fears—with one another. This means L. is a good listener as well as talker, which, to put it another way, means he's very good at foreplay.

4 Clearly, L. also shares the responsibilities of cooking, cleaning, errands and child care, which is another kind of . . . what?

Yes, you in the back of the room there.

That's right.

Foreplay!

In other words, a romantic act can be as small a thing as remembering her shoe size.

Do the dishes. Here's where we get to some concrete answers to the question: What do women want?

In one survey, 61 percent of women said they would rather see a man wash dishes than see him dance naked.

And the guy who does the dishes is a heck of a lot more likely to enjoy a night of passion than the guy who comes home and sits on his duff.

"Women have said to me, 'If I'm tired because of taking care of the kids, and he comes home and asks what's for dinner and then watches TV while I run around doing things, there's no way in the world. Either my sex is going to be mechanical, or there will be none,' " says Dr. Benokraitis.

Dr. Gray concurs. In *Mars and Venus in the Bedroom*, he reports that "doing dishes is great foreplay," because when a man does the dishes it makes his wife feel loved, and when she feels loved, "naturally, she begins to feel turned on."

Come clean. You can show her you love her by a thousand random acts of caring. Do the laundry. Bathe the kids. Clean the toilet. Mop the floor. Shop for groceries. Take out the trash. These are all "events" for the romantic athlete.

Is one of the kids yelling for Mom in the middle of the night? You get up instead.

Did the cat throw up on the living-room rug? Don't stand there and announce it. Clean it up.

According to Dr. Gray, "Romance is anything that helps her to feel that she is not alone and that someone is there for her. Any little thing he can directly do for her says

questions about my husband, I could probably not only tell you but tell you how those things have changed over the years," she adds.

that he cares and creates romance."

"Once a woman feels heard and seen, whatever a man does is like foreplay," Dr. Gray adds. "It just builds. She begins to think, 'Oh, he knows what I'm going through, and now he's helping. He's responding to my needs.'"

Just do it. Now, there's an art to the doing of these sorts of things. First of all, you do them graciously and without being asked.

Second, if you make a big production out of doing them—"Yo! Look at me! I'm doing the dishes!"—or if you do them grudgingly—"Oh, all right, I'll do the damn dishes."—it defeats the whole purpose. Which is, you will recall, to show her how much you love and care for her.

And third, you don't do them in the expectation of some sexual quid pro quo. "That," says Dr. Gray, "would not be romance. That would be a business deal."

"And if you do it without asking," Dr. Gray adds, "you get double bonus points for that."

Words of Love

If romantic athletics was an Olympic event, Zdeněk Fibich would be a gold medal winner and world record holder.

Who?

Fibich was a Czechoslovakian composer who lived during the last half of the nineteenth century, at the height of the Romantic movement. When he fell madly in love with Anezka Schulzová, one of his piano students, Fibich wrote more than 376 piano pieces to her, each one a musical portrait of an emotion Anezka made him feel, a memory they shared or some particularly pleasing aspect of her anatomy.

He wrote, for example, a series of compositions describing Anezka wearing different

Are You a Porcupine?

When men think of a huddle, odds are they picture beefy guys in pads and cleats circling around to plot the next gridiron play.

The famous German philosopher Arthur Schopenhauer conjured a few different images. Instead of Bears or Lions, he envisioned . . . porcupines.

We are like porcupines, he said, who are trying to survive a cold winter by huddling together for warmth. But of course each time we huddle we prick each other with our quills.

Deborah Tannen, Ph.D., University Professor of linguistics at Georgetown University in Washington, D.C., says that's the way it is with men and women. We waver between the need to be intimate with one another and the need to be independent.

clothes. He wrote a piece about Anezka asleep. He wrote pieces describing her hair, her tongue, her hands, seven pieces portraying her breasts, and even one about the nail on her little finger.

Perhaps it goes without saying, Fibich's passion was returned. There's a lesson here, guys.

Tell her she's beautiful. What? You say you're no composer? You don't have to be. You just have to show that same kind of attention to detail.

She needs to hear that she's attractive, that you find her beautiful, that the turn of her calf makes you tingle, that you sometimes stop in the middle of your workday to daydream about the nape of her neck.

Tell her again. She needs to hear this from you on a regular basis, not just when you're first courting her or trying to get her into the sack.

Why do women need to hear this stuff?

Unfortunately, Dr. Tannen says, women tend to need more intimacy and men more independence.

Which means men often run from their beloved's embrace.

Of course, you need your space. Both of you do. This isn't a formula for self-suffocation.

But if you can resist that urge to run out and adjust your carburetor, and instead sit down and just talk with her—about matters of consequence or nothing at all—you may be surprised at how much easier spending time together gets with just a little practice. And you may also be surprised by new levels of passion in the bedroom.

Because listening, more than anything else, is foreplay.

Consider the images that the media bombards them with day in and day out.

"The images of women are typically around 19, that is, young. They're always gorgeous, according to White notions of what gorgeous is, and they're always very, very slim and sexy. And now with the craze on having big breasts, they also have a lot of cleavage," Dr. Benokraitis says.

From their first Barbie on, little girls are given the message that this is the way they're supposed to look. And, of course, few women do.

"Most of the women that are in those ads don't look like that in real life," Dr. Benokraitis says. "Most women don't even come close. So women from the time they're very little feel very inadequate. They feel very insecure."

And again. That's why you can make a mighty difference in your relationship if you take the time to tell her how much she sends you.

"If men realized the enormous pressure that women feel about not being this 19-year-old image on the cover of *Vogue* or *Seventeen*, they could do all kinds of things," says Dr. Benokraitis. "Even just saying, 'You know, I'm really glad I know you. I think you're great. I forget to tell you how important you are to me.' If men complimented women without emphasizing the physical part of it, that would endear them to women to no end. I guarantee it."

Pay Attention!

Just about everybody has had the experience of sitting next to a "one-way" couple in a restaurant. They might be out on a first date; they might be wearily married. But the one thing they most certainly are is a one-way street conversationally. And often as not, it's the man who is doing the talking. On and on he drones while his partner chews her arugula.

Men do this sort of thing a lot. Which is a shame, really, given that a woman's most erogenous zone is *your* ear.

She wants you to listen to her. Really listen. It doesn't matter what she's talking about: It could be how she scored a cut-price pair of Gucci pumps at the mall. The important thing is to look her in the eye and give her your full attention as she talks to you.

"Men, there's a billion-dollar industry out there. It's called therapy. And 90 percent of the people who go to therapy are women. And why is that? Because women will *pay* to have somebody listen to what they're feeling," says Dr. Gray. In fact, he says, "what women are looking for in their relationships most of all is a man who will be attentive, who will take the time to listen."

Indeed, you can do all the dishes you want, but if you don't listen to her, says Dr. Gray, you're just wasting your time.

Communication: The Key to Great Sex

Don't Fumble for Words— Talk with Her

On the football field chicanery and deceit are not only allowed, they're acclaimed and admired. Whatever it takes—play action pass, quarterback sneak, double reverse, fake punt, the "fumblerooski"—the object is to get into the end zone and score a touchdown. And the problem with many men, says linguist Suzette Haden Elgin, Ph.D., director of the Ozark Center for Language Studies in Hurtville, Arkansas, and author of *Genderspeak*, is that they view relationships in much the same way. The bedroom is the end zone. And scoring a touchdown involves . . . well, it's pretty obvious, isn't it?

Women, however, tend to abide by the lessons of the classroom, not the gridiron, says Dr. Elgin. In school you learn that teamwork on tests is cheating. If you do exactly as you're told, you'll get an A. Kindness is encouraged. Truthfulness is rewarded. Loudness and aggressiveness—also known as horsing around—are punished.

"We just don't play by the same rules," Dr. Elgin says. "How often has a woman accused her man of lying when he has simply omitted all the facts?" For example, since she didn't ask, he didn't feel the need to tell her he was out with another woman the night before. On the football field it's okay to pretend you don't have the ball when you do or that you do when you don't. That's how the game is played, men say. In the schoolroom a false statement is a lie. And conveniently leaving out important facts is still a lie.

Bridging the Gap

So the problem in relationships is the same faced by some major universities: how to get football players into the classroom. Dr. Elgin says it can be done.

"To couples who say every time they try to talk it turns into a fight, I suggest they stop in the middle of conversations when the other person is using words they don't understand and ask, 'What do you mean by that?' "

Dr. Elgin says men must understand that, for women, "talking is more important than sex. Men who use talk as a move to get a woman in bed will be horrified when it turns out she is interested in conversation as an end in itself. Men think women should recognize it as only another play that gets them closer to the end zone. But for women life is not a succession of plays. It's all connected. They take it all seriously."

And men should, too. Talking with your partner and communicating your feelings is the most stimulating foreplay a man can perform on a woman. Great sex will be a mere residual benefit compared to the great sense of intimacy you'll feel.

To that end, the following advice from some of the country's leading relationship experts should help you quit fumbling for the right thing to say.

Be honest. "Honesty can be an incredible aphrodisiac," says Sheila Rogovin, Ph.D., a couples psychotherapist based in Washington, D.C. She tells the story of one man who hid from his wife the fact that he had lost his job. Eventually, their sex life deteriorated into abstinence. When he finally confessed, the sex heated up again.

"I see much of male armor as a facade behind which beats a heart as vulnerable as any woman's," says Dr. Rogovin. "The men I see professionally feel they have to be 'male' in various stereotypical ways. The cost of keeping up that strong, silent, competent face can be terrible."

If confiding in your mate is difficult, she suggests talking to a friend, relative or professional therapist. "Communicating with some neutral person can sometimes vent steam and ease the pressure," she notes. "Most of us have more people resources than we realize. Use them."

Say what you mean. Consider this a corollary to the above. "Too often a man will say, 'I love you' or 'You're the most beautiful woman in the world' when he means, 'Let's go to bed,'" says Sonya Friedman, Ph.D., author of *Secret Loves* and *On a Clear Day You Can See Yourself.* "Don't say, 'There's no one I'd rather be with for the rest of my life' when you mean, 'There's no one I'd rather be with for the rest of the evening.' Women can take the truth."

Write it down. If you can't say it, put it in writing—on a piece of paper, on a chalkboard or even on e-mail, says James W. Pennebaker, Ph.D., professor and chairman of psychology at Southern Methodist University in Dallas. "Writing gives men in particular a less threatening medium of communication that allows them to say things that may be hard to say out loud," he says.

Women appreciate your taking pen to paper—or, in these modern times, keyboard to computer—because it shows that you've taken

Get It Out in the Open

One of the reasons it's so tough to be a man today is that from day one we get hammered with all sorts of "reasons" to be ashamed of ourselves, says psychotherapist Dr. Samuel Osherson, author of *Wrestling with Love: How Men Struggle with Intimacy.*

"Many men feel a lot of shame about performance and how well they're doing, and they often feel like they're not living up sexually," says Dr. Osherson. Problems can start at an early age, with boys comparing penis size in the locker room, and go through "feeling like you're not as tough as the other guys on the basketball team if you lost your virginity later," he says.

Our typical male reaction to these perfectly normal experiences is to try to cover them up and hide them away. But because so much of our sexual education is wrapped up in these experiences that leave us feeling insecure or shy, and because those feelings "carry over now into your relationship, it's important for couples to find some way to talk about the ways in which they don't feel sure about themselves," Dr. Osherson says. "It can often be helpful just to talk about some of that."

some time to think out your feelings and made the effort to express them. Don't worry about grammar or syntax. And don't bother stealing ten-dollar words from your thesaurus. That won't impress her. It's not a Ph.D. thesis you're writing. It's a message from the heart; you're allowed poetic license.

Avoid a hostile takeover. Passive aggressiveness is a clinical term for people who have indirect and inappropriate ways of expressing hostility, says Scott Wetzler, Ph.D., chief of the division of psychology at Albert Einstein College of Medicine in New York City and author of *Living with the Passive-Aggressive Man.* That hostility is a thin veil concealing insecurity and low self-confidence. "Passive-aggressive people have a fear of dependency, and since sex makes us dependent, it's a problem area," he says. Passive-aggressive men will avoid showing their vulnerability by having many sex partners or none at all. Or once in bed with a woman they will get so inhibited, they'll have sexual dysfunctions such as premature ejaculation or impotence.

The first step in dealing with this tendency is to recognize the behavior and where it comes from, he says. The next is to confront it. "Get more comfortable with your dependency and vulnerability in relationships," says Dr. Wetzler. "Pursue exactly what you fear. Recognize your dissatisfaction with your current situation and the potential gratification of success. Don't walk out on a verbal confrontation with a woman. Engage in the competition. What's wrong with getting into a fray? Do battle. Get into it with her. Face up to your fears. Open your heart." That doesn't reflect a weakness. It reflects a strength.

Be an active listener. That's a nice way of saying, "Shut up and let the other person talk."

Good talking frequently means good listening. "That's sexy to women," says anthropologist Helen Fisher, Ph.D, research associate at Rutgers University in New Brunswick, New Jersey, and author of *Anatomy of Love.* Look in her eyes. Encourage her to talk by using short verbal cues that tell her you want to hear more: "Really?" "Yes?" "Uh-huh." And, most important, don't interrupt. Sit on your hands. Bite your tongue. Count to a hundred. Do whatever it takes, but let her talk. Ask questions and actually wait for her to respond. Nothing turns off a woman in conversation or in bed more than being cut off.

Make small talk. Talks don't have to

Hey! Listen Up!

Take an informal poll of your women friends, and you will find that a lot of them agree with Harriet Schechter, co-author of *More Time for Sex: The Organizing Guide for Busy Couples*, when she says, "A man who listens is the sexiest man."

Seems simple enough, right?

But it isn't. Witness the fact that one of the more commonly heard complaints by therapists is, "He doesn't listen to me."

So here's an experiment, suggested by Dr. Patricia Love, author of the book *Hot Monogamy*, that you and your mate might want to try. Tape your next conversation. Just turn on a tape recorder and forget it's there. Just don't be

be big and meaningful all the time, suggests Dr. Lonnie Barbach of the University of California at San Francisco Medical School and author of *The Erotic Edge: Erotica for Couples* and *For Each Other: Sharing Sexual Intimacy.* She notes, "Even at the most mundane times—making pasta, for example—there should be a discourse that's going on that has both parties feeling respected, feeling good about each other, feeling important to each other, feeling connected. That's what leads to great love-making later on." Studies show that couples who spend 20 minutes a day in face-to-face communication stay together longer than those who don't, she says.

Talk with your body. Women are better at reading body and facial language than men, according to Tomi-Ann Roberts, Ph.D., assistant professor of psychology at Colorado College in Colorado Springs.

Dr. Elgin agrees. "Men are not aware that their body language will betray them," she says. It's been estimated that 65 percent of all the information we transmit in English is through our tempted to use the tape in a debate, she cautions.

When you play it back, you may be surprised (and embarrassed) at the number of times you hear yourself interrupting her in midsentence or changing the subject.

If taping seems a little . . . uh . . . intrusive, Dr. Love suggests a couple of questions you might ask your partner instead. "Ask her, 'Do you feel heard by me?' and also at the end of a conversation, question, 'Did it feel like I was listening?' "

If she says no, don't get defensive.

What's important is not whether you thought you were listening, it's whether she thought you were listening to her.

body language. So when you're in conversation with a woman, respond with an open face and a relaxed demeanor. Crossed arms and legs say, "Do not enter." Mirror her body language; it's a subtle way of "keeping in time with each other's bodybeat," says Dr. Fisher. "You can signal that you are relaxed and comfortable with yourself—appealing attributes that say you are available for a relationship—in the way you walk and carry your torso. That's sexy, too."

Voice your true feelings. One of the most reliable ways to detect what a person is really trying to tell you is from the inflection in her voice. "When a person is agitated, the pitch will go up," says Dr. Elgin. Or it could indicate an intention to deceive.

Men make the mistake of trying to hide their true feelings by training their voices. "That's wrong," says Dr. Elgin. "That's acting. And more likely than not, you'll get caught because you have so little control over your voice." Her advice: Say true things. Don't say, "I'll give you a call next week" when you have no intention of calling. Just say, "I had a nice time"—if it's true.

Sex Talk

Now that you know talk is not cheap when it comes to the art of seduction, you're ready for the advanced training. The secret is timing. Knowing what to say—and when—can make or break an evening with a woman. The object: not to put your foot in your mouth. The reward: emotional and sexual satisfaction for both parties. Here are some tips from Dr. Elgin.

Be consistent. The man who is hoping to spend Saturday night with a woman should communicate well with her Monday through Friday. "If you say hurtful things during the week, she'll remember them come Saturday," says Dr. Elgin. "She will take them into the bedroom with her—if indeed she takes you with her."

Remember, to women it's not a play-by-play situation. Relationships are part of a continuum; they don't happen in a vacuum. Also, don't start a deep and meaningful conversation just before you plan to get into bed with a woman. She'll want to continue talking. That's a good thing, but be ready to shift your priorities. One good evening of conversation could turn into a lifetime of great sex.

Tune out when you're turned on. Women should take with a grain of salt anything a man utters as he nears orgasm, Dr. Elgin says. "Talk at that moment is irrelevant," she says. A man trying to think of clever things to say or to monitor his impetuous verbal outbursts will probably not be concentrating on the important matter at hand. By the way, a woman should be given the same slack during the sex act.

Be real. Hold her close, look her in the eyes and earnestly say, "Thank you, that was wonderful." But only if you mean it. Don't forget: If it's not genuine, your body will betray you. And if it truly was wonderful, you won't need us anymore. The right words will come naturally after that.

Turn-Ons and Turn-Offs

Tune In to What She Likes

At a well-wined dinner party not too long ago, the conversation turned—as it will at well-wined dinner parties—to sex.

In this particular instance it turned to the things men do that turn women off. At the most raucous point in this mostly raucous discussion, a woman asked, "Have *you* ever had sex with a man with a beer belly?"

No, we conceded, we couldn't say we had.

But the point was well-taken: Certainly one of the biggest turn-offs for women is a man who doesn't maintain the property. This extends beyond mowing the lawn on Sundays. It includes such matters as dress, personal hygiene and general housebreaking—like not hanging your jockstrap from the shower knob.

Most guys, of course, have at least some animal magnetism. That's how they got into a relationship in the first place. But the fact remains that your sexiest qualities—the ability to listen, a steely gaze, a gentle touch in bed—count for little if you combine the manners of Archie Bunker with the physique of the Michelin tire man.

Animal House

In a bit we'll turn our attention to what really turns women on. But first we'll look at a few of their turn-offs—those mindless little things we do every day that absolutely, positively stop them cold.

If your idea of the good

life is shaving every third day and changing clothes once a week, you're almost certainly spending a lot of time alone.

"Hygiene," says Dr. Lonnie Barbach of the University of California at San Francisco Medical School. "I can't tell you how often that comes up." As far as women are concerned, the clean man is the erotic man, she says. "So shower, brush your teeth and shave."

Harriet Schechter, co-author of *More Time for Sex: The Organizing Guide for Busy Couples*, says it's not always the big things that turn women off, like making rutting noises when you climb into bed. It's often the little things, stuff you're not even aware of.

Like using up all the toilet paper and not replacing it.

Like leaving globs of toothpaste in the sink after you brush.

Like lounging around the house in a ten-year-old T-shirt with Swiss cheese ventilation.

It all comes to manners and consideration. Do things you know she'll appreciate will get you points later on; ignoring the finer points of civilized living means you'll spend a lot of nights sleeping alone.

While you're at it, "wear sexier things when you're at home together," Schechter says. Sexier just means nicer. Hey, you dress up to impress complete strangers. Why not for your loved one?

How to Turn Her On

But enough about turn-offs. We (and you) could write a whole book about those without giving it too much thought. The more difficult question is, how do you turn her on?

Talk to her. Really listen. Dr. Barbach has spent a lot of years listening to women and men talk about what turns them on. She says the number one turn-on for women—no surprise here—is a man who will listen to her and connect with her.

"It's the relationship," says Dr. Barbach. "The feeling that you're cared about, that you exist, that it's not just your body that they're interested in. Listening, sharing."

Dr. Barbach often advises couples to spend time just lying in bed and talking before they get into anything physical. Cuddling and sharing stories will add warmth to any encounter—and turn up the heat later on.

Touch her. Women even more than men love to be touched. No, that doesn't mean touching her *there*. "It's touching of the entire body," Dr. Barbach says. "Kissing and all of that before going to the crotch. It's slowing down the initial physical lovemaking before getting very specifically genital."

Do what she likes. Of course, the best way to find out what turns your partner on is to ask her—and then do it.

"One of the major complaints that I get from women is, 'He asks me and I tell him, but he never does it. So why bother?' Or, 'He does it for two seconds, then moves on to something else.'"

Do something special. Don't just turn out the light, climb into bed, pull the covers over you and roll over on your partner. Women appreciate a man who takes the time to set the mood, who does something to give them a romantic feeling. This can be done with "candlelight, flowers, perfume, cologne on the man or something that makes this moment seem just a little bit special," Dr. Barbach says.

Wrap it up. Speaking of flowers, it's worth noting—when it comes to gifts—how big a thing a little thing can be.

"You can take a little nothing and wrap it

How to Be an Unforgettable Lover

You say you want to be the kind of lover that a woman never forgets? You want her to talk about you, tell her friends about you, maybe even scrawl your name on restroom walls?

Well, read on. Here's a list of tips culled from the files of the country's best-known sex experts.

- When she tries to talk to you, ignore her, make fun of what she says or, better yet, change the subject to something that interests you. Hey! How about those Reds?
- Let her do all the work around the house. After all, you bring home the bacon, right?
- Never praise her, compliment her or tell her you love her.
- Touch her only when you want to have sex.
- If you're feeling horny, just grab at her breasts or crotch and say, "Let's do it, baby!"
- If she says she doesn't feel like it, either sulk or nag her until she gives in.
- When she does, get yourself inside her as fast as you can and pound away until you reach orgasm.
- Ask her if she came. If she says she didn't, act hurt. Tell her that other women you've been with said you were the best.
- Roll over and go to sleep.

Follow these simple rules, and we guarantee you'll be the one man she never forgets. Or forgives.

very nicely, which makes it very special, or you can give them this really beautiful pin and just put it in their hand," Dr. Barbach says. "It doesn't have the same effect.

"There's something about the specialness of the presentation," she adds. "It's not only that you went and got her this thing that she'll really love but also the unwrapping of it: 'Here, I've made it beautiful for you.'"

Pleasure: Ladies First

'Tis Better to Give Than to Receive

"He had now fixed, nailed, this tender creature with his home-driven wedge . . . she felt the melting symptoms from him, in the nick of which, gluing more ardently than ever his lips to hers, with eyes lifted up in a trance, he showed all the signs of that agony of bliss being strong upon him, in which he sent his soul, distilled in liquid sweets, up the body of that charming creature and gave her the finishing titillation: inly thrilled with which . . . she answered it down with all the effusion of spirit and matter she was mistress of, whilst a general soft shudder ran through all her limbs, which she gave a stretch-out of, and lay motionless, breathless, dying with dear delight; and in the height of its expression showing, through the nearly closed lids of her eyes, just the edges of their black, the rest being rolled strongly upwards in her ecstasy."

So when's the last time *you* made a woman's eyes roll up into her head?

Come Together?

If you believed half of what you read in fiction, such as this passage from the Victorian erotic classic, John Cleland's *Fanny Hill,* you might wonder why you, too, can't dispatch women with a few well-chosen thrusts of your mighty "home-driven wedge."

In fiction, in the movie theater and on the television screen, men and women—who often have met mere moments before—come together fast, with their limbs thrashing about

and sweat pouring off their brows. These fictional characters present us with what clinical psychologist Dr. Bernie Zilbergeld calls "the fantasy model of sex."

"It is a model of total unreality of how bodies look and function, how people relate and how they have sex," Dr. Zilbergeld says. And, unfortunately, for lack of better models, many of us "learn" much of what we know about sex from this model. Which, says Dr. Lonnie Barbach of the University of California at San Francisco Medical School, is "like learning to be a doctor by watching *General Hospital* or learning to be a lawyer by watching *Perry Mason.*"

And perhaps the most damaging piece of misinformation contained in the fantasy model of sex, says Dr. Barbach, is that it "dictates that a sexual experience must keep building in intensity until it peaks in the ultimate simultaneous orgasm."

Double Your Pleasure

The idea that simultaneous orgasms are the ultimate in sex is damaging because it puts enormous pressure on women and men to emulate it: women, by trying to accelerate their arousal to the speed of men, and men, by trying to slow their arousal to the speed of women. This, says Dr. John Gray, author of *Men Are from Mars, Women Are from Venus* and *Mars and Venus in the Bedroom: A Guide to Lasting Romance and Passion,* can turn sex into a lot of stress instead of a lot of fun.

When it comes to coming, says Dr. Gray, "there's a concept that bigger is better. Two orgasms at the same time is bigger, and so therefore it's better.

"I remember seeing in a movie, *Siddhartha,* where an Indian boy becomes spiritual, and then he meets this woman and they have sex," he says. "They're having sex and when the orgasms come, simultaneously, they actually get thrown across the room from each other."

Dr. Gray laughs.

"In a sense, that's what happens when you have an orgasm at the same time. Your own orgasm is so intense that you're kind of brought back to yourself as opposed to really sharing it with your partner."

For that and several other reasons, it pays for gentlemen to observe the simple admonition: Ladies first.

To begin with, Dr. Gray says, "the experience is much different if a man is there when she has her orgasm. She gets to experience her orgasm fully. And then you have your orgasm, and she gets to fully experience your orgasm. It's like having two orgasms."

And two for you, too.

Also, for you, instead of that terrible pressure to pace yourself with your partner, there is the wonderful pleasure of making her climax and then coming after.

Dr. Gray says it boils down to basic biology. That is because of the differences in the way men and women are aroused, he says. "The hormone secretions during orgasm are very different for men and women," Dr. Gray says. "In men, the pleasure hormones in the body are released very intensely, which allows you to peak, then have an orgasm. After you have an orgasm, they disappear.

"But when women have an orgasm, the pleasure hormones take a lot longer to rise up. When they get to the peak and she has an orgasm, they stay there, and that's when she can enjoy sex the most, after she's had her orgasm."

Practicing Polarity

When you were a kid, it seems some adult was always harping on you and your squabbling siblings or friends to "take turns." Well, Dr. John Gray, author of *Men Are from Mars, Women Are from Venus*, believes couples should do precisely that when it comes to sexual pleasure.

Dr. Gray recommends that lovers practice what he calls "polarity sex," in which each partner takes turns pleasing the other.

It can begin with her arousing you for a bit, but when you reach the point where you think, "If I keep going, I'm going to have an orgasm," you "put your orgasm on hold, put it on a shelf and focus on giving to the woman for whatever time it takes—15, 20, 30 minutes—to bring her to orgasm."

Then, and only then, you enter her.

"She feels the longing inside for you to fill her up," Dr. Gray says. "That's the time, after orgasm, to gently, slowly penetrate her. It's a time when she can respond pleasurably to your gentle movements in her vagina more powerfully than at any other time."

And when you enter her after she's had an orgasm, you don't have to worry about how long you're going to last. Both of you can give yourselves over fully to the pleasure of intercourse.

Because "to a woman, it doesn't matter how long a man lasts if he first satisfies her," Dr. Gray says.

"Intercourse for a woman before orgasm is much less stimulating than after she's had an orgasm," Dr. Gray says. "After an orgasm the vagina expands, then contracts. Once it's contracted, sex will satisfy her at a much deeper level."

Overcoming Inhibitions

You Can Work It Out

The lights are dim, the music is soft, the mood is set like a Broadway stage. The foreplay is titillating, the sex sublime. And yet . . . something is holding you back—or maybe it's holding her back.

It's the thing.

You know what we're talking about—that thing that makes one of you crazy for sex, that drives one of you wild. Problem is, the thing may be driving a wedge between you because one of you just can't bring yourself to tell the other that the thing he or she likes so much makes you uncomfortable as hell.

Now, the thing could be anything—maybe it's role-playing or phone sex; maybe one of you wants to try something new or something you did with a previous lover, something that involves cucumbers or whipped cream, handcuffs or vibrators, talking dirty or contorting into positions you haven't seen this side of Twister. Whatever it is, you're uncomfortable at the thought of it. Your partner's desire for this variety of sex play washes over you like a tide of passion, and you're standing on the beach, watching the sand erode under you, feeling the panicky sensation of being pulled into something that's way over your head. And if you're not careful, you could be drowned by your own inhibitions.

Relax, take a deep breath, try to tread water with us for a moment. Experts tell us there's nothing unusual about being inhibited when it comes

to certain aspects of sex play.

"Even the most uninhibited person usually draws the line at some point—there's something that they simply won't do," says Carol Cassell, Ph.D., a sex therapist in private practice in Albuquerque, New Mexico, and author of *Tender Bargaining*. And in that sense, inhibitions are good. They're a moral compass: Without them, we'd quickly find ourselves in jail, afflicted with some horrible disease or up to our armpits in a cesspool of depravity.

Breaking Loose

That said, you never, ever see the words "inhibited" or "repressed" on anyone's Top Ten list of desirable qualities in a lover. So if you're concerned about it, maybe you and your lover should work to loosen up some inhibitions, the ones that keep you from exploring and enjoying sex to the fullest. Here's how.

Name your demons. If you want to lose inhibitions, you first have to figure out what they are.

"Talk to yourself, acknowledge your inhibitions, ask yourself, 'What's stopping me?' " says Carol Queen, author of *Exhibitionism for the Shy* and San Francisco–based leader of seminars on sex and eroticism. "From there, you can break down the things you'd like to change, address their small parts and make those small changes first."

Talk it out. Communication is often the first and worst inhibition, especially for men.

"Sex is the most natural thing in the world, but we don't talk about it like it's natural. Sometimes we don't talk about it at all," says William Hartman, Ph.D., co-director of the Center for Marital and Sexual Studies in Long Beach, California. "Talk to your partner. If you feel uncomfortable even talking about what you or she wants out of sex, go ahead and admit it."

Adopt as your personal mantra that old Beatles hit "We Can Work It Out." Once you find you can talk about it, you may find that you've won the battle. Once one inhibition falls, others will soon follow.

Question authority. If you're like most people—that is, brought up in a world where talking or thinking about sex was taboo—chances are you have a little tape loop in your head that runs incessantly anytime a partner suggests something outside of the norm. "No matter what we do, we have to fight the past, when we were told that sex was bad, that we had to wait, keep our flies zipped and our legs crossed," Dr. Cassell says. "It's old programming, and the first step is to recognize it as such and question it."

Don't spring surprises. One chronic challenge with inhibitions in a sexual relationship is that one of you is ready to charge forward and the other isn't, creating all sorts of uncomfortable pressure that's as conducive to sex as sandpaper sheets.

Let's say you happen upon a book or magazine article that contains an exciting new sexual scenario you would absolutely love to try. But it does seem a little, well, kinky. Don't just spring it on your partner and expect her to be as excited as you are. She may be scared to death. "It creates a threatening environment that only reinforces inhibitions," Dr. Cassell says.

To avoid surprises, talk it out with your partner—be very clear about what it is you want to do or try—and don't broach the subject 30 seconds before you jump in the sack either.

Wait until you're both ready. If you're the one feeling inhibited, don't let yourself be intimidated into doing something you don't want to do. "Don't be afraid to put on the brakes. Take things at your own speed," says

---

Turn On the Lights

It's automatic. Before you climb into bed, you turn out the lights. Why not leave them on, if sleep isn't exactly what you have in mind?

Sex with the lights on is one of the most basic inhibitions, often shared by both men and women. "People are worried about how they look. Women especially are concerned that their bodily imperfections are going to be highlighted," says sex therapist Dr. Carol Cassell.

Solution: For starters, don't focus so much on her genitals. Work first with other areas of the body. Kiss her neck, her breasts and gradually work your way down. She can do the same. And if you both have concerns about taste, experiment with flavored massage oils or food, like whipped cream. (Be sure to wash thoroughly after using these items, though. When left on too long, they can irritate sensitive skin.) "In her case, she can use a flavored condom," suggests Arlene Goldman, Ph.D., coordinator for the Jefferson Sexual Function Center in Philadelphia.

Dr. Cassell. "By the same token, be patient with your partner if she's slow to respond to your ideas."

Use your imagination. If your partner is suggesting a variation she might enjoy, when you talk about it, be sure to mention something you'd like to try. "It's a two-way street— remember that you deserve pleasure, too," says Queen. If there's an equal exchange of sex ideas, you'll both be broadening your horizons.

Enter laughing. "Go into any experimentation with the idea that it's just that—you're playing around, you're testing boundaries. If you go in thinking this new variation will be the best sex you've ever had and it turns out to be a disappointment, that's only going to strengthen inhibitions," warns Dr. Cassell.

When to Go to Bed with a Woman

It's Not as Simple as It Seems

This should be a very short chapter.

You know she wants to. She knows you want to. So you do it. Right?

But of course it's not that simple. In fact, knowing when to go to bed with a woman can be hellaciously complicated.

First of all, there's all that conflicting social pressure, says social historian Dr. Peter N. Stearns of Carnegie Mellon University and author of *Be a Man! Males in Modern Society.* Should you prove your manliness by scoring, or prove yourself sensitive and sensible by *not* scoring?

You are, after all, constantly bombarded by TV and movie images of men who take control and take their women fast and furiously . . . at least until the commercial breaks. Then you are hit with dire warnings of the consequences of reckless sex.

"On the one hand, we have a highly charged sexual culture. Every other TV show seems to be talking about jumping in the sack and sexual performance and all that stuff," Dr. Stearns says. "On the other hand, there are tremendous pressures on men to restrain themselves sexually because of fear of disease and because of fear of offending women."

A further complication is that most of us find it so hard to talk about sex, says clinical psychologist Dr. Bernie Zilbergeld.

"Communicating is extremely difficult. To put it out there, who you are and what you want . . . none of us really wants to do that because we're afraid who we are and what we want might not be accepted," he says.

And so you play a lot of games of cat and mouse, being less than honest because you're trying to show her your best side while you figure out, without coming out and baldly asking, what she wants.

All of this uncertainty and trying to live up to those fantastic media-made expectations can result in sex that is not particularly fun and relationships that should never have become relationships in the first place.

The First Time

Anyone with any sexual experience can tell you that the first time is notoriously overrated. Take one woman who is afraid she won't please him, add one man who is afraid he won't please her, and you have a formula for serious stage fright. After all, you're supposed to be a love machine, right? And she's supposed to make you see stars.

No surprise, then, that the first time is sometimes about as much fun as getting a root canal. "Don't rush into sex," advises Dr. Zilbergeld. "Go slowly and get into sex only when you're comfortable with your partner."

Here is some expert advice to help you figure out when the time is right.

Take your time. Who says you have to have sex on the second date? Or on any particular date? If you're feeling the least bit like sex is somehow required of you, then you're putting unnecessary pressure on yourself. Or your partner's putting unnecessary pressure on you.

Either way, it's probably

not the best time to have sex. Sex should never feel compulsory, for either of you, and if it does, it's not going to be much fun. Better to give the relationship time to develop. When you feel comfortable and secure with one another, the sex will follow.

Take a reality check. Before going to bed with a woman, it's always a good idea to pause for a moment—or even for a few days, weeks or months—and ask yourself these questions: "Is this the real thing?" "Am I accepting my lover for what she is, or am I creating a 'dream date' that's about as real as the movie of the week?"

If you expect your lady to cook your dinner, entertain your boss and clean up your dirty laundry, and also, while we're at it, to bear a striking resemblance to Sharon Stone, you're almost certainly in la-la land and are heading for a fall.

Take a moment to apprise your emotions. Is this something you both really, truly want to do, or is it just that you're on your seventh martini? Or maybe you're on the rebound from someone else. Either way, recognize that personal vision isn't always 20/20—and it always helps to take a second look.

Talk about it. Then talk some more. Just 30 years ago, people often met, dated and mated without talking about sex at all. These days, it's not only okay to talk about sex with your date, it's become a part of the etiquette of survival.

"At the very least, people are talking about AIDS and condoms and how many partners they've had and all that," says Dr. Zilbergeld.

Tell the truth. With any new relationship there's always a certain amount of game-

In Video Veritas

In the classic film *The Seven Year Itch*, the very married Tom Ewell tries using Rachmaninoff's second piano concerto to seduce the very zaftig Marilyn Monroe while his wife is out of town.

But what gets Marilyn hot is not Rachmaninoff; it's "Chopsticks."

"I can feel the goose pimples!" she coos.

Which leads to a passionate performance of "Chopsticks" on Tom's piano, which leads to Tom's tackling Marilyn on the piano bench, which leads to them toppling onto the floor.

This, class, is a good example of how to tune in to your partner to learn what really turns her on. But it is also a classic example of how not to behave with a woman, says clinical psychologist Dr. Bernie Zilbergeld.

"Lying, saying you're interested in marriage when you're not or you'll respect her in the morning when you won't, is really not okay," says Dr. Zilbergeld.

The fall from the bench restores Ewell's conscience, and he says to Monroe, "This is terrible. There's nothing I can say, except that I'm terribly sorry. Nothing like this ever happened to me before in all my life."

"Really?" she says. "It happens to me all the time."

playing, Dr. Zilbergeld says. "We're trying to gauge what will fly here, what's acceptable," he says.

Put your cards on the table. Take the risk and tell her how you really feel, Dr. Zilbergeld says. "And if she says the timing's just not right, then so be it."

Keeping Love Fresh

Tune In to What Turns Her On

Live with someone long enough and you'll start to look like her. Worse still, she'll start to look like you.

This, anyway, is the common wisdom: that as you and your soul mate grow old together, you will grow to resemble one another. (And then, as you grow older still, you will both begin to resemble your living room furniture.)

In fact, scientific studies have shown that couples *do* tend to look like one another, but not because they become more alike over time. It's because they start out that way.

Either way, you can't help but come to the spooky conclusion that the more she looks like you, the more having sex with her will be like having sex with . . . uh . . . yourself. And, hey, didn't you mate in the first place because you were tired of that?

Wake Up

Many couples in long-term relationships become so "comfortable" with one another and so much a part of one another's routine that they no longer really notice one another.

"It's like the brain sort of goes to sleep," says Dr. Patricia Love, author of *Hot Monogamy.* "You know, if you live by the railroad tracks and a train goes by, you don't even wake up."

When your sex life becomes as predictable as the

5:15 from Altoona, then, to paraphrase bluesman B.B. King, the thrill is most definitely gone.

That's why the first rule of romance is what Dr. Love calls mindfulness. "It's really about being conscious," says Dr. Love. "Instead of going through each day in a rote way, you make your best effort to see your partner through fresh eyes."

Fanning the Flames

You've woken up next to the same woman since disco was all the rage. How do you see her through fresh eyes? First, you need to . . .

Stop! In the name of love. Put aside whatever you're doing and tune into your partner.

"If you want to create ongoing romance," says Dr. Love, you have to "find out what says 'I love you' to your partner and do it." And to find that out, you have to learn "to see the world through your partner's eyes.

"I often say the biggest problem in relationships is what I call self-centeredness," says Dr. Love. "And what I mean by that is believing that I have the only reality, that my reality is your reality. If I'm turned on, you must be turned on, and if I'm not turned on, what's wrong with you that you are turned on?"

So your goal here is to step outside yourself and try to truly understand your partner. What sort of things truly please her?

Surprise her. Once you know what really sends her, you can use this knowledge to surprise her by doing things that you know will especially please her, things that are anything but routine.

You could do anything from writing a poem to fixing her a pot roast for dinner. The key is that what you do should be tailored to your partner.

"It can't just be hearts

and flowers all the time, unless that is exactly what your partner wants," Dr. Love says.

Remember, hearts and flowers are generic romance, romance for everywoman; what you're seeking here is romance for your one and only.

"Romance is proof positive that I understand," Dr. Love says. "It is an acting out of the understanding. It is concrete proof that I understand you, that I have been watching you and paying attention to you and I really see myself in relationship to you."

Get adventurous. There probably isn't a sex therapist alive today who doesn't recommend that couples keep their sex lives fresh by getting out of bed and doing it . . .

   a) on the kitchen table
   b) in the shower
   c) in the car in the driveway
   d) in the "no-tell motel" down
      the road
   e) all of the above

The point here isn't so much a change of venue as to use your imagination and have fun. If the two of you are particularly good at fantasizing and talking about your fantasies, you can stay in bed and pretend you're on the pitcher's mound of Yankee Stadium.

Meet again for the first time. Most of our imaginations, though, need a little help from the real world, some props, if you will.

Dr. Lonnie Barbach of the University of California at San Francisco Medical School suggests a couple might want to pretend that they've just met.

Arrive separately at a bar or hotel and strike up a conversation, the sort of conversation that two people that have just met might have. Flirt. Seduce her. Take her to a hotel room and ravish her. Given what you know

---

Start Dating Again

You say you and the missus settle down for sex every Saturday at precisely nine o'clock after you've put the kids to bed? And sex is beginning to feel a lot like the old in-and-out?

You, friend, need to get out and date again. No, no, no, not someone else. Her!

One of the most important things you can do to keep love fresh is to go out on regular dates with your partner, says Dr. John Gray, author of *Men Are from Mars, Women Are from Venus.*

Dr. Gray says he and his wife "have date nights booked up a year in advance. And once a month we do an overnight outside of the house away from the kids.

"And that," he says, "is one of the most important things. I cannot stress it, emphasize it more: Leave the kids behind and get to a hotel room. If you can't afford a hotel room, go camping. Get away from your normal environment."

Getting away, he says, allows you to get away from the cares of the household and focus your attentions on one another.

Bottom line: "You have to make your partner more important than your work," Dr. Gray says. "And you have to do things that say she is more important."

---

about her now, it should be even better than the first time.

Don't forget the cardinal rule of romance, though: Tune into your lover.

"Fantasies just don't work for everybody," says Dr. Barbach. For some people, "playacting would be just weird. They'd feel ridiculous, stupid and awkward and anything but erotic."

Making Time for Sex

Know Whether You're Coming or Going

A few years ago Harvard economist Juliet B. Schor, Ph.D., wrote a book called *The Overworked American* in which she calculated that the average American worker slaves away about 329 more hours per year than did the average medieval peasant.

That's because the average medieval peasant took so many holidays that he tended to work only two-thirds of the year, and while his work day generally ran from sunup to sunset, he broke it up with breakfast, lunch, dinner, assorted refreshments and an afternoon nap.

Meanwhile, his average medieval significant other stayed home to cook, clean, rear the children and slaughter the livestock.

Today, the average significant other often goes off to a job of her own. But she still has to cook, clean and rear the children when she gets home.

American men *are* working harder, doing about 160 more hours of work a year than they did at the end of the 1960s, according to Dr. Schor. But women are working harder still, having added about 300 hours of work a year to their schedules.

And you wonder why so often she says she's too tired to fool around. Part of the problem, says author Harriet Schechter, is that men still don't pitch in on the home front as much as they might.

So if you want her to have more time for you, you have to give her more time. Or as Schechter advises men: "If you want to get down and dirty, get up and clean."

Schechter should know. She's the founder of The Miracle Worker Organizing Service, which has helped thousands of couples and businesses to organize their lives.

With many couples, time that might better be spent romantically is spent instead fighting over who is or is not doing his or her fair share of the dishes, laundry, child care or _____ (fill in the blank).

"Women will make assumptions about what needs to be done and who is going to do them, and then they'll get all bent out of shape because the guy hasn't figured it out," Schechter says. "And how are they going to figure it out unless you've discussed it?"

Make a Time Budget

Step number one is to stop fighting and start talking. Each of you needs to sit down with a list of all the things you do in a week—everything from sleeping to running errands to looking for lost things—and figure out how much time you spend doing each of them.

This may lead to some revelations.

You: "Whoa! Do you really spend that much time doing chores?"

She: "Do you really spend that much time watching the box?"

Okay, now you need to make a list of chores that you both think need doing (there

may be quite a bit of discussion about what belongs on that list) and how these things ought to be done.

"You have to agree on standards," Schechter says. "I might think that doing the dishes means washing the dishes right after a meal, drying them and putting everything away, whereas my husband's view of doing the dishes is to let them pile up for a few days until it's a satisfying experience. And then wash them and leave them in the drainer." Which means, Schechter says, "you have to be willing to compromise a little bit."

Here are some ideas that are guaranteed to help you make time for sex.

Turn off the tube. We like to complain that our bosses rob us of our leisure, but in truth we often rob ourselves. We have become slaves to our appliances, and our chief master is none other than Mr. Television. Outside of work, Americans spend more waking hours glued to the tube than doing anything else.

In one study, in which 2,500 adults were asked to rate their favorite things to do and then to keep diaries of how much time they spent doing them, the average person spent 2 hours and 17 minutes a day watching television and 1 minute having sex. This is ironic, given the fact that by far the favorite activity was having sex.

Don't answer that! Other appliances control us as well. Some of us never hear the waves break on the sand because we can't seem to go to the beach without a boom box. Some of us are unacquainted with birdsongs because we are unable to walk in the woods without a personal stereo on our head or cellular phone pressed to our ear.

Some of us lead lives of noisy desperation.

And speaking of phones, Schechter says, "you don't have to have that Pavlovian response" every time it rings. Instead, screen your calls with an answering machine. And whatever you do, she says, "don't have the phone ringer on in the bedroom . . . because that can really ruin things for your love life." Ask yourself who's in charge here: you or your television, boom box,

personal stereo or telephone.

"It's really about stepping back and saying 'I don't have to do that,' " Schechter says.

Start a daily ritual. Just as you may already set aside a certain time each day to work out or to walk the dog, you should set aside a

Dad? Mom? Whatcha Doin'?

Remember how, when you were a kid playing doctor with the girl next door, you had to sneak around so your parents wouldn't catch you?

Now you're a parent yourself and guess what? You have to sneak around so your kids won't catch you.

Kids. One of the great mysteries of life is that any couple ever manages to have more than one. From the moment they arrive, passion goes out of fashion, bedtime becomes deadtime and sex . . . well, isn't that what got you into this mess?

So how do you find time to make time when there's no time that isn't Howdy Doody time?

Hire a babysitter and hit a hotel, says Dr. John Gray, author of *Men Are from Mars, Women Are from Venus*, or wake up your lover in the middle of the night. But the first can put a quick dent in your wallet and the second a quick dent in your forehead.

So here's a better solution: Saturday morning cartoons. That's right. Plug 'em in. The wonders of animation can amuse the kids and reanimate your sex life.

"Use the television as a tool," says author Harriet Schechter. "If you're going to have TV, use it effectively."

And with such blessed inventions as VCRs and videotapes, the kids can watch a movie any time.

P.S. Don't forget to lock your bedroom door.

time when you and she can massage each other's feet or take a shower or just be together and talk.

This time should be as inviolable as your workout time. After all, what could be more important than spending a little time with your main squeeze?

"It's the idea of taking time that is your time together," Schechter says. "You don't have to do the same thing all the time, but as long as that is time that you both look forward to and it's kind of a little oasis in your day, that's really important."

Hit the sack. Schechter also suggests that you follow her "Rules to Go to Bed By." You should, she says, take time to go to bed early, clean, comfortable, happy and prepared.

Obviously, the most important of these is the first: Plan to meet your mate in bed a half-hour earlier than usual.

"I've had some people say to me, 'Isn't planning your sex life a little bit compulsive?' I don't think so. People plan everything else in their lives, and they expect their personal lives to take care of themselves. And that, obviously, isn't working," Schechter says.

"It's really about putting that as a priority on your overall list and saying, 'Okay, I'm going to consciously make time for this.' And it works."

It's good to arrive in bed clean, she says, which is to say fresh from the shower (no law against sharing one) and comfortable (wear silk or flannel or your birthday suit: whatever you feel good in).

The "happy" part is the mood you bring to bed with you. Schechter suggests you each take a few moments to clear your minds, and if something's troubling you, clear the air.

And be prepared.

Time-Saving Tips

If you want to make time for sex, first you have to make time. Follow the advice below and we'll soon have you humming, "Time Is on My Side."

Use automatic deposit. It's the 1990s. The time it takes you to drag your sorry paycheck to the bank, fill out the right color deposit slip and stand in line while the one teller on duty handles the little old lady who's cashing in her entire penny collection could be put to much better use. You say it only takes ten minutes? Wise up. That's how long it takes the average guy to make love.

Put things back where you found them. You're running late for the office—again. And you can't find the damn car keys. The time—and energy—you waste running around the house like a madman, cursing and screaming and looking for someone to blame, could be avoided if you just hang your keys on a nail beside the front door.

Kill two birds . . . No, not literally. But double up chores whenever possible. How many times have you run out to the hardware store for paint and then had to turn right around and go to the package store next door for a case of beer? Keep a magnetic note board on the refrigerator and scrawl an ongoing list of errands. Before you head out, check the list to see if you can combine at least two errands.

"Stock your nightstand with everything you could possibly need or want during romantic interludes: contraceptives, lubricants, massage oil, towels, tissues, toys, snacks . . . anything you wouldn't want to have to look for later."

Good night.

Part Three

The Skillful Lover

What Makes a Man

The Mechanics of Manhood

It is a paradox of manhood: We want to know what we're talking about, but we often talk about things we know nothing of. That is often the case when we talk of cars, women, politics, sports. And so it is with the penis.

Many of us brag and banter about it, but most of us know more about the plumbing in our kitchens than the plumbing in our bodies.

Meet Your Body

The only thing we get when we enter the Boys Club at birth is a pair of testicles and a penis. No briefing. No instruction manual.

Although it makes sense to know our bodies, few of us do, or at least as well as we should. Consider this shocking statistic: 83 percent of men over age 50 know the function of a woman's ovaries, but only 42 percent know the function of their own prostate gland.

Here are the components of the male machinery and a primer on how they work.

The Testicles and Scrotum

In ancient times men swore on the testicles of the men they made promises to. That's where we get words like *testimony*, *testament* and *testify*. Today, testicles aren't bandied

about so publicly, but their import remains in colloquial references to the "family jewels."

Testicles *are* jewels. To men wanting families, they're priceless. To boys wanting mustaches and muscles, they're treasured. Each of your two testicles weighs about 22 grams, or as much as a palmful of paper clips. Each averages 1¾ to 2 inches long, and 1 inch wide. In most cases, the left hangs lower than the right and is slightly smaller, presumably so they don't smash together when you close your legs. The testicles' main function is to produce sperm and androgens (male hormones), the most popular of which is testosterone.

What fine jewels wouldn't be held in a delicate pouch? This is the scrotum, a very thin, fibrous, nearly fat-free sac of skin along the root of the penis. The scrotum holds the testicles outside your body because sperm forms best at temperatures two to three degrees lower than body temperature. To control testicular temperature—and in response to exercise, arousal and ambient temperature changes—muscles called the dartos muscle in the scrotum and cremasters above the testicles can shrink or enlarge the scrotum and thus lower or raise the testicles. Peek down your trunks next time you dive into a cold pool and you'll see what we mean.

The Penis

The penis takes the spotlight in the lineup of male genitalia. Few other organs in the human body have endured the same myths and misconceptions, legend and lore, fame and misfortune as the world's first phallic symbol.

Physiologically, the penis hardly lives up to the hype. Quite simply, a penis exists for two reasons: It gives you something to aim when you pee, and it allows you to deposit sperm far enough inside a woman to ensure procreation. Most penises are 2½ inches limp (flaccid) and 5 to 7 inches hard (erect). And despite what society may have you think, clearly most men—as many as 98 percent—fall within the normal range size-wise. (For details on the long and short of this matter, see Sizing Yourself Up on page 4.)

On the exterior the penis is a wrinkly, lifeless fellow when flaccid and a rather impressive vein-embossed companion when erect. Its skin is fat-free and chock-full of nerve endings. Starting at the tip, all penises have a head, or glans. Head shape and size differ from man to man. The head of an uncircumsized penis wears a hood, a thin piece of skin called the foreskin, or prepuce, which obscures the head most of the time. (Circumcision is the name of the operation that removes the foreskin.)

The tiny piece of V-shaped skin on the underside of the head is the frenulum. It and the head, especially the corona, or ridge, are among the most sensitive parts of your equipment.

Finally, there's the shaft, the part of your penis that makes up the bulk of its size. Women tend to find the thickness of their partner's penis more stimulating than the length.

For everything you need to know about how erections work—and how they can work better—see Lasting Longer on page 90.

Pubic Hair

Pubic hair comes in all shapes and sizes, depending on your race, heredity and the amount of testosterone coursing through

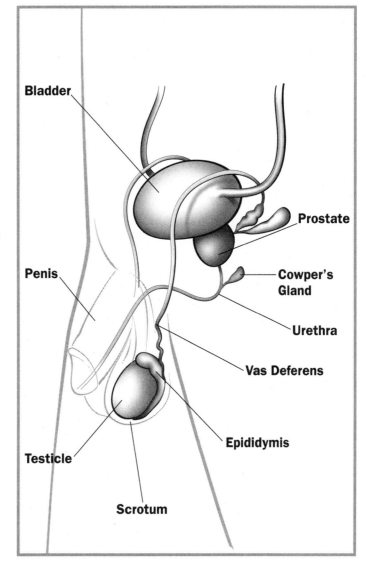

your veins. In men, it typically surrounds the penis, dots the scrotum and sweeps upward in a narrow band toward the belly button, a strip of hair colloquially called the happy trail.

Functionally, pubic hair doesn't have much use in sex, short of serving as a reminder of our evolution. It can be shaved off, a practice embraced by some adult movie stars. Just never use a depilatory—they can burn—and be prepared for an uncomfortably itchy period as it regrows.

The Prostate and Cowper's Glands

The prostate and Cowper's glands are men's internal sex organs, yet most men know little about them except that prostates are prone to cancer and that they often swell up with age, causing frequency of urination and poor bladder emptying.

The prostate is a chestnut-size gland that weighs about as much as a testicle. It collars the neck of your bladder.

The Cowper's glands are two pea-size glands at the base of your penis. The Cowper's glands and prostate generate fluids that mix together with sperm to create semen. Incidentally, because one out of every eight of us will be diagnosed with prostate cancer, you should schedule a full prostate exam every year starting at age 40.

The Tubing

Tubing in the male genitals mainly consists of the epididymis, the vas deferens, the seminal vessels and the urethra.

Feel that bulge at the back of each testicle? It's your epididymis, a comma-shape coil of tube that's up to 20 feet long when straightened out. The epididymis stores sperm that has developed in the testicles. At the end of the epididymis is the vas deferens. It shuttles sperm, via the spermatic cord, into your pelvis, until it joins the back of your bladder with the seminal vessel.

The seminal vessel is a soft cord

The Male G-spot

While the prostate is best known as a center for pain and cancer in your golden years, it also is gaining a reputation as a site for sexual pleasure. Some even call the concentrated bundle of nerve endings the Male G-spot.

Much to their chagrin, some men have discovered the erotic power of the prostate while bent over an examining table in a sterile doctor's office. As the doctor inserts a gloved, lubricated finger through the rectum and probes the back wall of the prostate, some men experience an erection that defies all efforts to restrain.

If you're uncomfortable with the thought of anyone—including your loving partner—inserting anything into that particular orifice, there may still be a way to tap this happy spot. Here's how.

Have your partner gently press the ball of her thumb into your perineum, the little island between your scrotum and your anus. A stroke or soft touch here, especially as you're building to orgasm, can put pressure on the prostate, which in turn stimulates the penis.

If you're not sure about the whole thing, you can try it yourself the next time you masturbate.

measuring a little over two inches in length and containing up to three milliliters (three-fifths of a teaspoon) of sticky fluid that forms a good portion of the stuff of which ejaculations are made. The ducts of the seminal vessels help form the ejaculatory duct, which runs through the prostate, where it enters the urethra. The urethra then expels ejaculation. It also expels urine.

A Man's Guide to the Female Genitals

Your Map to the Unknown

The female body is a new world, an anatomical landscape so markedly different from our own. Where we grow scads of hair, women grow none. Where we show sinewy muscle, they show suppleness. Where we have angles, they have curves.

The first time each of us pioneered this territory is an indelible part of our personal history. Remember stroking a woman's sloping waist for the first time, or delighting in the silky softness of her breasts? We were sensual de Sotos, exploring unexpected new territory.

Whether you've played gender geography one or one million times since that first time, there's still a lot of unmapped territory to explore. Barroom bragging aside, we men do not know the female body half as well as we think we do. Fortunately, working toward that wisdom is one of the great pleasures of life.

Meet Her Body

Two plumbers are in a hospital lobby awaiting news of their newborn babies. The nurse comes out and tells the first plumber it's a boy.

"That's great," he exclaims. "All the pipes are in plain view."

The nurse leaves and

returns moments later to tell the other plumber his baby is a girl.

"That's better," the second plumber beams. "Master plumbers leave *no* pipes sticking out."

Part of the allure of the female genitalia is that they're tucked away from view. No pipes are sticking out. And while that doesn't make her plumbing superior, it does make it mysterious. Yet the blueprint for a woman's piping is not much different than your own. Here are the parts you need to know.

The Vulva

A woman's vulva is essentially everything that meets the eye when she's naked. It includes the outer lips (labia majora), the inner lips (labia minora), the tip of the clitoris and the vaginal opening.

The labia majora, Latin for "larger lips," are the ones you'll see first. They're made of fibrous, fatty tissue and run from the anus to the top of the vulva, where they fuse.

The labia minora, or smaller lips, are skin folds just inside the labia majora. They're fat- and hair-free but contain a large number of lubricating glands. Along with vaginal secretions, they form a waterproof barrier into the vagina.

Just as no two penises are alike, the lips of a woman's vulva vary greatly in size, shape and color. But they all have one thing in common: During arousal, the lips will swell with blood, change color and thicken by as much as 300 percent.

The Clitoris

The clitoris is enshrouded in almost as much mythology as the penis and, believe it or not, functions in much the same way. Situated at the top of the vulva, just inside the labia minora, the clitoris is built much like a miniature penis.

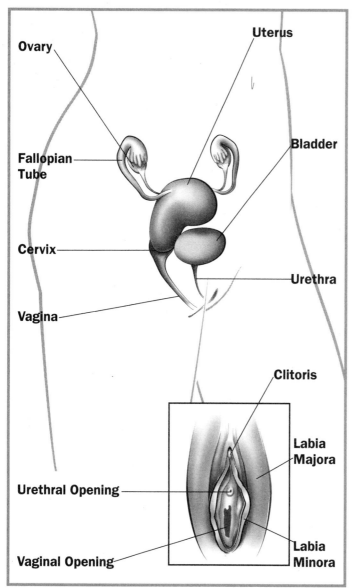

Ovary

Uterus

Fallopian Tube

Bladder

Cervix

Urethra

Vagina

Clitoris

Urethral Opening

Labia Majora

Vaginal Opening

Labia Minora

Pubic Hair and the Mound of Venus

A woman's pubic hair is largely a decorative triangle of hair that sprouts at puberty. Interestingly, it's generated by a woman's comparatively minute amounts of testosterone, the male sex hormone.

The Chinese thought pubic hair revealed a lot about a woman's sexual demeanor: Black, feathery hair meant an obstinate woman; brown, gold-tinted hair a generous woman; thick, bushy hair a passionate woman. They were right in a sense, because a good hormone doctor can tell a lot about a person's sex hormones from their pubic hair distribution.

Otherwise, it's not clear how accurately you can judge a woman's sexual appetite—or her true hair color, for that matter—by pubic hair alone. The only thing pubic hair definitively says is that she has entered puberty.

As for the Mound of Venus, that's actually a pad of fat just above a woman's vulva. It covers the point where her pelvic bones join. Also called the *mons pubis*, it acts as a cushion during sex.

The Vagina

Picture the cardboard tube inside a roll of toilet paper. Now imagine it slightly shorter and made of muscle. What you'd have is a crude vagina.

Despite its mystique—and despite its vital role in the process of childbirth—a vagina is nothing more than a fibrous, muscular tube, measuring 3¼ inches long on average. The vagina lining is thick and folded horizontally and vertically. Each fold is called a ruga. The lining also contains a coat of

But unlike the penis, which holds a day job pulling urination duty, the clitoris exists solely for sexual pleasure. Its head is covered by a sensitive membrane that's awash in receptive nerve endings. Its body is ¾ to 1¼ inches long. It doubles in size during arousal, just like the penis. Also like the penis, clitoral shape and size differs from woman to woman.

muscle, which runs longitudinally and contains a plethora of blood vessels.

One of the reasons why penis size isn't as important as many men mistakenly think is the way nature designed the vagina to accommodate almost any man. It changes size by shrinking and expanding. Incidentally, the vagina's flexibility enables women to give birth—a crucial characteristic for an organ expected to pass something the size of a small watermelon.

Inside the Vagina

At the end of the vagina is the cervix. You may have discovered it at one point by thrusting too vigorously during sex, much to the painful chagrin of your partner. During arousal the cervix pulls up and back, out of harm's way.

Though if a woman has a retroverted or tipped uterus, the cervix stays where it is, suspended in this ever-widening vaginal cavity—where the man's penis may batter it, sometimes painfully, during intercourse.

That's why some deep-penetration sex positions can be painful for a woman if you're not careful. Physiologically, the cervix is a gateway to the uterus, or womb, the muscular pear-shaped headquarters of gestation.

At the end of the uterus are two curving tubes called the Fallopian tubes. They shoot off to the left and right and end near the ovaries, a woman's equivalent of testicles.

From a frontal view, the uterus, Fallopian tubes and ovaries are shaped like a little ram's head, with the uterus being the head and the tubes and ovaries being the

The Female Ejaculation

When you think of the differences between male and female orgasms, odds are the first thing that spurts into your mind is, well, spurting.

That ain't necessarily so. It turns out that a woman may also have the anatomical equipment for ejaculation. Experts are split on this point, with the existence of the G-spot being the main bone of contention.

During intercourse or other forms of stimulation, proponents say the G-spot may be sufficiently stimulated to trigger the release of a clear, odorless fluid. However, skeptics in the medical community say it's nothing more than urine. To them, "female ejaculation" is simply stress incontinence.

Lab analyses have failed to provide conclusive evidence for either side. Whatever the fluid is, a Masters and Johnson Institute survey of 300 women found that only 5 percent reported ever having ejaculated during sex.

However, another survey found that slightly more than half of the women said they had ejaculated at some time during sex, although only 14 percent reported it was a regular part of orgasm. (For more information on the G-spot, see Erogenous Zones on page 78.)

horns. As you probably learned way back in your junior high school health class, ovaries produce eggs roughly once a month. The egg then travels down the Fallopian tube and into the uterus.

Once it reaches its destination, the egg either meets a friendly sperm or is eliminated in menstruation.

Erogenous Zones

A Touch of Heaven on Earth

Even if you didn't know the difference between an end zone and an erogenous zone in your high school football days, you probably learned Lesson Number One when you played two-hand touch for the first time with your girl-friend. Lost in the depth of her gaze, you stroked her hair as if trying to touch each silky strand one at a time. You delicately traced her crescent brows, the rise and fall of her cheekbones, the slope of her nose, the pink fullness of her lips.

A few rose petal–soft kisses later, you lowered your mouth so your lips lingered on her chin. You inched along her jawline, leaving a trail of nearly imperceptible kisses in your wake. Then, just as you began to nuzzle her ear, she gasped so hard you weren't sure if you were offsides or on your way to a touchdown.

But you soon found out, didn't you?

human behaviorist Ashley Montagu said in his book *Touching: The Human Significance of Skin,* "The language of sex is primarily nonverbal . . . in no other relationship is the skin so totally involved as in sexual intercourse."

Men and women share many erogenous zones. Both of our faces, for example, respond splendidly to soft kisses, delicate caresses and lingering licks. That's why your high school sweetheart gasped when you kissed her neck and ears. But if, somewhere along the line, you stopped paying attention to those small caresses that once drove your woman wild, you have badly underestimated their power.

"Although we in the massage industry have worked very hard to get away from the illicit image of massage, you can't deny that there's a very sensual component to touch, especially in erogenous zones," says Ralph R. Stephens, a massage expert and spokesman for the American Massage Therapy Association headquartered in Evanston, Illinois.

"Touch signals many things. It shows acceptance, affection, appreciation—it comple-ments feelings of love and caring," Stephens says.

The Body Electric

"Erogenous zones are parts of the body directly wired for sexual stimulation," says Erica M. Goodstone, Ph.D., a sex therapist in private practice in New York City.

On a physiological level, these "zones" are nothing more than patches of skin packed with sensitive nerve endings. Because of this, "we have more sensory awareness in these areas," Dr. Goodstone says. On a philosophical level, however, erogenous zones are intimate areas that allow us to communi-cate with our partners in a way that transcends words. As

Zoning Regulations

If you must know just one thing about erogenous zones, it's this: Not everyone is a natural. You or your partner might balk at this type of intimacy. Many men, for instance, aren't touch-oriented because we've been con-ditioned to avoid it. Likewise, some women avoid sensual touching because of poor body image or past sexual abuse.

According to marriage counselor and sex therapist Anne Hooper, author of *The Ultimate Sex Book,* here's how to deal with this touchy subject before it becomes an issue.

- Establish ground rules. Decide what body parts, if any, are off-limits.
- If she's nervous or uncomfortable with sensual touching, encourage her to express these feelings early on. Then provide her with plenty of patient reassurance.
- Notice body language. Yours and hers. Look for tenseness, nervous breathing and other signs of stress. Breathe deeply and rhythmically to relax body and mind.

The Top Ten

Here are the ten most sensitive, sexual hot zones on the human body, along with a brief description of what works best to arouse your partner.

- Face. Particularly the eyes, lips and ears, which respond well to licks, kisses and hot breath.
- Scalp. Massage or stimulate by running your fingers through her hair.
- Neck and shoulders. Among the most sensitive of zones. Kiss, lick or caress the neck. Gently rub and massage the shoulders.
- Chest and breasts. A center of sexual pleasure. Stroke, massage, kiss. The breasts also can be lightly squeezed or kneaded.
- Nipples. Extremely sensitive in men and women. Stick with gentle lip and tongue touches; also try blowing on them or fondling them with your fingers.
- Abdomen. Very responsive to light stroking and soft kisses.
- Waist. Often an unexplored zone that can yield pleasurable results. Use firmer strokes, like holding and molding her hips in your hands.
- Thighs. Particularly the inside of the thigh. Use light caresses and counterclockwise circular rubbing.

- Back of the legs. The fleshy hamstrings are very sensitive, as is the area behind the knee. Use light combing strokes with your fingertips and gentle caresses.
- Buttocks. Use more forceful, deeper touches on the butt cheeks, and sprinkle in some kisses, kneading or light spanking.

Find Your Own

Just like on the music charts or best-seller lists, your personal favorites may not make the Top Ten. The entire body is an erogenous zone, and there are plenty of other possibilities to attend to. Don't be afraid to explore uncharted territory.

"If you take a little time and experiment with her body in a playful way, you can discover your partner's own special erogenous zones," says Cathy Winks, co-owner of Good Vibrations, a retail and mail-order adult store in San Francisco, and co-author of *The Good Vibrations Guide to Sex.*

"You don't have to be a skilled shiatsu masseur," Winks says. "There are lots of nonprofessional ways to touch each other. Just relax and don't be too concerned with being perfect."

Here are some other tips to hot-wire your sex life.

Handle with care. Winks says you don't have to be a pro. But what *should* you do to keep from feeling so amateurish? According to the American Massage Therapy Association's Stephens and Dr. Goodstone, you can't go wrong as long as you touch with love.

Generally, though, erogenous zones are so sensitive that you are wise to explore them slowly and with a tender touch. This defies our own innate sense of touch turn-on because most men enjoy fairly overt, direct stimulation.

Give her some fancy footwork. No, you don't have to be Fred Astaire. Massage experts called reflexologists believe that every part of the body can be stimulated through the foot. This is especially true for women whose feet are powerful erogenous zones. "Even if it's not a direct sexual turn-on, everybody loves their feet rubbed," Stephens says. "If you want to please your mate, it's hard to go wrong doing this."

Massage the foot first with the sole facing up. Add just a dab of oil or talcum powder for lubrication, and stretch the toes gently apart, lightly bending them backward and forward. Knead the sole with your knuckles, working from the heel to toe. Then make firm, circular thumbs strokes from toe to heel. Flip the foot over so the sole is facing down, and apply firm, gentle pressure to the valleys and tendons on the top of the foot. Then tug each toe gently, and finish with some deep, relaxing strokes in the arch.

Find the "key" to sexual pleasure.

In the days of old, when knights were bold, the honor of a fair maiden was protected by a chastity belt. Only her true love could be entrusted with the key. Turns out that's still true.

The word *clitoris* comes from a Greek word meaning "key," and it's no coincidence: To many women, the clitoris is the key to sexual ecstasy. "One of the most common myths about women and sex is that they should reach orgasm through intercourse alone, without clitoral stimulation," Winks says. "The truth is, there are very few women who don't require at least fairly overt clitoral stimulation to reach orgasm."

Start by caressing her whole body and concentrating on the other erogenous zones. When you reach her genitals, don't get down to business too quickly. The clitoris is like a miniature, highly sensitive penis, and it often needs a slow, gentle, patient hand to stimulate it properly. But once you're on the right track, Winks says, you'll know it.

"If you have her communicate what kind of stimulation she wants or needs in order to climax, it will save you a lot of guesswork," she

suggests. "But as a rule, most women respond best to direct, prolonged clitoral contact."

Play in the minora league. As part of his pioneering sex research in the 1950s, the late Dr. Alfred C. Kinsey had five gynecologists using glass, metal or cotton-tipped probes explore the genitals of almost 900 women to find out which areas were most sensitive. It certainly comes as no surprise today that 98 percent of the women were aware when the probe gently touched their clitorides.

But it may surprise you to learn that the same number—98 percent—reported they were sensitive to the probe's contact with the labia minora, the delicate inner lips that surround the clitoris. "As sources of erotic arousal, the labia minora seem to be fully as important as the clitoris," Dr. Kinsey wrote.

Indeed, Dr. Kinsey found that 84 percent of the women in the study who masturbated did so by stroking both the labia and the clitoris. You should do no less with your partner.

The G-spot: The Hottest Hot Spot?

The G-spot has taken on almost mythic proportions in the annals of sex. Proponents say it is the most powerful and mysterious of erogenous zones. And the hardest to find.

Some medical experts say it's hard to find because it simply doesn't exist. They say that while there is no question some women have a region in the anterior wall of the vagina that is sensitive to touch, there is no conclusive scientific evidence that there is an anatomically distinct entity.

While scientists and doctors continue to debate its existence, here's what we know: Named after Ernst Grafenberg, a German obstetrician/gynecologist who discovered it in the 1940s while researching birth control, the G-spot is defined as a conglomeration of nerve endings, blood vessels and glands amassed around a woman's urethra on the inside, front wall of her vagina. Even proponents concede it apparently does not exist in all women. And when it does, they say, it's indistinguishable from surrounding tissue until she becomes deeply aroused. Then it swells and protrudes, until it feels like a firm, fleshy knob.

Some experts say the G-spot acts as a magic sex button for some women and is responsible for female ejaculation, a phenomenon not unlike our own, except that a woman ejaculates clear fluid, not sperm.

If you and your partner are curious about the G-spot, by all means, check it out. But keep in mind this important word of caution from Dr. Goodstone: "Remember that there hasn't been enough research to say whether the G-spot exists for all women. So if a woman can't find her G-spot, it doesn't mean there's anything wrong with her. Maybe she's not relaxed enough. Maybe it doesn't exist in some people. Maybe it atrophies if it hasn't been touched. We just don't know enough to say."

Here are two ways to attempt to locate and stimulate the G-spot.

Get on your knees. Ask your partner to lie down on a bed with some pillows under her hips, so that her legs are spread and her bottom is slightly raised. Straddle her torso, facing her feet, so that you're supporting most of your body weight on your knees. With a slow, gentle touch, stimulate your partner's clitoris. When she's really aroused, slip two fingers into her vagina, keeping your hand palm up so that your fingertips can brush against the front, top part of her vaginal wall. If she has the G-spot, you'll feel a small knob of firm flesh about the size of a bean or two. As you stimulate her G-

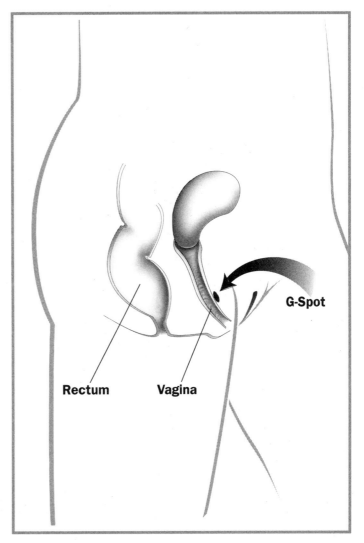

G-Spot

Rectum   Vagina

spot, don't be surprised if she explodes with ecstasy and gushes fluid. Many women say orgasms stimulated from the G-spot are more intense than clitoral orgasms.

Position yourself for success. Another way to stimulate the G-spot is to use proper positioning. Certain sex positions allow better G-spot stimulation than others. Your best bets are most woman-on-top positions and nearly all rear-entry ones. These allow your penis to contact the vaginal wall head-on, so to speak, thus stimulating her G-spot better.

Masturbation

The Benefits of Solo Practice

In a classic episode of the sitcom *Seinfeld*, comedian Jerry Seinfeld and friends make a bet about who can last the longest without masturbating.

"Are *you* the Master of Your Domain?" Jerry would intone, meaning have you lost the bet. Amazingly, no one uttered the m-word itself during the entire episode. Yet through innuendo, insinuation and implication, the message (and punch line) was loud and clear.

Masturbation is like that. It's a universal phenomenon that crosses cultures, spans generations and transcends civilizations. We all do it. We all know it. We rarely talk about it.

Look at the numbers.

- 60 percent of all men 18 to 59 said they had masturbated within the last year, according to the landmark 1994 *Sex in America* survey conducted by University of Chicago researchers.
- 15 percent of the American readers of *Playboy* magazine do it daily, according to the magazine's 1995 international sex survey.
- 48 percent of single men and 68 percent of divorced men do it daily to weekly, according to the *Janus Report on Sexual Behavior*. Forty-four percent of married men do it once a week or more.

"Masturbation is fun. It's a healthy, sexual thing to do," says Betty Dodson, Ph.D., a New York City sex educator, therapist and author who has been called the mother of mas-

turbation for her hands-on clinics on perfecting self-gratification.

You're living in special times. You needn't worry about someone chopping your hands off if you're caught, well, red-handed in the bathroom, because experts sing the praises of masturbation.

"Madonna's done it on stage in concert," says Dr. Dodson. "It's pretty much in the forefront of our sexual consciousness."

If masturbation has become mainstream, some experts say, it is a good thing. The act has many benefits. Physiologically, masturbation rids your body of older, slow-moving sperm cells that aren't as likely to impregnate a woman as their younger, feistier counterparts.

Perhaps more important, masturbation is great practice for sex with a partner. It shows you how to touch sensuously, how to pace yourself, where your body is most responsive. And solo sex teaches you ejaculatory control, which makes you a better lover, says Marilyn K. Volker, Ph.D., a sex therapist in private practice in Coral Gables, Florida.

The Basics

If you are morally opposed to masturbation, we respect your opinion. But you still might benefit from the following advice by sharing the information with your partner. Having her stimulate you by hand is a common form of foreplay and even sexual pleasuring among couples. It certainly increases intimacy. If you are open to masturbation, chances are you have much to learn to make it both more enjoyable and educational. Here are ways to achieve both.

Linger leisurely. Masturbation is a gift to yourself. Take your time. Make solo sex as sensual as sex with a partner. "You certainly don't want to clock it, but if you're reaching orgasm in a few minutes, you're not getting much out of it," Dr. Dodson, who wrote *Sex for One: The Joy of Selfloving*, a book on masturbation, says. "Ten to 15 minutes of stimulation at the least shouldn't be a big deal."

To be a black-belt masturbator, Dr. Dodson says you're looking at "an hour or more alone." Don't be in a hurry to climax. Simply enjoy the sensation of touching yourself. You'll heighten the intensity of orgasm when you finally get one by building it gradually.

Please the senses. Some therapists suggest setting the mood for masturbation by finding something to appeal to all your senses. Ears: soft music. Nose: sweet incense. Sight: flattering candlelight.

If you're in your living room, for example, light a few scented candles, play some of your favorite music, watch a few arousing movies, sprawl on the couch. Nibble on lush fruit. Treat yourself to a glass of fine wine or an imported beer.

Use the right lube. Lubrication is important. Without it, you run the risk of rubbing yourself raw. It's effective for touching the rest of your body, too, since a good lube has a soothing massage effect. Apply just enough to ease friction, but not so much that you're awash in it. About a quarter-size dot or two is probably sufficient to start. Add more as necessary.

"Lubrication is a necessity, but as for the type, that's largely up to you," Dr. Dodson says. Forget spit or petroleum jelly. There's a raft of affordable lubricants designed for sex. "I prefer a good unscented massage oil," she says. "Water-based lubricants, like K-Y Jelly, are pretty thin. They're best if you're using a condom. If you're alone, treat yourself to a thicker lubricant."

Be like Eric Clapton. Rock 'n' roll Hall of Famer Eric Clapton goes by the modest moniker of "old slowhand." Take a tip from the virtuoso guitarist and become a slowhand yourself. Before you touch your penis, caress your entire body gently and slowly, exploring it as if for the first time.

When you get down to business, keep the rhythm slow and sensual. Vary the pacing and remember that your most sensitive spot is your frenulum, that V-shaped piece of skin on the underside of your penis, where the glans meets the shaft. Knowing this can help you speed up or slow down climax, depending on what you had in mind.

Concentrate on *other* body parts. A successful solo session titillates your entire body—not just the parts between your legs. "Get into the erotic sensation. Good masturbation is a whole mind and body experience," Dr. Dodson says.

Need more impetus? "When you masturbate quickly and ejaculate in seconds, you're training your body to react that way during sex, too," she adds. "If you can control yourself in masturbation by concentrating on your whole body, you'll do the same in sex and have a better chance of making your lovemaking last longer."

Concentrate on erogenous areas, like the nipples. Up to 60 percent of men get nipple erections when aroused. Other hot spots to dally over: the chest, thighs, buttocks, waist and back of legs.

Pay attention to the lesson at hand. Learn what works and what doesn't when it comes to arousing yourself, Dr. Volker says. By approaching masturbation as a lesson in love, you'll better communicate your turn-ons and turn-offs to your partner, thus enhancing your sex life together.

Try an occasional nightcap quickie. When you're home in bed but office woes are keeping you awake, quick masturbation might be the ticket to swift slumber. "For some people, having an orgasm loosens them up and relaxes them," Dr. Volker says. "A short, fast quickie may indeed work when you're stressed or tired."

Foreplay

Give It Star Billing

Picture your sexual arousal as a Porsche 944: It blasts from 0 to 60 in four seconds, leaving skid marks and a cloud of dust in its wake. A woman's arousal is more like a Cadillac Coup de Ville, with leather seats, tilt steering and cruise control. Speed doesn't matter. It's the ride that counts. And the slower, more luxurious the ride, the better.

Taking things slowly is what foreplay's all about. And it's not just for the woman.

"If a man's interested in getting more out of sex—more pleasure, more sensation—the idea is to make it last longer," says Dr. Betty Dodson, a New York City sex educator, therapist and author. "One of the secrets to that is in the buildup."

Foreplay is about giving yourselves time to clear your minds and focus on nothing but each other. Your bodies. The here and now. Forget the kids. Forget the bills. Forget the boss. It's just the two of you, and every moment together should be an eternity.

Far-fetched? Only in movies? Maybe. But consider this: Three-quarters of men climax every time they have sex, while just 29 percent of women can say the same. Moreover, 8 percent of women rarely or never climax, compared to 2 percent of men. What these numbers suggest is that men are revving their sexual engines at excessively high rpm's, at least from a woman's point of view.

"One of the most important things a couple can realize is that a man and woman's sexual response cycles differ," says sex therapist Dr. Marilyn K.

Volker. "Many men enhance their sexual response by holding back longer."

An All-Day Feeling

Foreplay is something to be savored, not merely endured. It takes time—at least 15 to 20 minutes—and it takes tenderness. But in a very real sense, experts agree, foreplay starts as soon as you wake up. Here's what they advise.

Make love all day. We're conditioned to think of foreplay—hugging, kissing, cuddling and so forth—as something that happens between the sheets. But the best foreplay is an all-day, ongoing affair, Dr. Dodson says.

By building anticipation throughout the day, you can make a smoldering fire that burns hotter—and longer—than a single flash of passion. Compliment her outfit as she leaves for work in the morning. Call her in the afternoon. Leave a love note on her windshield. Surprise her with roses.

Set the mood. Good foreplay is synonymous with setting the mood. This sounds like a no-brainer, but remember to lower the ringer on the telephone, let the machine take your calls, dim the lights and play some soft music. Light candles and burn incense, if you like. Get comfortable.

"Believe it or not, just relaxing, focusing on the moment and breathing evenly and deeply will help you last longer through the night," says Barbara Keesling, Ph.D., a sex therapist in Orange, California, and author of the best-selling *How to Make Love All Night (And Drive a Woman Wild)* and *Sexual Pleasure.*

Make a clean start. A shared shower or bath is a powerful precursor to lovemaking. To make showering sexy, don't rush. Lather her body slowly and deliberately, spending extra time in the erogenous zones, like her breasts, buttocks, back and stomach. Also wash her hair, giving her scalp a sensuous massage at the same time.

Touch her. Not just in one place, but all over. According to a survey on sensuality conducted by the Revlon company, 55 percent of women ranked touch as the most sensual sense, as compared with 42 percent of men. According to Ashley Montagu, author of *Touching: The Human Significance of Skin*, "Touch is the true language of sex."

Ask her to lie down and close her eyes. Straddle her hips and gently caress her face, breasts and stomach for 15 minutes. Trace the contours of her body. Outline her brows, cheekbones and lips. Run your fingers through her hair. Circle her breasts with gentle, nearly imperceptible strokes of your fingertips. The more she feels loved, the more she'll love you in return. For more information on touching, see Becoming a Handy Man on page 86.

Kiss her. Then kiss her some more. Author Jen Sacks, in an article about kissing in *Men's Health* magazine, writes: "Kissing is one sure way to get me, and all the women I've talked to, very, very ready.... One serious kiss from a man gets me farther than 20 minutes of attention to the more obvious places."

She recommends:

- Spending time on her lips. Bite them softly or lick them gently. Touch the corners of her mouth with your tongue. Kiss her with different grades of intensity before heading inside.
- Opening her mouth gently but firmly with your own. Play with her tongue. Refrain from sticking yours all the way down her throat.
- Moving your jaw a little from side to side and concentrating solely on her mouth.

Revealing Moments

In one of the largest, most rigorously controlled sex surveys of all time, researchers asked women to name their favorite turn-ons. A whopping 81 percent said watching their partner undress was somewhat to very appealing. It even beat out receiving oral sex.

If you want to treat your partner to her own private striptease, here are some moves, suggested in Dr. Glenn Wilson's *The Intimate Touch: A Guide to More Active Lovemaking for You and Your Partner*, that you may want to try.

- Undo your tie slowly and deliberately. While maintaining eye contact, drape it around her neck and pull her close for a passionate kiss.
- Unbutton your shirt slowly, revealing half your chest at a time. Turn your back, slip your shirt half off and show her your shoulders. Then turn around, slip your shirt off and let it drop to the floor.
- Never, ever fold clothes as you undress. This isn't the time to keep your wardrobe neat.
- Kick off your shoes with flair. And remove your socks beforehand. A naked man wearing socks looks silly, not sexy.
- Let her unzip your zipper—but don't let her touch anything else. At this point the pot should be simmering, not boiling over.
- Pull your pants down one leg at a time. Or let them fall naturally by thrusting and gyrating your hips.

Don't think about what comes next—enjoy the moment.

Treat sex like a business. Dr. Volker advises: "How do you find out what a customer wants? You ask. How do you keep your customer happy? Give her what she needs. How do you avoid competition? Keep your 'product' new and exciting."

Becoming a Handy Man

Mastering the Magic of Massage

At this very moment, whether you know it or not, you have in your possession a sex organ so large it doesn't fit in your pants. It can be soft or hard. Smooth or rough. Saggy or taut. It changes color like a chameleon. Stretches like a rubber band and wrinkles like a raisin. It's a sexual medium so powerful that merely touching it can make you moan in ecstasy, gasp with desire or sigh in serenity.

This marvelous sex organ is not between your legs, and it's not between your ears (that's the most *important* sex organ, not the largest). This sex organ surrounds you: It's your skin, and it's your ticket to steamy sex and rich romance.

Sensuality That's Skin Deep

The skin is our largest organ, weighing six pounds and covering some 20 square feet of surface area in the average man. Packed into each square centimeter are 12 feet of nerves, 3 feet of blood vessels, 10 hair follicles and 100 sweat glands. The epidermis, or outer layer, wears away monthly, and, in a lifetime, we can rub off nearly 40 pounds of dead skin cells.

More important, there are anywhere from 14,000 to 18,000 nerve receptors in each square inch of skin—and they provide an awful lot of sexual stimulation if you let them, says Ralph R. Stephens, a massage expert and spokesman for the American Massage Therapy Association.

"Most people assume skin is nothing more than some durable covering that holds us in and keeps other things out," Stephens says. "But while it's true that our skin is a barrier, it also connects us to our environment.

"The skin tells our mind what's going on around us. Touching it signals approval. It makes us feel safe and accepted. Wanted."

As Bertrand Russell said, "Our whole conception of what exists outside us is based on the sense of touch."

What You Knead to Succeed

Learning to please the skin is easy: Just touch with love and tenderness. You don't have to be a touchy-feely kind of guy to master massage. When you do, you'll find yourself a sensual King Midas, making everyone that you touch feel golden. Here's how to get started.

Drop your guard. As men, we're socially conditioned to be a bit standoffish when it comes to touch and other expressions of intimacy. But that doesn't mean our partners feel the same way. And it doesn't mean even the most inveterate Lone Wolf can't develop that tender Midas touch.

"The secret is that the more you touch, the easier it becomes," says Anne Semans, co-owner of Good Vibrations, a retail and mail-order adult store in San Francisco, and co-author of *The Good Vibrations Guide to Sex*.

"Having someone else's hand on you always feels different at first, but once you get comfortable with it, it feels very, very good."

Our advice is to take it slow and easy at first. Start by touching nonthreatening areas, like her neck and shoulders. Enjoying touching means feeling at ease with yourself and your partner. In time this will build intimacy and increase your comfort level around each other's body.

Set the scene. Once you're comfortable with touching and being touched, go for a more extended session. Do this in a soothing environment. That means turning off the TV, dimming the lights and letting the answering machine take your calls. Play soft music, burn some incense or scented candles and make sure there's a big bed, comfy couch or plenty of plush pillows handy. Also, adjust the room temperature: Make sure it's your magic fingers causing those goose bumps and not a cold draft.

Massage with oil. Dry, smooth skin can be caressed without painful friction or snagged hair. But serious touching, particularly massage, requires lubrication. Use a commercial massage oil, available at health food stores, or make your own. Just use pure oils, like almond or peanut oil. To increase the ambience, add a few drops of concentrated peppermint or strawberry essence for a delicious, lingering aroma. Other scents that work well include lavender, mandarin and Roman chamomile, which some experts claim calm the body.

To use oil, put a quarter-size dab of it in the palm of your hand, then rub your hands together so it warms up. Don't use oil on clothing or near the eyes, ears or nose.

Use different strokes. The most common massage stroke is *effleurage* (ef-FLER-ahj), which uses the fingers and palm in long, gliding strokes that go toward the heart. Then there's *petrissage* (pe-TREE-sahj), a squeezing/compressing/kneading motion that rolls muscles. It works well on shoulders, the sides of the back and the triceps. Also try deep friction strokes to reduce stress and improve circulation, and soft, light strokes for a more arousing feel.

"Finger pressure should always be

Just a Touch

Who knew something so little could mean so much? Consider this simple experiment on the amazing power of touch.

Researchers exploring the psychological benefit of touch asked a librarian to lightly touch the hand of every other person who checked out a book. The scientists then surveyed library customers as they left, quizzing them about the librarian's attitude. Overwhelmingly, those who were touched, even lightly on the hand, reported a much more positive experience. They said the librarian smiled, was friendly and seemed warm and approachable *even though her expressions and actions were identical for every customer.* In contrast, those who weren't touched described the librarian in neutral terms; some even said she was cold or unfriendly.

The moral to this story?

"Little touches can mean a lot," says sex therapist Dr. Erica M. Goodstone.

---

appropriate," Stephens says. Brisk, assertive strokes are better for invigorating; deep, slow strokes for relaxing; and gentle, nearly imperceptible strokes for sexual stimulation.

Finish strong. The end of a massage is as important as its beginning. If you've spent the last half-hour stroking your partner into deep peace, don't abruptly wrap up by flicking on Monday night football or blaring the radio. Instead, try this special finishing technique used by the pros: Cover your partner with a towel or blanket to keep her warm. Briskly rub your hands together for several seconds until they're hot. Then gently cup her eyes with your warmed hands so she can relax for several moments. Then creep away quietly so she can come to her senses at her leisure.

His and Hers: The Differences in Orgasms

A Scientific Look at Love's Hot Spot

Remember the first time you were with a woman as she climaxed? You probably weren't sure what happened—maybe you even had to ask. Her orgasm seemed much more visceral than yours. More mysterious. Holistic. It seemed so . . . magical.

As for yours, there was little mystery involved. A 21-gun salute—at least in your younger days—and then find a towel.

The differences in male and female orgasms, however, are not as profound as they may have once seemed. All orgasms are magical in their own right. Experts still aren't exactly sure what they are or where they come from. But there's no reason to believe hers is any more mysterious than yours.

that it resembles the high-power surges that occur during epileptic seizures.

Researchers who study human sexuality acknowledge that while they can identify some of the physical events that accompany orgasm—increased brain activity, muscle contractions and so on—there's no way to predict what an individual will actually feel.

In one study, a number of women reported climaxing, even though the machines measuring their responses drew a blank. Similarly, men who climax without the usual ejaculation say the sensations they experience are just as powerful as when they have a "wet" orgasm.

One thing that's certain, however, is that the urge to climax is among our most powerful drives. In laboratory studies, scientists wired rats so they had the ability to tickle their pleasure centers at will. The animals became so intent on getting pleasure that they literally lost interest in the basics, like getting enough food or sleep.

"Orgasms are pretty enigmatic," says sex therapist Dr. Barbara Keesling, author of *How to Make Love All Night (And Drive a Woman Wild)*. "We think there's an emotional component, a physical component and a genital component. But there's a lot we don't know."

The Big O

Despite the obvious involvement of the genitals, it's almost impossible to tell where orgasmic sensations begin and end. The actual event, however, appears to originate north of the belt, in a part of the brain called the limbic cortex, or the pleasure center. At the moment of orgasm, the limbic cortex positively sparkles with electrical activity. Indeed, this synaptic firestorm is so intense

His Orgasm

If you ever doubt the extent to which men and women view the world differently, check out the nearest magazine rack. You'll spot dozens of covers featuring women, most in various stages and degrees of undress. How many naked guys do you see up there?

Any art director can tell you—and doctors concur—that the quickest way to a man's groin is through his eyes. That's where arousal often starts: an attractive skirt on a spring day; your lover modeling thigh-high, fishnet stockings; a steamy encounter on a sexy video.

As arousal continues—progressing to touching, foreplay and intercourse—a man's penis fills with blood and gets erect. The scrotum thickens, and the testicles draw in close to the body. Breathing, blood pressure and heart rate increase, and the skin may flush red.

Orgasm occurs for most age groups within five minutes after arousal starts, but Dr. Keesling and other experts say any man can train himself to last longer. Before climax a man reaches a "point of inevitability." This is when the train is coming and you're on the tracks—and there's not a thing you can do to stop it. This orgasmic point of no return generally lasts two to three seconds and is accompanied by the gathering of prostatic fluids as the body prepares to ejaculate.

During ejaculation there is a series of four or five powerful contractions in the penis, about one every 0.8 second. The anus also contracts rhythmically. The result of each ejaculation is one to two teaspoonfuls of semen and more than one hundred million sperm cells.

After orgasm a man enters a *refractory*, or cooling-off, period, where he loses his erection and must wait until the next one comes along. This can take as little as 5 to 15 minutes in a teenager or as long as a day in a 60-year-old man. Some experts believe that any man can learn to substantially reduce or even eliminate his refractory period, making it possible to enjoy several orgasms in a row.

Her Orgasm

Although men generally regard the female orgasm as being more intense or at least different from their own, studies suggest the two events are very much alike, says Dr. Keesling. Indeed, when people write about

their orgasms but don't specify their sex, there's no sure way to tell whether the description is by a man or a woman. "Many men describe their orgasms in sensuous ways we'd normally think of as female," says Dr. Keesling. "I think there are fewer differences in male and female orgasms than we might want to believe."

While men are often aroused by visual cues, a woman's turn-ons are likely to involve such things as romantic, sexy talk, or perhaps a sensual massage. As excitement builds, her lips redden, her pupils dilate and her nipples become erect. Her breathing, heart rate and blood pressure rise. Blood rushes to the vagina, expanding the thick, wrinkly walls until they're taut and firm. At the same time, she starts getting wetter.

As a woman nears orgasm, her clitoris behaves similarly to a penis. It fills with blood, becoming erect and exquisitely sensitive. Direct stimulation, say with the tongue, fingers or even a vibrator, can trigger orgasm faster than indirect stimulation, such as vaginal intercourse.

During orgasm the clitoris contracts under its hood, so it's hard to say exactly what it does. But the outer third of the vagina contracts 3 to 5 times (and sometimes as many as 10 to 15) in 0.8-second intervals.

Some women experience long, powerful, slow waves of contractions. Others experience faster, more intense peaks. Many experience both, depending on the type of stimulation they're receiving and the mood they're in.

The most obvious difference between men and women, orgasmically speaking, is that women have no refractory period and can often climax repeatedly. Yet many women report that having one orgasm (or two or three) is no less enjoyable or satisfying than having more. In bed and out, quality beats quantity.

"I've heard of one woman who had 150 orgasms in a row with a vibrator," Dr. Keesling says. "That might sound impressive, but why would you want to do that? I can't believe she got out of bed the next morning."

Lasting Longer

Take Control of Your Lovemaking

Right or wrong, it's a mental barometer against which every man measures his sexual performance: How long can I last?

Sure, you've listened to the experts' soothing advice that you no longer have to be a stoic superstud in bed. You've read about everyone being responsible for their own orgasms. And you know all about the virtues of fantastic foreplay and random acts of sexual kindness. Yet for many men, the mark of a successful sexual encounter boils down to how long the clock was ticking before he went off.

"One of the biggest differences between men and women during sex is that women are more sensually focused, while men are more performance focused," says sex therapist Dr. Barbara Keesling, author of *How to Make Love All Night (And Drive a Woman Wild)* and *Sexual Pleasure.*

"Women approach sex more from an enjoyment perspective, rather than a task-oriented perspective," Dr. Keesling says. "This task-oriented approach is a hard thing for many men to break out of because it's been their way of looking at sex for years."

Can you blame us? We live in a society that often equates power and speed with superiority, and superiority is what ensures self-survival. It's what makes us successful at work. It's what makes us number one on the basketball court. It's what makes us men.

That's all well and good, Dr. Keesling says, but remember that sex isn't like life's other activities. In an almost Zen way, it's an activity that you only do well at when you stop trying so hard. Lasting longer in bed, she says, boils down to knowing when to relax. It's rhythm. It's timing. It's knowing when to thrust and, more important, when not to.

Is learning how to last longer worth breaking decades of social conditioning? You bet. From a purely selfish standpoint, lasting longer means more pleasure. "I think learning ejaculatory control can be one of the most important sexual techniques a man can master," says Dr. Betty Dodson, a New York City sex educator, therapist and author.

"Lasting longer lets you control your lovemaking, instead of it controlling you," she adds. "It makes sense, because lasting is the part that feels so good. Once you ejaculate, most of the show's over." Moreover, consider that a mere 29 percent of women claim to achieve orgasm "always," while a whopping 75 percent of men say the same.

How Long Is Long Enough?

As a starting point to lasting longer, it helps to know how long a "normal" bout of lovemaking lasts. If you're thinking, "until I'm done," you're probably not alone. It has only been in recent years that attention has been paid to female orgasms. "It wasn't too long ago that people thought women weren't orgasmic at all," Dr. Keesling says.

Researchers have tried for years to define "normal." Famed sex experts William H. Masters, M.D., and Virginia E. Johnson, of the former Masters and Johnson Institute in St. Louis, put the limit for a "normal" man's staying power at whether he reached climax before his partner around 50 percent of the time or less. Other experts said a "normal" man should last 50 thrusts. Even Dr. Alfred C. Kinsey, the most famous sex researcher, noted that 75 percent of men ejaculate within two minutes after penetration,

making three-quarters of all men dysfunctional by yet other standards that said we should last a minimum of two minutes.

Experts today say the numbers game is hogwash. Although an estimated 20 to 30 million men can be technically classified as having a condition known as premature ejaculation—coming too quickly—what really matters is not what the stopwatch says but what your partner says. If you're satisfied and she's satisfied, it doesn't matter if you can clock yourself with a chronometer or a sundial. Of more than 3,000 American adults questioned in the 1994 *Sex in America* survey conducted by University of Chicago researchers, roughly 70 percent say their lovemaking sessions—at an average of six or seven a month—last 15 minutes to an hour. A little under 20 percent go more than an hour, and about 13 percent last less than 15 minutes.

Anatomy of an Erection

Besides knowing how long other people are lasting in bed, lasting longer means knowing how your body works. This means knowing what gives you an erection, what keeps your erection and what kills your erection. Despite what it feels like, a stiff penis doesn't begin below the belt—it starts above the collar, in your brain. Some type of stimulus—usually something visual, like a miniskirt or low-cut blouse—triggers your brain to firm things up downstairs.

After the brain becomes intrigued, it sends arousal signals racing down the spinal cord to the genitals. The signals immediately cause blood to stockpile in your otherwise flaccid fellow. This extra blood—20 times the normal amount—gathers in three spongy chambers in the penis: the corpus cavernosa, two large chambers on the top and sides; and the corpus spongiosum, a smaller chamber on the underside that contains the urethra and forms your penis head, or glans. To keep all this blood from escaping, "erection" nerves emit a chemical that neutralizes "flaccid" nerves.

When the "flaccid" nerves are turned off, the blood pools, resulting in a towering tribute to your sexual interest.

In addition to causing an erection, all that raging blood in your body pools in your skin, making you flush and perspire. Because you're pumping more blood and becoming worked up, you'll start breathing faster, your heart will pump harder, the skin of your scrotum will thicken and your testicles will draw in closer to your body.

Then the fun begins. Once you're erect and inside your lover, you're immediately engulfed in a cascade of exquisite sensation. You feel the tight warmth of her blood-swollen vaginal walls. You slide against the wetness of her natural lubrication. You might even bump against the one-way exit of her vaginal canal, the cervix. These sensations don't even include what's going on outside her body—the delicious kissing and licking, kneading, caressing, heavy breathing and moaning that's also assailing your senses and sending your brain—and body—into stimulation overload.

With all this going on—uncontrollable contractions, the sensation overload, the feelings of delight—it's no wonder it's so hard to stay hard. Ejaculation, which usually occurs 10 to 15 minutes after arousal, happens when you're stimulated to the "point of no return"—the time when your body's sex system is on automatic pilot and you're just along for the ride. At this point your body has churned up seminal fluids to the base of your urethra, the tube through which you urinate. When the grand finale arrives, muscle contractions drive this fluid up through the urethra and out of your body. This happens in a series of four or five contractions that occur every 0.8 second, generally lasting four or five glorious seconds in total.

When There's a Problem

Saying how things are supposed to work is the easy part. Saying why they don't work—or at least not as well as you would like—is a bit more difficult. The causes behind a man wilting prematurely in bed vary. But it's safe to say that it's usually just a matter of conditioning for most men. In a small percentage of cases, psychological distress may be an issue. And the 20 to 30 million men who ejaculate sooner than they want to—maybe you're one of them—should not resign themselves to the nearest monastery. It's not a disease and it's not a scarlet letter of masculine imperfection. It's very common and, more important, very treatable.

"All those old rules with number of thrusts or minutes or partner orgasms really put a lot of pressure on men," says sex therapist Dr. Marilyn K. Volker. "The good news is that, with time and practice, any man can learn the basic skills for extended lovemaking."

The pattern for Speedy Gonzales lovemaking is established early in life, experts says. It's often a learned response that comes from a lifetime of masturbating in a hurry. Since most guys started masturbating on the sly, say in bed at night or while taking a shower, their strategy was to get off as quickly (and quietly) as possible. Making it last meant risking getting caught.

"This type of masturbation builds a sexual response pattern in the mind," Dr. Dodson says.

A similar type of conditioning may have unwittingly come from your first relationships: Since you probably weren't living on your own at the time, sex was something you probably rushed so you didn't get caught. Maybe you were in a car, parked on a side road. Maybe you were in your living room and your parents were sleeping upstairs. There's nothing like that to force your body into warp nine when you should be at cruising speed.

A Primer on Impotence

Impotence—the inability to get or keep an erection—is the scourge of man's sexuality. It's his greatest fear. After all, an erect penis has long symbolized power and fertility, masculinity and strength. Even our primate cousins will demoralize would-be competitors by holding up their erect penises in a prosimian power struggle.

"Anything that deals with the penis in a pejorative way is a sure way to emasculate a man," says sex therapist Dr. Marilyn K. Volker. "Not being able to get or keep an erection can bring a man to his knees."

Most of us experience periodic bouts of temporary impotence caused by fatigue, stress or too much alcohol. But chronic impotence—affecting roughly ten million men—can be caused by something psychological, such as performance anxiety, depression or stress, and was once believed to be the root of all impotence.

Eighty percent of all chronic impotency—and most cases for men 50 and over—are physical in nature, like a testicular injury or poor penile blood flow. Diabetes, alcoholism and multiple sclerosis also contribute to impotency. And a number of prescription drugs, especially those used to treat high blood pressure, can be the culprit in some cases. Psychological causes, such as anxiety over performance or penis size, can come into play as well.

Luckily, impotence needn't mean the end of your sex life. Here are some tips to keep in mind.

Stay in touch. Intercourse is only one element of

Loving Better

It's probably safe to assume that we all want something that feels as good as sex to last as long as it can. It's human nature. Here's how lovemaking. **There are plenty of other things to do, like intimate touching or massage, that are just as pleasurable.**

See a pro. **Don't let a chronic case of impotence erode your confidence. See a urologist for a full physical checkup, and consider visiting a sex therapist if you suspect psychological anxiety is at work.**

Work it often. **Regular use of your machinery prevents it from breaking down. If you're not impotent now, having a regular—preferably frequent—sex life, alone or with a partner, will help keep the pump primed permanently, says Richard A. Carroll, Ph.D., director of the Sex and Marital Therapy Program at Northwestern Medical Center in Chicago. "This is, in part, because having sex and orgasms stimulates testosterone production," he says. "There's a feedback cycle here. If you're sexually active, you'll keep producing testosterone.**

There's also a psychological factor. If you're happy and are enjoying your sex life, you'll keep at it."

Consider other options. **Your doctor can tell you about a host of medical treatments for chronic impotence, including:**

• **Self-injection therapy: Here you take a needle and inject drugs like papaverine directly into your penis for a firm erection that lasts 15 to 30 minutes.**

• **Prosthetics: Prosthetic devices, the so-called gold standard treatment, are permanent erection-producing implants. One type is a flexible rod that's inserted in your penis to keep it semi-rigid; the other type is a true pump, which enables you to pump up an erection at will.**

last longer and vowing to work at it. Anne Semans, co-author of the comprehensive *The Good Vibrations Guide to Sex*, suggests you view it in a financial frame: The more time you spend on your investment of lasting longer, the more "interest" your lovemaking will accrue, and, ultimately, the bigger return you'll get when you finally cash in.

Practice, practice, practice. At the outset, lasting longer isn't something you'll do in one night, one week or even one month, Dr. Volker says. It's a skill that takes time and effort and practice. But at least the practice is fun.

If you're opposed to masturbation for religious or other reasons, the next bit of advice isn't for you. But if you're open to the idea, Dr. Dodson says masturbation is an excellent way to build control, "providing you're not masturbating like a teenager in the shower." Rather, take your time. Explore what types of strokes work best and what rhythm keeps you in control. (For more information, see Masturbation on page 82.)

Know the real score. It's a classic, albeit worthless, guy myth: Concentrating on baseball scores, or any similar mundane data, will distract you enough to avoid orgasm. Dr. Keesling suggests leaving baseball trivia to the sports almanac.

"It's bull," she says. "And doing math problems in your head doesn't work either. I don't know why people try it."

As a sex surrogate for 12 years—yes, that means she had sex with her patients to counsel them—Dr. Keesling says baseball stats and math problems aren't the least of it.

"I know some men who have trained themselves to think of something disgusting, like

to extend your lovemaking from a sprint to a marathon.

Make a commitment. The most important step you can take toward lasting longer is attitude, admitting that you want to a disgusting accident scene, so they won't ejaculate," she says. "Can you image their partners looking up and seeing the look on their faces? To me it's like, 'Go ahead and ejaculate. Don't put yourself through that.' "

Relax and enjoy it. There's a strange paradox in sex, one that's responsible for many of us ending faster than we'd like: The more we try *not* to ejaculate—the more we try to distract ourselves, the more we tense up—the more likely we are to climax.

"It's ironic, but if you focus on how good you're feeling, how good your partner is feeling and on your enjoyment, it keeps climax from coming so quickly," Dr. Keesling says. So instead of tensing up to mute those wonderful sensations, slow down, relax and embrace them. Enjoy them with every slowly passing second.

Take a breather. "The only time we ever think about breathing is when we have trouble doing it, yet conscious breathing can be a powerful aid in sexual growth," says sex therapist and educator Marty Klein, Ph.D., of Palo Alto, California. He suggests the following two breathing exercises to promote intimacy and to keep your erection around longer.

- Slow breathing: Deliberately slow down your breathing during sex so it's deep and relaxing. Although this is contrary to what your body is telling you, slow, relaxed breathing will delay ejaculation by reducing tension and anxiety.
- Coordinated breathing: Exhale deeply as you thrust slowly into your partner, and inhale as you withdraw. Coordinating your breathing with your movement enhances pleasure and intimacy.

Pump your PCs. No matter how many times you may hit the gym, no matter how many Cybex stations you work out at and no matter how much you can bench-press, you'll never hit the muscles that really count in sex.

The Big Yawn

" . . . because the only people for me are the mad ones, the ones who are mad to live, mad to talk, mad to be saved, desirous of everything at the same time, the ones who never yawn . . . "

—Jack Kerouac, from *On the Road*

The famous Beat writer might have had a different view on yawning if the drug clomipramine had been around when he was getting his kicks.

Clomipramine (Anafranil) is an antidepressant that carries an unusual, albeit rare, side effect: It brings on unexpected orgasm every time you yawn. The earth-shaking reaction happens in just 5 percent of users. Fluoxetine (Prozac) may also cause a similar response. Normally, antidepressants inhibit orgasm.

According to one of the first published case studies

They're the pubococcygeal (just call 'em PC for short) muscles, and no amount of weight lifting in the world will build them up.

"A lot of guys wonder how porn stars can get an erection on demand. It's PC muscles," Dr. Dodson says. "I've had the chance to check the PC muscles of some porn stars, and I almost swooned."

The PCs are a group of muscles on the underside of your body, running from your pubic bone to your tailbone. They're the same muscles you use to stop the flow of urine. But with the right conditioning, they can slow or stop ejaculation, enabling you to enjoy all the pleasure of sex while keeping your erection standing proud.

To get your PC muscles shipshape, you need to build your basic fitness. To do this, you'll have to perform what's called Kegel exercises, named after the 1950s gynecologist who used them to help women with incontinence. For the next three weeks, contract your PC muscles three times a day, 20 to 25 times at a on clomipramine's side effect, one married woman in her late twenties, who was taking it for depression, asked if she could continue on a long-term basis. She'd enjoyed the drug and even gave herself orgasms by yawning deliberately, according to the November 1993 issue of the *Canadian Journal of Psychiatry*. In another case, a twentysomething married man had to wear a condom continually to prevent embarrassing ejaculations every time he yawned.

As word of the drug's curious side effect spread over the Internet, cybernauts had a field day. One writer suggested clomipramine could have fascinating social implications if its orgasm-inducing abilities became widespread: People would flock to academic lectures, tune in to politics and seek out the most boring people at parties.

clip. Unlike any other exercise in the world, you can do this anywhere without anyone knowing, including while working at your computer or sitting in front of the TV. Just smile. No one will be the wiser. (Caution: Just don't get too ambitious—like all muscles, overdoing it can make you sore. And trust us—you don't want to be sore there.)

Step it up. After a few weeks to a month of general PC conditioning, try these advanced Kegel variations. Pick one and stick with it for another month or so. At the end of two to three months, you should notice a dramatic improvement in your muscle control and staying power.

- Extended Squeeze. Hold each contraction for two to three seconds. In time, progress slowly to the point where you're holding each contraction for ten seconds.
- Flutters. Rapidly work your PC muscles in a series of three fast and tight Kegel contractions. Once this becomes easy, build up to flutters of five and ten contractions.

- The Big Squeeze. Contract your PC muscles for as long as you can and hold it. Because this can wear the little guys out quickly, don't do repetitions of this exercise. Just three times a day should be sufficient.

Stop right there. The start/stop technique is a delaying tactic pioneered by James Semans, M.D., a urologist at Duke University School of Medicine in Durham, North Carolina, in the 1950s. To do it: Wait until you're almost at the point of ejaculation—just before that "moment of inevitability." Then stop all stimulation. Just lie still and breathe. Let the arousal pass. A minute or two later—when you've recomposed yourself—start thrusting again, stopping each time you approach that inevitable moment. If it helps, gauge your arousal on a scale of one to ten, with ten being climax. You'll probably be operating in the area of six to seven at the beginning of your thrusting. When you reach eight and are closing in on nine, stop.

Assume the position. Proper sexual positioning can spell the difference between a short roll in the hay and a leisurely one. Why? Some positions better lend themselves to the long haul. For example, despite its pervasiveness, the missionary position (man on top) allows the most sensitive parts of your penis to be most easily aroused by a woman's vagina. Opt instead for woman-on-top positions or side-by-side sex, which is less intense stimulation-wise.

Wrap it. Even if pregnancy is the farthest thing from your mind, and you've been in a monogamous relationship for years, there's something to be said in favor of the slight desensitizing nature of condoms. Some extra layers of latex might be just what you need to help you last longer. So if you want an easy way to stay stronger longer, put on two condoms. Some men find the latex layers and the firmness of the condom ring keep them erect.

Multiple Orgasms for Men

It Ain't Over 'til It's Over

When it comes to climax, male orgasm is a bittersweet finale to the delightful symphony of sex. Orgasm means electric tingling sensations, wracking waves of intense muscle spasms and a feeling of celestial light-headedness. But, for most guys, it also means an ensuing intermission in lovemaking, if not the end of the concert.

It needn't be this way. Men usually think orgasm and ejaculation are one and the same. But they aren't. Ejaculation is the expulsion of semen. Orgasm is the apex of sexual excitement. Some experts say the two can—and should—be separated to make each sensation more intense and pleasurable.

In other words, you can teach yourself to experience numerous orgasms before ejaculating. Here's how male multiple orgasms work: A refractory period—the penis's natural downtime—usually follows ejaculation. By learning to hold back ejaculation, you enjoy several "mini-orgasms" first. When you finally ejaculate, it will be more intense and satisfying than ever before.

"The problem is, so many men assume the two are synonymous that they fail to explore their own bodies enough to find out," says Dr. Betty Dodson, a New York City sex educator, therapist and author of *Sex for One: The Joy of Selfloving*, a book on masturbation.

Are male multiple orgasms real, or are they faddish doppelgängers of regular orgasms? Studies, what few exist, suggest they're real. But not everyone agrees. Male multiple orgasms were first documented in American literature in 1886 by researcher R. von Krafft-Ebing in *Psychopathia Sexualis*. Krafft-Ebing and subsequent sex researchers of the 1930s and 1940s considered it a dysfunction.

Since then, researchers have tried to quantify the phenomenon. Groundbreaking sex researcher Dr. Alfred C. Kinsey verified the existence of male multiple orgasms, but he failed to answer how and why they occur. Masters and Johnson, however, offered a dissenting view. Their studies showed that men who claimed to have had multiple orgasms were actually contracting their own rectal sphincter in a way that mimicked orgasm.

An illuminating 1989 study by Marian E. Dunn, Ph.D., of the State University of New York Health Science Center in Brooklyn, questioned 21 men ages 25 to 69 who claimed they had experienced multiple orgasms. Dr. Dunn found that 13 of the men had multiple orgasms all their lives, while 8 started after age 35. Two of those men consciously taught themselves to do it, while the other six serendipitously encountered it on their own.

What does this mean for you? The bottom line is that, whether they're clinically defined as multiple orgasms or merely as a roller-coaster series of sexual peaks and plateaus, men can experience greater pleasure and last longer. Interested in learning how?

The Joys of Multiplication

There are two reasons you should open your mind to the possibility of multiple orgasms: yourself and your partner. "It helps you understand your partner's sexuality better so you don't just roll over and go to sleep after

Round One," says sex therapist Dr. Barbara Keesling, author of *How to Make Love All Night (And Drive a Woman Wild)*, a how-to manual on the male multiple orgasm. And multiple orgasms feel good; they allow you and your lover to enjoy longer lovemaking.

Here's how to get started.

Find somebody to love. Unless you're flying solo, practice only with the right partner. In that 1989 survey, researchers found most of the multi-orgasmic men required a familiar, sexually responsive partner and a nonthreatening, stress-free atmosphere. Dr. Keesling says working with a partner can be rewarding and erotic. "Sex doesn't happen in a vacuum. Working together can be satisfying and educational for both of you," she says.

Know that time is on your side. You might think your ability to climax more than once receded along with your hairline. But evidence, both empirical and clinical, suggests the ability of men to experience multiple orgasms only gets better with age.

"The men I know who had the most success with multiple orgasms were in their mid-thirties, forties and fifties," Dr. Keesling says. "Men in their early twenties generally have a shorter refractory period, so it seems they're not as interested in having multiple orgasms."

Work it on out. Multiple orgasms start with conditioning of the PC muscles. If you think we're telling you that only politically correct guys are multi-orgasmic, you haven't been paying attention. We're talking about the pubococcygeal muscles. (For more on them, turn back to "Pump your PCs" on page 94.)

Don't expect to qualify immediately for the sexual Olympics. World-class marathoners started off jogging to build up their basic fitness, and world-class lovers have to apply the same principle. To achieve a basic level of PC fitness, do this: For the next two to three weeks, contract and release your PC muscles—just like you would if you were trying to stop urinating—20 to 25 times, three times a day.

Pump it up. Once you've achieved basic PC fitness, push those muscles to the next level by holding each contraction for two seconds. After two weeks of this, hold contractions for five seconds. A few weeks later, do your 20 to 25 reps at ten seconds each. By then, Mr. Happy should start feeling like Mr. Olympia, and you're well on your way to multiple orgasms.

Build muscle for brains. Pumping the PC muscles is only half the battle: Your mind needs a workout, too. Next time you're between the sheets, alone or with a partner, mentally rate your arousal level on a scale of one to ten. One means you're not aroused, ten is orgasm.

Don't split hairs when it comes to this. There's no right or wrong. A four for you might be a six for the next guy. The goal is to recognize how close to or far from orgasm you are, so you can respond accordingly. "The numbers aren't points. Ten doesn't mean you win," Dr. Keesling notes. "This is a scale to help you identify arousal level and control climax."

Put it all together now. Once you've built rock-hard PCs and can judge your arousal level accurately, you're ready for the real thing. If you're with a partner, start by thrusting slowly, building your arousal to a low level, say, a four. Before your excitement mounts, pause, tighten your PCs and breathe deeply. Your arousal should subside a point or two.

Resume thrusting until you're at level six. Then pause again, tighten your PCs and breathe deeply, feeling your arousal again sink a notch or two. Continue these peaks and valleys until you're hovering around an arousal level of nine. Then push the envelope to 9.1, 9.2 and so on, peaking and relaxing, until you're at the brink of ecstasy: 9.9.

At that point, slam on your PC muscles *hard*, open your eyes and take a really deep breath. If you've trained your mind and muscles enough, you'll experience all the wonders of orgasm without ejaculating.

When you're done, relax a few minutes before continuing. You've earned it. What you do from there is up to you.

Positioning Yourself for Great Sex

Ways to Keep Love Alive

Sexual positions have been a part of the sexscape ever since the first couple got bored with the same-old, same-old in bed. Then imaginations went wild, and our procreative partnerships were limited only by our creativity and physical ability. This fascination with sexual positions has persisted through the years—and why not? It's only when you can ad-lib after mastering the basics that the fun really begins.

"Experimenting with sexual positions is an excellent way to keep love alive. Every relationship is kept fresh by some amount of sexual variation," says sex educator Judy Kuriansky, Ph.D., host of the popular *LovePhones* radio show in New York City and author of *Generation Sex* and *How to Love a Nice Guy.*

Variations in sex positioning date back to antiquity. The first, and perhaps best-known, book on positions is the ancient Indian text the *Kama Sutra*, written some 2,000 years ago. It details numerous poses. Even ancient Rome—the same society that brought us toga parties and orgies—had some positioning provisos: According to philosopher Lucretius, having sex like animals—that is, more or less doggie style—assured conception "since the semen can more easily reach the proper place."

But, Lucretius added, "It is absolutely *not* necessary for wives to move at all" during sex. He believed prostitutes writhed about during sex to avoid pregnancy and to "make the lovemaking more enjoyable for men, which obviously isn't necessary for our wives."

Different Strokes

Lucretius may have missed the boat on the whole movement thing, but he was onto an important concept: Different positions result in different outcomes. Some couples thrive on seeing how many positions they can think up. Experts have even explored the anatomical options in the name of science by (unsuccessfully) trying to count the total number of sex positions. One Indian sexologist tabulated it to be 529—but he treated even the most minor variation, like a change in the bend of an arm, as an entirely new position. What you need to know is not how many positions exist, but that experimenting with all or any of them can boost your sex life.

"Sexual positions can also be a matter of practicality. If a guy is a sports guy and he has torn some cartilage, for example, he might need to adjust for that in bed," Dr. Kuriansky says.

That said, here are the three primary position "genres," if you will, with the distinct advantages and disadvantages of each.

Man on Top

These positions include the traditional missionary position, which famed sex researcher Dr. Alfred C. Kinsey once estimated was the only position used by 70 percent of the adult U.S. population. But despite its ubiquity in our culture today, the pose wasn't common abroad or throughout history. Pacific Islanders, for example, laughed hysterically when they were taught the missionary position by visiting missionaries. (Hence, its name.) And the oldest known cave drawing depicting sex shows Fred Flintstone preferred *Wilma* on top. (But he was probably fantasizing about Betty the whole time.)

Still, there's much to be said for old faithful. The advantages are that these poses allow for great intimacy. Since you're facing each other, you can kiss, caress and whisper sweet nothings without being contortionists or throwing your back out. Doctors also say man-on-top positions best ensure pregnancy, since a woman's vagina is inverted and retains sperm best in this position.

Man-on-top positions also put you in total control, meaning you're in charge of rhythm, timing and thrusting. While novel at first, this can become a mixed blessing, says sex therapist and author Dr. Barbara Keesling. That's because being the top man can put pressure on you. If you're worried about performance, being the perpetual master of ceremonies can hamper your fun, especially when you want to just lie back and enjoy sex passively, Dr. Keesling says.

As for drawbacks, man-on-top positions make you climax more quickly because your penis receives maximal stimulation this way. But despite getting the goose off quickly, these positions do little for the gander: Man-on-top positions are *least* likely to arouse women, because they're indirectly, if at all, stimulating her clitoris. Worse yet, you're not at liberty to lend a hand for some manual assistance.

Woman on Top

Some guys balk at woman-on-top positions because they're intimidated. While woman-on-top positions put her in a "superior" position—they let her determine penetration depth, thrusting, rhythm and movement—they're nothing a sexually confident man should be afraid of, experts say. As we mentioned before, the earliest known cave drawing, found 3,200 years ago in the Ur excavations of Mesopotamia, shows a woman on top.

Woman-on-top positions give her maximal stimulation, since you're hitting her clitoris more directly. If that doesn't work, you can always use your hands. And you're more likely to last longer in these positions if you generally climax too quickly. Plus, if you're ever down

with erection troubles and can't keep it rock hard, she can stuff your semi-erect penis into her vagina and still wind up feeling dandy.

Rear Entry

Rear-entry positions are a mixed bag for some couples: Some love 'em, some hate 'em. Although they've been around since antiquity—and are documented in the *Kama Sutra, The Perfumed Garden* and other ancient love manuals—these positions are still considered perverse by some because they're believed to be animalistic or to mimic male homosexual intercourse. While it's true that nearly everything from poodles to pythons mounts in rear-entry positions, there's nothing homosexual about them. Sex preference is a matter of partners, not positions.

Despite the biases, there are compelling benefits to rear-entry positions. For him, the sight of upraised buttocks is usually a turn-on—it works for our monkey brothers, who know a female is ready to mate when she lifts her bottom. But the real gem of rear entry for men and women is the potential for gratifying, deep penetration. In rear entry you're able to hit the nether regions of her vagina, and it's your best bet to discover for yourself whether the mysterious G-spot really exists.

One drawback is that it's easier for a man to slip out of rear-entry positions. They're also not very intimate, since you're facing away from each other. Plus, they emphasize a dominant role for the man, which is something some couples, women particularly, don't feel comfortable with.

Positions for Play

On the following pages are detailed instructions and illustrations for 18 sex positions. We've included the three basic categories—man on top, woman on top and rear entry—as well as two other groupings: exotic and adventurous. These two categories include a grab bag of some innovative and athletic variations, including side-by-side sex, standing sex and some configurations you may never have imagined.

Man on Top
Missionary

If sex was weight lifting, the missionary position would be the bench press. It's a mainstay in our society and the ideal pose for pregnancy. Lie between her spread legs, so that you're lying on top of her and are face-to-face. While supporting your weight on your elbows or hands, insert your erect penis up into her, so it's parallel to her vaginal walls. Variations can include her wrapping her legs around your waist to change the shape of her vagina, which will alter the sensation for both of you.

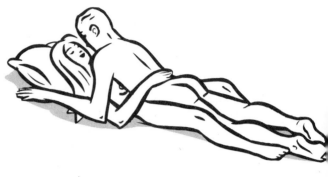

Man on Top
Seated Missionary

This is a good position if you want to rest your elbows or if you feel that you are crushing her in the standard missionary position. Sit between her legs, with her knees bent, while keeping your legs spread wide. Ease yourself into her vagina by wriggling toward her and leaning forward. The limited thrusting power is compensated by more direct penetration.

Man on Top
Knees to Chest

This is a more advanced missionary position that requires some flexibility on her part and some strength on yours. Enter her as you would in the standard missionary position, but instead of her simply spreading her legs, have her lift her knees to her chest and hook her ankles over your shoulders, while you support your weight on your hands. This gives you greater penetration and stimulates the back walls of her vagina.

Man on Top
Cross Buttocks

This is another good position to take your weight off your partner. It's also enjoyable for her because it stimulates the side of her vaginal walls, something she doesn't normally feel. Insert yourself into your partner in the missionary position, but lie across her pelvis, slightly askew, while still supporting your weight on your elbows.

Woman on Top
Reverse Missionary

This position is identical to the traditional missionary, but she's on top. Also, her legs are spread and yours are closer together. Now you're the passive partner, and she supports her weight on her elbows. This position gives you greater ejaculatory control and is ideal if she's much lighter than you. Variations include alternating whose legs are spread or spreading both of your legs at the same time.

Woman on Top
Woman Astride

These positions have plenty of advantages, including deeper penetration and more exquisite sensations for both of you. You also get a full view of the action and can touch her clitoris and play with her breasts. Enter this position by getting in the woman-on-top missionary first. Then have her draw her knees up until she's in a kneeling position, straddling your hips and sitting atop your pelvis. If need be, she can relieve some of her weight from your pelvis by leaning back and supporting herself on your thighs.

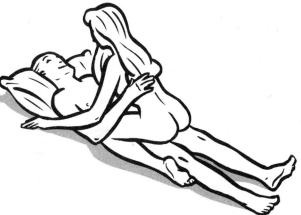

Woman on Top
Woman Astride, Facing Away

This position gives you a pleasing view of her zaftig buttocks. And since neither of you is looking at the other's face, you're free to close your eyes and fantasize. As in the previous position, the woman is straddling your body on her knees, but facing toward your feet; optionally, she can squat over you. The advantage for her is deeper penetration and control. The benefit for you is that she can caress your thighs and scrotum, and you can caress her buttocks and back. To take a bit of pressure off your pelvis, she can lean forward on your thighs or backward on your chest.

Rear Entry
Classic Rear Entry, Kneeling

Also called doggie style, this position allows for sensuously deep penetration, which you'll both enjoy. It also is said to be best for hitting the elusive G-spot and allows you to stroke her clitoris, breasts, hair and back—all powerful erogenous zones. Position yourself so you're kneeling behind your partner, who should be before you on her hands and knees. While kneeling, insert yourself and remain between her legs either upright or leaning over so your body drapes over hers. Take care while thrusting, since her wide-open vagina may allow you such penetration that you'll hit her cervix, something she can find painful.

Rear Entry
Rear Entry, Standing

This position is similar to classic kneeling rear entry, with the obvious difference being that you're both standing, which allows more thrusting latitude. Another plus is that you can caress her clitoris for extra stimulation. To get in position, stand behind her and have her bend over at the waist, keeping her upper body parallel to the floor. Hold her hips for support and enter from behind. You can make up for any dramatic differences in height by bending at the knees or by having her stand on something stable.

Rear Entry
Seated Rear Entry

This is a low-energy position for you in which she's in control. While you sit on a chair or the edge of the bed, she squats down on your erect penis. She controls movement and penetration, which can be quite deep and pleasurable for both of you. You're free to caress her breasts and upper body. Either one of you can fondle her clitoris for an extra zing. This position is good for surreptitious sex outside the bedroom.

Exotic
Spoon

The spoon position is the classic Sunday morning sex position: It's highly romantic and allows for a slow, luxurious ride in which you're both likely to last a long time. Spooning is also good if the woman is pregnant or if the man is on the heavy side. Plus, it's an ideal position to fall asleep in after sex. Enter the spoon while you're both on one side, facing in the same direction. Have her draw her knees up slightly, then tuck up behind her pelvis so you can enter from behind. By adjusting the lean of your bodies, you'll vary the angle of entry and your latitude to thrust.

Exotic
Spoon, Facing

This is a variation of the traditional spoon, and one that can be assumed from man-on-top or woman-on-top missionary positions without interrupting intercourse. From the missionary position, simply turn onto your sides in unison, using your arms to gently support your upper bodies. To start directly from this position, face each other on your sides and have her slightly lift or bend her leg while you enter.

Exotic
Squatted Kneeling

This is one of many kneeling positions, all of which are more athletic than some of the more familiar poses. The upshot of kneeling positions is that they allow your penis to better stimulate her clitoris and labia. In this position, you're squatting on the balls of your feet, with your legs spread apart about shoulder-width apart. She sits in your lap, facing you, straddling your legs with hers, while mounting your erect penis and bringing your upper bodies close together. By bouncing on the balls of her feet, she controls penetration and depth, but you both enjoy lots of intimate skin contact. This isn't a long-distance position and shouldn't be attempted by anyone with bad knees or a bad back.

Adventurous
Man on Top, Facing Away

Although this position limits movement for you both, it gives her full access to your scrotum, buttocks and anus for added teasing and pleasing. Have her lie down with her legs uplifted and spread. You then lower yourself between her legs, with your head going in the direction of her feet, entering in reverse. Your weight is resting on your elbows, which gives you leverage to lightly thrust backward.

Exotic
X Position

Another easy-rider position, this was called "a winner for prolonged slow inter-course" by Alex Comfort, M.D., in his best-selling book, *The Joy of Sex.* Start fully inserted, with her facing you in the woman-astride position. Clasp your hands in hers and move them out to the sides of your bodies. Then she lies back between your legs, which should be adjusted so that they "scissor" each other. Slow, leisurely wriggling movements will provide enough stimulation to make up for the lack of thrusting power. Either of you can sit up to change positions without disturbing the action.

Adventurous
Woman on Top, Leaning Back

This is a variation of the woman-astride position, and one that's sure to give you both novel sensations. From the facing woman astride position, she gently lies back until she's lying down between your legs. Although this limits your thrusting power, it allows either of you to caress her clitoris for added stimulation. If her knees ache, she can straighten her legs without interrupting. An interesting variation of this when she's on top, facing away: As before, she lies backward gently, until she's lying on top of your chest. This lets you stroke her clitoris and breasts.

Adventurous
Standing Wheelbarrow

This athletic variation is about the only position you literally can do on the run. Enter her as you would in standing rear entry, but lift her up by the pelvis and have her grip your waist with her legs. You'll be in a position similar to the "wheelbarrow" races you played in school—which were never this much fun. Because she'll be supporting her weight on her arms, she'll need to be strong. And although you'll both be able to stroll around the house in this position, it isn't something you'll want to do for an extended length of time.

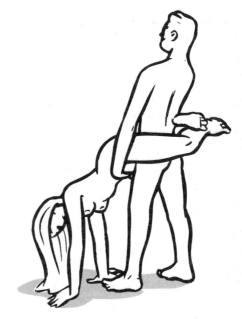

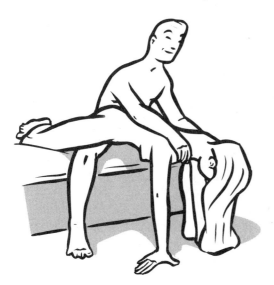

Adventurous
Seated Wheelbarrow

Great for a close-up view of the buttocks, this position is nearly identical to the Standing Wheelbarrow, except the man sits in a chair or on the edge of the bed. It likewise allows for limited movement but good penetration. And although it's not as strenuous on her as the Standing Wheelbarrow, it isn't something for marathon lovemaking.

Oral Sex

Becoming a Silver-Tongued Devil

It's the sort of thing you might read in *Ripley's Believe It or Not*, circa 2053: "Strange but true! Even though oral sex was known to be one of the most effective ways to bring a woman to orgasm, many men of the late twentieth century still did not practice it on a regular basis!"

And it *is* unbelievable, given what we've known at least since sex researcher Dr. Alfred C. Kinsey, circa 1953: Most women need clitoral stimulation to climax, and one of the best clitoral stimulators around is none other than Mr. Tongue.

So it comes as no surprise that when University of Chicago researchers polled more than 3,000 American adults about their sex lives for the 1994 *Sex in America* survey, they found that the thing that women enjoy most in the bedroom, second only to intercourse, is . . . you guessed it.

"A man could absolutely get a woman to be putty in his hands if she enjoys oral sex and he offers it," says sex educator, author and radio talk-show host Dr. Judy Kuriansky.

And more men than ever before are doing just that.

The Girl Most Likely To . . .

But while oral sex has become much more popular than it was in your grandfather's day, it still has not become a routine part of most couples' boudoir repertoire.

This appears to be more a function of education than anything else, say the researchers who did the *Sex in America* survey. For example, the survey showed that the woman most likely to be receptive to being on the receiving end is, first and foremost, well-educated, having a master's or other advanced college degree. (She is also single, White or Hispanic, between the ages of 25 and 34, and the woman most likely to return the favor.)

So let's go to college. We'll start with Latin 101. Oral sex on a woman is called cunnilingus (cun-eh-LING-ges). It comes from the Latin word *cunnus*, for vulva, and *lingere*, "to lick."

Because cunnilingus appeals to all five senses, it's incredibly intimate. You see up close the details that make her vulva unique. You smell the bouquet of her natural, musky odor. You feel the warm, soft fleshiness of her most private parts on your tongue. You taste the sweet sting of her vaginal fluids. You hear her moan or scream in joy.

Class, ahem, dismissed.

Biology Lab

Some men may avoid cunnilingus because they believe that the genitals are dirty, say Dr. William H. Masters, Virginia E. Johnson and Dr. Robert C. Kolodny, of the former Masters and Johnson Institute, in their seminal work, *Masters and Johnson on Sex and Human Loving.* Actually, daily bathing and good hygiene keep everything remarkably clean. So much so, in fact, that mouth-to-genital contact is really no different, germ-wise, than kissing.

Women also may worry that their genitals smell or taste bad. Or they feel vulnerable. So the first thing you need to do, if you and your partner haven't

done it before, is talk about it. You may find, of course, that she simply doesn't want to do it, and nothing will change her mind. Respect that.

Of course, you may not want to do it either. Oral sex isn't a required course. But if you do (and she does), then you'll need to do your homework.

A Higher Degree of Ecstasy

Good cunnilingus is a skill, and like any skill, it improves with practice. Here's how to become an erotic artisan of the highest degree.

Tease to please. Don't move in downstairs without giving the land-lord plenty of notice. Women, as a rule, don't like men—even the men they love—jumping at their genitals. So work your way down there gradually. Kiss her neck, scratch her back, stroke her buttocks, nibble at her toes, and every now and then just brush past her genitals. By the time you home in on her clitoris, she'll be dying for you to touch her there.

Reassure her. And when you get there, let her know how much you enjoy it. Say something like, "You taste so good, I *love* doing this to you."

Practice patience. Don't expect her to climax instantly. Slow and steady wins the race, so take your time, and while you're down there, try some of the following patented techniques.

- Tongue flicks: Gently flick the tip of your tongue along her clitoris.
- Tongue thrusts: Roll your tongue and thrust it in and out of her vagina.
- Labia licking: Lick the inner and outer vaginal lips from bottom to top. Then circle the clitoris with your tongue and do the other side.

- Lapping: Rhythmically lap her vulva, especially her clitoris, as though you were tasting ice cream. Use the broad side of your tongue—long and slow.
- Love nips: Gently nip her thighs, but don't bite her genitals.
- Sucking: Suck on her upper, inside thigh. Also works well when done lightly on the clitoris and labia.

Do what she likes. The most important technique, however, is just to find out what feels good for her. Should it be gentler? Faster? More to the right? Let her know that you could use some tutoring here.

Study hard and the next thing you know, you'll both be getting that advanced degree.

Anal Sex

Proceed with Caution

Here's an experiment you can try at home: Next time you have some friends over for dinner, just say—apropos of nothing—the words "anal sex." Or better yet, jocularly toss off this question: "Anyone here ever had anal sex?"

After your guests blush and titter and shift uneasily in their seats (and your mate shoots you a look that says, "What planet are you from?"), you can explain that this was just a little sociological experiment to gauge how people react to this particular subject.

Yeah, you're right. You probably don't want to do this. Nor do you need to. You already know this is a delicate subject.

While Americans have become relatively comfortable with the idea of oral sex, there is still a lot of fear and loathing attached to sexual explorations of what Chaucer called the nether eye.

"There's a scary number of sex manuals that don't even bring anal sex up. There's a feeling it's a perversion," says Cathy Winks, co-author of *The Good Vibrations Guide to Sex*.

Many may feel that it's a perversion, but a surprising number of us have tried it—at least once. When University of Chicago researchers interviewed 3,432 American adults about their sexual practices for the 1994 *Sex in America* survey, they found that a quarter of the men and a fifth of the women had tried it.

They also found that while many have tried it, few make it a habit, leading them to conclude that "lifetime experience with anal sex may

be for most people an isolated experimental incident."

If you're thinking of trying such an isolated experimental incident, here's what you should know.

The Health Risks

Short of shooting up with someone else's needle, unprotected anal intercourse is the most effective way to transmit the HIV virus that causes AIDS.

So the first two rules here are:

1. Know your partner's sexual history. Be sure you're both monogamous and HIV-free. And remember: "Often histories are not told quite truthfully," says Stephanie Sanders, Ph.D., associate director of the Kinsey Institute for Research in Sex, Gender and Reproduction at Indiana University in Bloomington. "Part of that may be deliberate, and part of it may be because of how we define sex. You know, people kind of relabel events sometimes."

2. Always use a condom. And not just to prevent AIDS. You can get bacterial infections if you contact fecal matter. And the condom will reduce friction and prevent tearing of her rectum, which is not as durable as her vagina.

One other thing: To avoid giving her an infection, you should wash your penis thoroughly after anal sex before you put it anyplace else, like in her vagina.

Common Consent

You're all psyched for an anal adventure. Like Roald Amundsen, you want to be the first to visit her South Pole. But is she ready for the visit?

Don't be surprised if she's not. When the *Sex in America* survey researchers asked women how they felt about being on the receiving end of

anal intercourse, only 1 percent of them said they found it "very appealing." (On the other hand, another, less scientific, survey of 100,000 female readers of *Redbook* magazine found that 40 percent of the women who had tried anal sex rated it somewhat to very enjoyable. Forty-nine percent didn't care for it, and another 10 percent didn't care one way or the other.)

How do you know if your partner is interested?

Start talking. Discuss it in a positive, nonthreatening way. Explain that it's a way for you both to expand your sexual horizons. Emphasize that the anus, especially the sphincter muscle, is both stretchable and loaded with nerves—meaning it can feel very good when stimulated properly.

If she says no, take that as an answer and forget about it. If she says she doesn't care one way or the other, check her for signs of life.

But if she says yes, then . . .

Make a clean start. Schedule a pit stop so she can empty her bowels. Then both of you should take a warm bath or shower to get as clean as possible—inside and out.

Lay on the lube. You'll need more lubrication than usual because the anus and rectum don't produce natural lubrication like the vagina. Apply liberally to yourself and to her before starting and add more as you go along. Use a water-based lubricant like K-Y Jelly.

Start slowly. Never jump into anal sex head first, so to speak. Take it slowly—tease her anus with your pinkie first. Then use your index finger. Then two fingers. After 10 or 15 minutes, rub her gently with the tip of your penis.

Then, ever so slowly, ease your way inside, one centimeter at a time. If she says stop, stop. If she says pull out, pull out. Once you're

Check Out the Lube Tube

You've taken all the precautions.

You've hired a private detective to make sure your partner hasn't had sex with anyone but you for the past 15 years.

You've dressed "Mr. President" in the best condom money can buy, a Spartan Meganater 2000, guaranteed for two years or 2,000 miles, whichever comes first.

And now you're lubing up for the big spelunk into her hitherto unvisited nether end.

Hey! Wait a minute! What's that you're putting on there?

If your lubricant has oil in it, you're in for condom erosion, which, putting it bluntly, means that within 60 seconds, your Spartan Meganater 2000 will have just about that many microscopic holes in it.

A lot of guys make this mistake, says Dr. Stephanie Sanders of the Kinsey Institute for Research in Sex, Gender and Reproduction. "People think if it washes off, it doesn't have oil in it, but that's not true," she says.

Bad (condom-eating) lubricants include petroleum jelly, Vaseline Intensive Care lotion, baby oil and Nivea. Good lubricants are *water*-based—no oil. Want to make sure? Read the ingredients or ask your pharmacist.

in, you can thrust in and out as you would in her vagina, but *much more gently.*

"Be very sensitive to the fact that men are far more interested in anal sex than women," says Dr. Judy Kuriansky, author of *Generation Sex* and *How to Love a Nice Guy.* "Many women will find pleasure in it. Many will just go along with it. Whatever you do, always, always go gently into that dark night."

After the Loving

Writing Your Own Happy Ending

A well-written story, some traditionalists maintain, should feature a beginning, a climax and an end. Think back and you'll probably recall an English teacher or professor telling you that once. The theory may not hold up for all great writing, but it certainly does for great sex. If you're trying to write the Book of Love, you need a good ending—not just a climax.

And there's nothing academic about it. In fact, it's one of the most practical aspects of a sexual relationship.

"The feelings at the end of sex are really the most important feelings. They're the last imprints you're walking away into the next sex scene with," says sex therapist Dr. Marilyn K. Volker.

"I think aftercourse, or afterplay, is still part of the sexual experience, and people should look at what it is they and their partner need or want," Dr. Volker adds.

If what you usually want is to roll over and go to sleep, you may be missing a golden opportunity to deepen your relationship with your lover—and put more passion in your sex life in the process. By focusing a bit on what happens after the loving, you may be able to write your own happy ending.

The ABCs of Afterplay

Pick up any sex book from 10 or 20 years ago and you'd be hard-pressed to find much, if anything, about afterplay. It's exactly that lack of

information and education that led James Halpern, Ph.D., and Mark A. Sherman, Ph.D., to write their book, *Afterplay: A Key to Intimacy*, in 1979. In the first chapter of their groundbreaking work, they note: "What we found was that the success of a sexual relationship is more closely related to satisfaction with afterplay than with any other phase of the sexual encounter—foreplay, intercourse, even orgasm."

The importance of afterplay appears to be twofold: physiological and psychological, with a strong emphasis on the psychological. We address these differences for men and women below with a brief breakdown on how afterplay spans the gender gap.

Afterplay for Him

Physiologically speaking, afterplay is when we enter detumescence. Detumescence is how our bodies bid adieu to arousal. For men it happens quickly, especially if we pull out of our partners immediately after climaxing. The blood rushes out of our penises, our erections falter and flaccidity overtakes us. Then we enter what's called a refractory period, which is our downtime between erections.

Psychologically, the significance of afterplay is less straightforward. While many men love to coo and cuddle in the warm afterglow of sex, many do not. In fact, many want to withdraw, physically and emotionally, from their partners. This withdrawal is partly because our penises are hypersensitive after orgasm, making excessive physical attention, especially on the genitals, annoying, agitating or even painful.

Then there's exhaustion. No, it's not in your head. There's a scientific explanation for that woozy feeling you get after sex. It works like this: During arousal, much of your blood flows into your pelvic area, and many of your muscles contract and tighten. When all is said and done, there's a tremendous release. That brings relaxation. Just clench your fist for 15 minutes and see how tired your hand gets once you open it. It's the same principle.

Afterplay for Her

The time it takes women to wind down after arousal is much longer. It may be 10 to 15 minutes before a woman's vagina returns to normal after sex. And although her clitoris retracts under its hood five to ten seconds after the last orgasmic contraction, the clitoral head remains relatively enlarged, taking 5, 10, maybe 30 minutes to shrink to normal size. If she didn't climax, it might take *hours* for everything to return to normal.

A woman's psychological needs also differ in afterplay, perhaps because her body is coming down from the mountaintop on a slow, meandering path, while ours is careening straight down the cliff. Usually, a woman wants to be held, cuddled or embraced after lovemaking. She wants to be caressed and coddled. She wants to lie between your legs, or have you lie between hers, perhaps while you remain inside her, even if you're flaccid.

Finding What Works

It may seem like men and women are at odds regarding where we're going after coming, but things needn't be so complicated. Just knowing the basics about intimacy and afterplay goes a long way. And there's no reason men and women can't strike a happy medium that keeps them both satisfied after lovemaking. Here are some things to keep in mind when the

And Now, a Word from the Experts

Dr. James Halpern and Dr. Mark A. Sherman pioneered one of the first in-depth looks at afterplay in their 1979 book *Afterplay: A Key to Intimacy*. The book, which is no longer in print, contains comments from women on the most ideal forms of afterplay, generated by anonymously surveying 234 Americans throughout the continental United States. Here are some of our favorites.

"Not to talk, but hold each other a short while and have my head or back rubbed."

"I would like to be held and caressed for an hour and then given a body rub with oil and hot towels."

"I like to be held and caressed either verbally or physically and to feel that it is important to my husband that it is me who is there."

"I would like my partner to tell me how much he loves me and how beautiful he thinks I am."

"I would want to be held close and told I was cared for, as well as how wonderful I was in bed."

"I like to share our dreams with each other."

"I enjoy hearing my partner say whatever trivial, ridiculous things come to mind—it's a time of lack of inhibition, a comfortable time to do whatever you feel like, to say whatever you feel like."

"I like dim lighting and red lights for atmosphere, because it makes it so much more cozy and intimate. Atmosphere is important. It kind of creates a mood. Your surroundings can make you feel sexier, and if you feel sexy, you can do anything."

"I especially like it to be warm and quiet, with no children around."

"I like to shower with my lover. I love to kneel down and wash him."

"I would like an opulent feast served by someone. I would like to share eating and drinking with him from the same plate and glass."

curtain is closing on the evening's adult entertainment.

Ask her. If there's one thing that's repeated throughout this book, it's the importance of communication. Why? Because it's the one thing that came up again and again with the experts. Afterplay was no exception.

"It's important to see what your partner needs," Dr. Volker says. "You should know your partner, know your partner's style, know what she wants.

"You really don't know all this on a first sexual experience, but if you want to build this kind of intimacy, you'll need to talk about it," she says. "Ask and find out what she likes best after sex."

Have it your way. True, afterplay builds intimacy and gives lovemaking a sense of closure. But "don't put too much pressure on yourselves," Dr. Volker warns.

"Afterplay should be as significant as the couple wants it to be," she says. "There's no problem with your rolling over and going to sleep if it's okay with the both of you."

Strike a deal. If you like to sleep after sex and she likes to cuddle, don't let your differences drive a wedge between your intimacy. Be like Monty Hall and make a deal. Agree that some times you'll cuddle, other times she'll let you snooze. You don't have to be Henry Kissinger to negotiate these deals with diplomacy.

Don't underestimate intimacy. "Too often the emotional and intimacy aspects of sex tend to get overlooked," says the Northwestern Medical Center's Dr. Richard A. Carroll.

"Instead, we tend to take a clinical or mechanical approach to sex, but we have to appreciate the psychological aspects of desire as well," he says. So even if intimacy after sex isn't high on your list of priorities, don't assume she feels the same way.

Relax and enjoy it. Another barrier that can keep a man from enjoying afterplay is a fear of intimacy. "Let's face it, we as men are not very well-trained to be comfortable with

emotional intimacy," Dr. Carroll says. "This fear often has instinctual and biological origins as well as societal origins."

Just knowing that it's okay to open up and relax when you're done "performing" can be a burden off your shoulders. After all, if you worked out hard in the gym, you'd have no problem sitting around swapping athletic war stories with the guys.

Kiss . . . Some men see kissing as a sign of weakness or as a show of "womanly" affection. But don't underestimate the power kissing can have, especially in building intimacy and bringing your afterplay to a satisfying conclusion. Eighty-five percent of all Americans interviewed in a sensuality survey by the Revlon company said passionate kissing was one of the most sensual activities around.

. . . and tell. Now that we just told you to kiss her, try using your tongue in a different way: Talk to her.

According to that Revlon study we mentioned, 72 percent of women said "being told you are beautiful" was a sensual turn-on. Need something to talk about? Forget quantum physics or existentialism. Stick to the simple things in life: Tell her how great she was, how happy you are, how nice she looks. Say it with meaning—and remember to mean what you say. True intimacy is based on honesty.

Try something different. We've told you some of the basics of afterplay. Now how about trying these variations, if you'd both enjoy them?

- Massage each other.
- Take turns reading to each other, perhaps from classic erotic literature like Anais Nin's *Delta of Venus* or Marco Vassi's *The Vassi Collection.*
- Watch TV or a movie in each other's arms in bed.
- Take a brisk walk together, or spend the next couple of hours working together.
- Prepare and cook dinner together.
- Lounge around in bed, playing cards, chess or checkers.

Part Four

The Playful Lover

Make Loving Fun

The Play's the Thing

Like any other fully functional, erection-sustaining, orgasm-achieving male, you probably already thought sex was pretty fun. But you also know that in an imperfect world, there's always room for improvement—even where sex is concerned.

"There are a lot of men who see the pleasure of sex in one dimension—revolving around orgasm," laments William Hartman, Ph.D., co-director of the Center for Marital and Sexual Studies in Long Beach, California. "They need to learn to take more time, add more dimension to sex for themselves and their partners. Sex play is a good way to do that."

As the experts explain, sex and sex play are two entirely different beasts. Sex is, well, sex, the physical act of lovemaking. Sex play, like foreplay, is the icing on the carnal cake, the accent piece that can give your love life a special resonance, inject it with a new thrill and give it years of uninterrupted excitement.

After all, the couple that plays together stays together.

Romping on the Sexual Playground

To take advantage of the passionate perks of sex play, you'll have to start playing around, incorporating fun and games into your amorous routines. Hard task, right?

If your notions of sexual variety revolve around a repertoire of positions and some skimpy lingerie, get ready for a mind-expanding tour through the many flavors of sexual fun. Maybe you'll want to begin by experimenting with a sex toy, reading some erotic fiction with your partner or priming the pump with a steamy movie or two. If you have a home computer, you might even want to explore the realms of virtual sex, interfacing with others in the racier climes of the Internet. As you get more daring, you may want to change the playing field, taking your sex out of the bedroom and into the kitchen, the den, the broom closet— maybe even out in a public place like a park or a rooftop.

Whatever you decide to do, keep your eye on the prize—having fun. "Some people are a little nervous when they decide to start experimenting and playing with their usual sexual routine," acknowledges Arlene Goldman, Ph.D., coordinator for the Jefferson Sexual Function Center in Philadelphia. "If you or your partner is a little squeamish at first, that's okay." But remember, you don't have to do anything you don't want to—sex play and experimentation shouldn't be work, it's meant to be good, messy fun. And here's all you need to keep it that way.

Rely on your rapport. Just as teammates on the sports field need to give each other clear signals to set up the next play, you and your partner need to be clear on what each of you wants to do—and how far you're willing to go.

"It can be very destructive for one partner to suddenly bring up a new twist on sex when the other person isn't ready," Dr. Goldman says. So before you start fooling around with the way you fool around, huddle up.

"Talk with each other— it's the first step to sharing your fantasies and then being able to act them out. It can be fun, too. You just might be surprised and delighted by what your partner has in mind. But you'll never know if you don't build that rapport first," he adds.

Advocate an adventurous spirit. One of the most important organs you can bring to the bedroom is the one between your ears, not your legs. "The more open-minded you are about sex play, the broader your range of pleasure and enjoyment will be," says Carol Cassell, Ph.D., a sex therapist in private practice in Albuquerque, New Mexico, and author of *Tender Bargaining*. Don't let yourself be intimidated. Don't be afraid to be a swashbuckler of sex.

"There's a bumper sticker I saw once that read, 'Feel the fear, and do it anyway.' Let that be your motto for sex play. And even if you're not quite sure you're going to enjoy something, ask yourself, 'Will it really hurt to try this?' Once you open your mind to it, you might actually enjoy it," Dr. Cassell says. Depending on how old you are, it hasn't been that long since you didn't think girls were all that interesting—look how wrong *that* notion turned out to be.

Keep your wits about you. As any scientist can tell you, sometimes experiments end in failure—but that doesn't mean you should abandon your research altogether.

"It's always a good idea to maintain a sense of humor when you're playing," Dr. Goldman says. "If you decide to try a new position or location that's so unworkable it is ridiculous, go ahead and laugh about it."

This is a tough trick for guys to master, she says, because we get so caught up in the need to make every sexual experience the best one possible. "By its very nature, that's not always going to happen when you're experimenting."

So be ready to laugh off any experi-

ences that don't match the dirty movie running in your head. "By trial and error, you'll learn what does work—and then you'll *really* have some fun," Dr. Goldman says.

Let the games begin.

Where the Toys Are

Being an upstanding citizen, you might feel just a tad self-conscious walking into your local adult store to pick up a toy or video. What if the boss drives by just as you're going in? What if you bump into the boss inside?

For those of you who consider discretion the better part of valor, do your sex shopping the Sears way—by catalog. Here is a list of reliable sex toy and information resources.

Access Instructional Media
16161 Ventura Boulevard, #328
Encino, CA 91436
1-800-772-0708

Adam and Eve
P.O. Box 800
Carrboro, NC 27510
1-800-274-0333

Alamo Square
P.O. Box 14543
San Francisco, CA 94114
(415) 863-7410

Eve's Garden
119 West 57th Street #420
New York, NY 10019
1-800-848-3837

Focus International
1160 East Jericho Turnpike
Suite 15
Huntington, NY 11743
1-800-843-0305

Good Vibrations/Down There Press
938 Howard Street
San Francisco, CA 94103
1-800-289-8423

Pleasure Chest
7733 Santa Monica Boulevard
West Hollywood, CA 90046
1-800-75-DILDO

QSM (Quality SM)
P.O. Box 880154
San Francisco, CA 94188
1-800-537-5815

Xandria Collection
165 Valley Drive
Brisbane, CA 94005
1-800-242-2823

Risky Business

Why Naughty Can Be So Nice

Steven Tyler, lead singer for the legendary rock band Aerosmith, didn't just write the hit song "Love in an Elevator" off the top of his head. He did field research first.

"Tyler really did it," wrote sex educator and radio talk-show host Judy Kuriansky, Ph.D., in her book *Generation Sex*. "As he told me, he and two girls were on the floor of an elevator, one girl was doing him while he was doing another, and when the door opened at the ground floor, they didn't even notice the people looking in."

Never mind the fact that it was a threesome, or in an elevator or in a public place. It's that last detail—the door opening on a lobby full of people—that sticks in the mind. And it's probably that fact, the danger of getting caught, that made the sex memorable enough to immortalize it in a song.

Caught with Your Pants Down

Don't believe us? Close your eyes for a second. Cast your mind back across the years to the Dawn of Your Sexual Being.

You and your sweetie are sitting in the basement rec room, enjoying fine, wholesome entertainment. But the veneer of your innocent behavior is cracking like an eggshell. Soon, your hands are exploring each other's uncharted territories. You fumble with buttons; you strain against the various elastics of her undergarments; you round the bases of love. But like the player who tries to stretch a triple into a home run, you're very much aware of the danger of being caught—as well as the

supreme satisfaction you'll feel if you can get away with it.

Then, somewhere in the distance, you hear the approaching murmur of voices, the sound of footsteps. She hisses in alarm, "Someone's coming!"

"That's for sure," you think.

If this trip down memory lane rings true, believe it, you are not alone. The theme of risky sex—sex with the fear of discovery—emerged over and over as part of a fax survey we conducted in *Men's Health* magazine that drew roughly 1,800 responses. When we asked men to report their most powerful sexual experiences, the overwhelming majority revolved around encounters in crowded bars, in extremely public places or with the authorities close by. What's wrong with us? Nothing at all, say the experts.

"The thing is that our bodies really don't know the difference between anxiety and arousal. The adrenaline is flowing, our pulse is pounding, our senses are heightened—it's the same thing whether you're horny or frightened," explains sex therapist Dr. Carol Cassell, author of *Tender Bargaining*.

Why that's so is not entirely clear. Part of the reason can be found in our primitive roots, when we had to be ready at a moment's notice for any number of stressful physical activities—running from that saber-toothed tiger, hunting down a woolly mammoth or taking the opportunity to advance the species whenever it presented itself. Life was a frenzied dance to stay alive and spread our seed.

But today, we don't often find ourselves in life-threatening situations, so the adrenaline fires most often when we're being sexually aroused.

Now throw in a monkey wrench, a potential threat—a cop catching you in the act on a park bench, for example. Our modern minds know this will not cause us to be killed, but our primitive 911 system doesn't.

High-Stakes Games of Risk

They gambled everything—their power, their money, their lives—for sex. Some were ruined; others were made legends.

Emperor Nero: One of ancient Rome's more depraved rulers, Nero's idea of daring sexual encounters included castrating young boys and marrying them in public ceremonies, having sex with his mother as they were carried through the streets in an imperial litter and dressing up in the skins of wild animals and attacking the genitals of helpless prisoners. In A.D. 68, the Roman Senate said, "Enough of this crap." They intended to strip him, thrust his head onto a wooden fork and then flog him to death. When he found out what was in store for him, Nero committed suicide.

Marquis de Sade: His name is synonymous with sexual cruelty, and with good reason. In 1772, he threw a party that turned into a public orgy after he served guests chocolates laced with Spanish fly—a deadly aphrodisiac that reportedly killed several of the revelers. He spent the rest of his life in and out of prison and passed the time writing erotic novels that featured bizarre sexual practices. He died in an insane asylum in 1814.

Grover Cleveland: Though renowned for his honesty and his reputation as a public reformer, Cleveland's race for the presidency in 1884 was marred by newspaper allegations that he'd carried on an affair with a widow and even sired a child with her. His opponents gleefully began chanting the slogan: "Ma, ma, where's my pa? Gone to the White House, ha, ha, ha!" He owned up to the affair, but voters still elected him president—and again in 1892.

Roman Polanski: Hollywood wunderkind and gifted director of *Rosemary's Baby* and *Chinatown*, Polanski wound up casting himself in the role of cradle-robber and statutory rapist when the 43-year-old director had sex with a 13-year-old schoolgirl in Jack Nicholson's Jacuzzi. Polanski was arrested and pleaded guilty, but before he could be sentenced, he jumped on a plane to Europe and has been wanted in the United States ever since. *Tess*, his first film after the incident, won three Academy Awards.

Gary Hart: The man who would be president. Young, good-looking, popular with the voters, Gary Hart was also popular with the women. When he started cavorting with model Donna Rice, word—and pictures—got back to the press, and this public servant became a public scandal. Hart dropped out of the 1988 presidential race—and right off the political radar screen.

Hugh Grant: Boyish British heartthrob Grant got caught with his pants down on Hollywood's Sunset Boulevard when police arrested him in the midst of oral sex with prostitute Divine Brown—just days before the opening of Grant's new family movie *Nine Months*. Grant pleaded no contest to the charge, got two years' probation and gave new meaning to the phrase: To err is human, to forgive Divine.

More adrenaline is released in response to the threat, but because we're already equating adrenaline with sex, we get even hornier at the thought of being caught with our pants down.

"Put simply: The risk of discovery becomes an aphrodisiac," says Dr. Cassell.

Enjoying Risk Safely

Not to throw a wet blanket on the flames of discovery, but remember: When we say risk, we're talking about risk within reason. "There are risks you don't want to dice with—diseases, for example. Always practice safe sex. The kind of risk involved in not practicing safe sex isn't exciting or arousing—it's dangerous and stupid," says Dr. Arlene Goldman of the Jefferson Sexual Function Center. And if you're caught having sex in a public place, you run the very serious risk of getting arrested for any of a number of offenses, only the least of which is indecent exposure.

Here are some ways to add to the excitement and generate the element of fun risk.

Turn on your love lights. On The Beatles' White Album, Paul McCartney asked the salacious musical question, "Why don't we do it in the road?" (After all, he assures the listener, "No one will be watching us.") But if you want to see how much fun sex with the risk of being seen or caught can be, you don't have to march right out into the street and get busy. Start out with something simple.

"Experiment with the feeling of being exposed to view—even if the only other person who can see you is your partner," Dr. Goldman says. The quickest way to do that? Flick on the light switch. This also is a handy exercise to help both of you conquer inhibitions and be more comfortable with yourselves.

Leave the blinds up. As Dr. Cassell says, the possibility of being seen in the midst of sex has arousing appeal—and you can do it right from the comfort of your own home. Just don't draw the blinds. Or move your action into that room with the big picture window. "For

some, it's very exciting to think someone on the street below or in the next building might be watching," Dr. Cassell says.

Engage in sex talk. One of the safest but most titillating ways to expose yourself in public without too much fear of discovery is by talking to each other about what you want to do. "Dirty talk can be arousing, and it's doubly so if you talk about it to each other in public—on the bus, in a restaurant, wherever," says Dr. Goldman. "Telling each other in public what you want to do in private can be very stimulating—and you never have to put yourself at risk for discovery."

Take your show on the road. You probably don't need us to tell you the appeal of having sex on the highway. It has everything going for it—cars, women and sex.

But while many couples have experimented with sex in a moving vehicle, remember that this form of public display holds more risks than simply getting caught. "When you're aroused, you start to block out surrounding information—such as traffic. If you want to have sex in a car, make it one that isn't moving—pull over," says Dr. Goldman.

Visit your parents' basement. Even if you've been married and out of the house for years, you might be able to capture that old forbidden thrill next time you visit your folks or the in-laws.

"Many of us, when we were adolescents, had our first sexual experiences on the sly—in the basement, in the backseat of the car. There was always the danger of the authorities showing up and catching us. And while that made sex very anxiety-ridden, it also made it more exciting because there was the extra thrill of getting away with something," Dr. Goldman says.

So the next time you go home for the holidays and everyone's tucked away in bed upstairs, sneak down to the rec room with your partner and revisit those forbidden joys of youth. Just keep your ears open for the sound of parental footsteps.

Location

Being in the Right Place at the Right Time

In the backseat of a Cessna 172 airplane.

In a deer stand next to a very busy walking path.

On a golf course in Bermuda—the only hole in one I ever had.

And where's the most unusual place you ever had sex?

When *Men's Health* magazine posed that question in a survey, the editors were impressed by the sheer daring, resourcefulness and creativity of their fellow men, as demonstrated by the above testimonials.

One thing's clear: Love and war have more in common than merely the idea of what's fair. Location, for example. As any general can tell you, the strategic placement of troops and fortresses makes all the difference between victory and defeat.

It's been said that one man in the right place at the right time can win a war; the same holds true for you soldiers of love. By changing the location of your, er, troop activity, you'll constantly keep the other side guessing, forever have them wondering what's next—and in so doing create a sex life of unbeatable flavor and diversity.

"The reason people like to have sex in different locales is the same reason why there are 31 different flavors of ice cream," says sex therapist Dr. Carol Cassell, author of *Tender Bargaining*. "Even though we all think we have a particular favorite flavor, the truth is, the best flavor of all is variety."

Getting Out of Bed

On top of the washing machine while it was running.

In the backyard, on a trampoline.

On the kitchen table.

On my front steps in broad daylight.

Variety, in case you hadn't figured it out by now, truly is the spice of life. And when it comes to your sex life, variety begins at home.

"Even if you have a favorite restaurant, it can get pretty boring if you go there every night. For the same reasons, that's why changing locations for sex can be good once in a while," says Dr. Arlene Goldman of the Jefferson Sexual Function Center. "The first step to creating diversity in your locations is just by getting out of bed. As many couples have discovered, any room in the house can be a bedroom."

We're not saying you need to be an exhibitionist or a sexual daredevil. Not at all. But if sex has become routine, one of the ways to break out of your rut is to change venues. And you don't have to leave the comfort—or privacy—of your own home. Here are some ideas recommended by our experts.

Make change. You don't even have to leave the bedroom to add some variety to your sex life.

"Remember that location is just another word for variety," Dr. Goldman says. "If you want to start spicing things up, you don't have to go right from the bedroom to the rooftop."

Take your time. "Start slowly, if that makes you more comfortable. Change the how and when before you change the where. Start by having sex in a number of different positions, or changing the time when you normally have sex. If you always have it on the weekend at 8:00 P.M., try first thing in the morning on a weekday," Dr. Goldman says. By gradually tinkering with your standard sexual formula, you'll both become more comfortable—and more adventuresome—with the idea of sex in the exotic locales beyond the bedroom door.

Schedule a moving day. If you're ready to start moving around the house, try making new rules for yourself. "For example, you could decide that, on certain days of the week, you can have sex in any room—except the bedroom," Dr. Cassell suggests.

In the bathtub with the shower running.

Under the dining room table.

Such fun restrictions force you to start using your imagination. You'll quickly find other places in the house that may be even more fun and exciting than your old four-poster playground.

Have fun with furniture. Once you've moved beyond the bed, try couches, chairs or tables—some survey respondents reported amorous encounters involving dishwashers and washing machines. (It probably should be noted that the encounters took place *on*, not *in*, those appliances.)

On the couch—at her parents' house.

On the bathroom sink.

Just as you set rules about the bedroom, do the same thing with your usual lovemaking surfaces. You could, for example, make it a rule that you can have sex anywhere but on the bed or the floor for the next week, suggests Dr. Cassell.

Explore nooks and crannies. While many men reported the bathroom or shower as a favorite alternative to the bedroom, explore other tight places for a change—closets, pantries and toolsheds are other good examples.

Flagrante Delicto

You and your lust muffin are acting out your fondest fantasy, doing the deed . . .

a) in the Pirates of the Caribbean ride at Walt Disney World

b) on the path overlooking Niagara Falls

c) at the top of the Empire State Building

And it is great, even better than you could have ever imagined it . . . until . . . uh-oh . . . is that . . . uh . . . the cops?

It seems only fair to warn you that this is a real possibility with a real penalty.

Sex in the Magic Kingdom? That could get you "fifty lashes from Goofy," says Orlando, Florida, police sergeant Mike Holloway. More likely, it will get you a $500 fine and/or 60 days in jail.

What about Niagara Falls, Ontario, mecca of horny honeymooners? You could be looking at a fine of up to $2,000 or six months in jail, says Niagara Falls Detective Staff Sergeant Paul White.

White says, however, that he hasn't heard of anyone being charged in years. "We have a zillion hotels, so it's really not a problem."

How about on top of the Empire State Building? According to sources in the New York City Police Department, "Merely having sex in public isn't necessarily a crime."

Which is to say, if you take precautions not to get caught, it's not considered public lewdness. If, however, you shamelessly do the electric slide on 5th Avenue, you could face up to three months in jail.

In short, you gotta do a lot to get noticed in the Big Apple.

Taking It on the Road

When I was younger, I had sex on my high school wrestling mats and on the after-school bus.

On the floor of my boss's office.

In an airport photo booth.

In the cupola atop the Texas State Capitol in Austin.

You may find that moving your love-making around the house adds all the variety you need or want. That's great. Remember, what's important is not that you experience some *Penthouse* Forum fantasy but that you and your partner develop a more intimate and satisfying relationship. If you feel you want to experiment more, you may want to take your show on the road or anywhere out of the house that suits you.

"Although it can be exciting to experiment with sex in different parts of the house, it can be even more arousing to move to a completely unfamiliar or unusual environment," Dr. Goldman says. From a romantic weekend getaway to a roadside quickie, having sex in a totally unfamiliar—and occasionally quite public—place can be extremely arousing. Here's how you can have fun out of your house.

Be a backseat driver. Cars and girls: Rocker Bruce Springsteen made millions of dollars off that simple formula. It's easy to see why, judging by the response to our *Men's Health* magazine survey. Cars, vans and pickup trucks were the hands-down, four-on-the-floor favorite place for sex outside the house.

Had oral sex in the backseat of a moving car, while another couple was in the front seat.

"It's fun and nostalgic at the same time. It takes you back to when you had to have sex on the sly—maybe the only place you had any privacy was the car," Dr. Goldman says. And these automotive encounters weren't limited to teenage-style gropings in the backseat. On the hood, with the top down, even in the driver's seat (watch that horn!) are just a few vehicular variances some guys try.

Perform some moving violations. As the number of men who reported having sex in their cars indicates, one way to make sure the earth moves for both of you is to take your antics on the road.

"Sex by plane and train—not just automobile—has always been a great turn-on, as any member of the Mile High Club can tell you," Dr. Cassell says. Some movers and shakers we surveyed reported great sex in as unlikely and uncomfortable vehicles as police cars, ice cream trucks, motorcycles—even on horseback.

Take it outside. "For some people, there's nothing that feels better or more natural than being naked and having sex outside," says Dr. Cassell. "I have a friend who says she can't hike with her partner without wanting to stop along the trail and have sex. Being outdoors is very primal and can make for a very powerful sexual experience."

Just remember: There's a huge difference between secluded woods and a public park. And be sure never to underestimate Mother Nature, as this man did: *Unfortunately, we did it in the middle of a patch of poison ivy.*

Get a room. Of course, for many civilized men, there's something just as primal about hotel rooms. Maybe it's something in the tap water or the air freshener, but hotels just seem to invite sex, whether they're the most picturesque bed-and-breakfast or a dingy no-tell motel with a quarter-fed mattress vibrator.

"It's familiar and foreign at the same time. It's fun to be in a strange place, to wake up in a strange bed," observes Dr. Cassell. Plus, you don't have to worry about changing the linens when you're done.

Go to work. When you or your partner get a promotion—especially one that includes moving into an office—celebrate it. Inaugurate the office—go in to work some weekend or after hours, lock the door and have at it. Some guys we surveyed even reported putting in a little overtime in their boss's office. That's your call, of course. Just make sure you consider one question in advance: Do I really need this job?

Welcome to Fantasy Island

Follow Your Love Map to Paradise Peak

You're at the beach, lying in godlike repose as life's rich pageantry unfolds before you. You're basking in the glow—of the sun, and also of the bevy of bikini-clad beauties bouncing by. You gawk at them, wearing your best I'm-not-gawking-at-you-miss-I'm-simply-staring-into-the-middle-distance look. They, on the other hand, are wearing next to nothing. Their skimpy swimsuits make Eve's fig leaves seem like a Sunday-go-to-meeting dress. An older guy might leer at them, then collect himself and say disdainfully, "Those outfits leave nothing to the imagination."

On the contrary, they leave everything to the imagination. Because that's what's running overtime right now. Admit it—at the mere sight of a bikini, the big-screen TV flickered on in your head, and your own personal beach/sex fantasy came on it for the umpteenth time. It's an all-star cast, full of beautiful, half-naked women, many of them famous celebrities, as well as luscious total strangers you may have glimpsed on a warm summer day 20 years ago.

But here they are now, young as ever, vying with the likes of Pamela Lee, Sharon Stone and Uma Thurman for the right to rub sunscreen all over your body. You assure them there's enough of you to go around, and there is. After all, this is your fantasy, and you're the young, svelte, well-muscled star, ready to make love with

any of them—or all of them—from here to eternity.

Okay, so maybe your fantasy isn't on the beach, maybe it's on a Manhattan rooftop, with a high-class call girl; or at a seedy biker bar south of the border, with a leather-bound mama who's had your name tattooed on her inner thighs; or it could be right in your own home with your very own wife, except you've both lost 20 years and ten pounds and you're re-enacting that first marathon weekend of sex. The point is we all have fantasies. And you know what? Even if those fantasies involve some pretty sick and adulterous things—things we'd never think of admitting, let alone doing— it doesn't mean anything is wrong with us. In fact, the more fantasies we have, the healthier we are, sexually speaking.

That being the case, men in general must have the healthiest libidos in the known universe. Surveys conservatively estimate that more than half of all men think about sex on the order of seven times a day. Some experts estimate we spend up to 10 percent of our time on fantasy island.

Mapping Your Heart's Desire

Experts say part of the reason we have some pretty creative scenarios rattling around in our heads is because we're playing out behavior we'd like to see in our mates.

"In everyone's head there is something called a love map—a template we've been building from birth, and it contains all the information we need to find the woman of our dreams," says Galdino Pranzarone, Ph.D., professor of psychology at Roanoke College in Salem, Virginia. As Dr. Pranzarone explains, that map doesn't just include the physical features we crave from our ideal woman; it includes behavioral information as well.

"If you want someone submissive or compliant, or domineering, that's all built into the love map. Also, if you desire certain sexual activity—you want someone who's only too happy to perform fellatio on you—that's part of the love map, too. If your partner doesn't happen to have a certain quality that's on the love map, chances are you're going to start fantasizing about it in an attempt to satisfy that requirement."

Playing Head Games

But fantasies are more than a way to play out all the permutations of our sexual wish list; they also keep us from getting into trouble.

"One very good reason for having fantasies is to explore an experience or situation that you might not want to explore in real life, for the very good reasons that they might be against the law or they might ruin your marriage or career," observes William A. Henkin, Ph.D., a certified sex therapist in San Francisco. "If these fantasies aren't hurting anyone, then there's no harm. Just the opposite, in fact."

Finally—and we can't say this often enough—try not to read too much into your fantasies.

"It's a mistake to try to make specific interpretations about the kind of person you are, simply on the basis of sex fantasies and daydreams," says Robert O. Hawkins, Ph.D., professor emeritus of psychology at the State University of New York in Stony Brook. "Fantasies don't mean anything. It's just a way your body arouses itself to enjoy sex more." Of course, it also helps a boring afternoon pass a lot quicker.

Same-Sex Scenarios

If they're going to fantasize about same-sex encounters, the tastes of most heterosexual men tend to run toward, say, the female cast of *Friends*, wrestling naked in a pit of Jell-O. But experts say that once in a while, some straight men may, to their shock and surprise, find themselves having a fantasy involving another man.

If, in the theater of your mind, you've ever found yourself wondering, "Hey, what's he doing here with me?" our advice is: Don't worry about it.

"It's perfectly natural for a heterosexual man to have a homosexual fantasy, no matter how unlikely he is to act on those fantasies," says the State University of New York's Dr. Hawkins.

It may be a fleeting image or dream, or something more complex—like maybe a threesome in which you're interacting with a woman as well as another man. Instead of being repulsed by the idea or wasting your time wondering if something is wrong with you—nothing is, by the way—just give it a mental shrug.

"It's all part of normal sexuality. Our fantasies are our mind's way of running down all the possibilities, evaluating what you would and would not do," says Roanoke College's Dr. Pranzarone. "Having a homosexual fantasy doesn't mean on some deep, dark level that that is what you want. Your mind is just flashing an image at you, and it's a reality check, a reminder to yourself: 'Oh yeah, I wouldn't do that.'"

Here's a glimpse at some of the scenarios for common fantasies many men experience. In all cases, you'll find these fantasies are pretty normal, insofar as they let us blow off some

A Homemade Fantasy

Take it from us—some of those stores and catalogs selling fantasy items, like latex rubber suits, leather dominatrix outfits and a selection of finer bondage devices, can be downright intimidating. Not to mention expensive. And what if the kids should chance upon the shoebox where you stashed the whip and the handcuffs?

If these are the concerns running through your mind, maybe you're better off improvising with stuff lying around the house. According to Jay Wiseman, author of *SM 101: A Realistic Introduction*, there are plenty of examples of seemingly innocuous items that can be subverted for sex.

Instead of . . .	Try using . . .
Handcuffs or chains	Clothesline, belts (no metal parts), adhesive or duct tape; softer restraints—old neckties or scarves
Whips or paddles	Hairbrushes or old leather belts
Nipple clamps	Clothespins
Latex or rubber suits	A big roll of plastic wrap

psychic steam and also deal with some issues we might not otherwise wrestle with. And where it's realistic, we've provided some suggestions for ways to make your dreams come true in ways that are safe and legal.

Strangers in the Night

Be it a chance encounter on the street or a scenario where you hook up with a hooker, fantasies about sex with total strangers satisfy our brutish urges to sleep with every attractive woman we see. But they also help us enjoy a little variety without ever being unfaithful to our partner. Unless you're a swinging single, though, we don't recommend trying this out for real. But

you can act it out—with your partner.

"You could role-play to spice things up. Pretend you're meeting for the first time; try to pick each other up," says sex therapist Dr. Carol Cassell. Go all out if you want—arrange to meet her at a bar, dress like a man on the prowl, show up, sweep her off her feet and right into bed at the motel across the way.

But come up with a new pickup line—just because your wife fell for it once doesn't mean she'll do it again.

Group Sex

We don't have to tell you the lure of fantasizing about having more than one woman at a time, but we will. "It's a way of reassuring yourself about your desirability," says Dr. Pranzarone. Plus, a three-or-moresome relieves you from the pressure of having to do all the work.

Some sexologists theorize that when you're imagining sex with more than one woman, you're subconsciously putting yourself in the role of one of the women—an attempt to get in touch with what your partner is feeling. "That can only make you a better, more attentive lover in real life," says Dr. Pranzarone.

Bondage

Fantasizing about tying up or forcing someone to have sex plays into the common male feelings of power. And some women have fantasies of being taken by force, although it must be made clear that this in no way implies they secretly desire to be raped, says Dr. Pranzarone.

A word of caution: Don't try to act this one out without getting approval beforehand. If your woman's skittish about bondage, offer to go first, she might enjoy it so much she'll be more than happy to comply when it's her turn.

Fantasy-o-matic

Is your fantasy well dry as a bone? If you need to prime the pump a little bit, try these ready-made scenarios on for size. For more fun, mix and match the categories.

You:	Her:	You wear:	Your opening line:
A powerful executive	A new secretary	A power tie and a smile	"Miss Jones, can you step into my office? I have some dictation for you."
A sheik	The latest addition to your harem	A towel on your head	"Dance for me, my love slave." (clap twice for effect)
A ski instructor	A snow bunny	Goggles and gloves	"Would you hold my pole for a minute?"
A bad boy	A stern headmistress	Your pants around your ankles	"Thank you, ma'am, may I have another?"
The lord of the manor	A French chambermaid	A monocle	"I say, *this* could use a bit of the old spit and polish!"
A knight in shining armor	The queen	A sword on your belt	"I am called Lancelot. Wouldst thou like to know why?"
A captured spy	An interrogator	A trench coat	"The name is Bondage. James Bondage."

And you don't have to hog-tie her—start out gently with loose restraints made of soft material, like scarves, bathrobe belts and that sort of thing.

Many experts agree that bondage has gotten a bad rap, conjuring images of a subculture of sick people who like to tie others up and force them to submit to their every whim. That's often Hollywood's view. In the movie *Basic Instinct*, femme fatale Sharon Stone ties her lovers to the bed—then jabs an ice pick into their hearts.

"Bondage is a word that is too often misunderstood. It's not necessarily about a very painful and restrictive experience," Dr. Henkin says.

Bondage is as much about trust and release as it is about having power over somebody. By agreeing to be restrained, you're putting yourself in someone else's hands. That takes a lot of pressure off you to be in control and do all the work, Dr. Henkin says. And it doesn't necessarily have to involve elaborate leather harnesses, chains and handcuffs. If your partner orders you not to move while she services you, for example, that's a form of psychological bondage.

Female Domination

Many powerful men, guys with lots of responsibility in their daily lives, find tremendous sexual satisfaction in being dominated by their women. Again, this is a perfectly healthy fantasy—it can be quite stress relieving and also a big turn-on, Dr. Pranzarone says.

"This is especially true for guys who are exerting power as part of their daily lives. It's no longer a thrill for them," he says. "What is thrilling is the sense of relief and release you get by turning over control to your partner."

Yes, you heard him right: Being dominated by your woman isn't going to rob you of one iota of your manhood.

"And it doesn't have to be anything terribly dramatic. When you think about it, a sexual position where the woman is on top is a kind of domination. And there are probably plenty of men who enjoy these positions who would say they weren't into domination at all," says Dr. Henkin. "It's really all a matter of perspective."

Turning over control to your partner can be more than a form of release—it may also be a way to break through some communications barriers.

"Some women have a very difficult time articulating what they want, what feels good to them during sex," points out Dr. Pranzarone. "If you play a submissive role—where whatever she says goes—your partner will feel more empowered. Some of the inhibitions may fall away, and she'll start to feel more comfortable about asking for what she wants." That's good, because it means a more equal and enjoyable sex life for the both of you. "Of course," Dr. Pranzarone warns, "you may end up unleashing a sexual dynamo whose appetites outstrip your own." Boy, *there's* a problem to have.

Spanking

Madonna, the Pretenders and Van Halen have all sung the praises of a red bottom. Two of America's greatest male icons—John Wayne and Elvis Presley—climaxed movies by flipping pretty women over their knees and spanking them into submission. And shock jock Howard Stern has parlayed bare-bottom spankings of beautiful women into number one ratings in major radio markets across the country.

It seems there's a whole lot of spanking going on. Including in the bedroom. Sadomasochistic practices also include whipping, pinching, tickling, rubbing ice or menthol rubs on certain sensitive parts of the body—you get the idea. These are fantasies you may be able to safely re-create—and many people do.

"It's a broad universe. And contrary to what most people think, it doesn't have to involve pain in the least," says Dr. Henkin, who has co-authored the book *SM/DS: Communica-*

Sex to Die For

It's America's dirty little secret: A man is found hanging from a rope tied around his neck. His pants and underwear hang around his ankles, and he's wearing women's clothing. Nearby is an open jar of petroleum jelly and some sex toys. It's not suicide, but it might as well be. It's autoerotic asphyxiation, and it's just as deadly.

Autoerotic asphyxiation is a bizarre and dangerous sex practice that combines masturbation with near-suffocation with the goal of a uniquely intense orgasm. As many as 1,000 people die each year from it. Researchers know little about this practice, largely because embarrassed friends and family hide evidence and deny what happened.

"This really strikes us as bizarre because it combines our own mortality with very extreme sex practices," says Sheila Garos, a doctoral candidate at Arizona State University in Tempe specializing in sex addiction, and author of one of the few academic journal articles detailing the practice.

According to Garos, in a typical scenario, a man ties a rope or cord around his neck just before he masturbates.

tion and Safety. "The reason so many people see it as painful is that since childhood we've come to associate intense sensations like slapping or spanking as shameful, painful, punishing things. But as adults, we're perfectly capable of recognizing that a slap to the ass isn't life-threatening or dangerous in any way. From there, we can override the message that tells us it's pain and reinterpret it as simply an intense sensation."

And one you might actually find pleasurable. After all, the areas around the thighs and buttocks are just loaded with nerve endings, and a spank can actually travel to your more erogenous zones, sexually stimulating you.

If you're still wary of the whole idea, think back over the course of your own love life. Chances are you've ended up with a few

As he nears climax, he increases tension on the rope by slowly hanging himself, cutting the blood flow to his brain. This reportedly intensifies orgasm and produces euphoric feelings. But lack of oxygen—especially during sexual arousal, when blood pressure and heart rate skyrocket—can cause blackout or instant cardiac arrest.

"Survivors who talk about this liken it to the rush you experience on a roller coaster," Garos says. "What they're not aware of is that you're manipulating a physiological reflex action when you do this, and unconsciousness is the result. You can also develop chronic brain damage."

As a sex practice, autoerotic asphyxiation has been around for a long time. It has popped up in many cultures and is mentioned in Marquis de Sade's *Justine* and Samuel Beckett's *Waiting for Godot*. The first documented death came in 1791, when famous London composer Frantisek Koczwara asked a local prostitute "to hang him for his sexual pleasure and cut him down in five minutes."

It turned out to be his last request.

scratches on your back after some scorching sex and never even felt them—or if you did, you never felt anything remotely like pain. If so, you've already been engaging in some light sadomasochism, and you didn't even know it, Dr. Henkin says.

Living in the Real World

Although we'd hate to discourage any man from making his dreams come true, please remember that having fantasies is one thing—living them is a somewhat trickier tiger to snag by the tail. Obviously, you don't really want to go running off with the boss's wife or kidnap that young hitchhiker you just passed and force her to become your love slave.

"But if what you are thinking or doing is not hurting you or me or the community, if it's not affecting your professional or social life adversely, then where's the harm?" asks Dr. Henkin.

You also have to know when to share your fantasy and, even more important, when *not* to. "Common sense dictates that there are some fantasies you just want to keep to yourself and replay them only for you, say, during sex when you want a little boost," Dr. Hawkins advises.

But if you want to act out some of your tamer fantasies, things that may not be as threatening to your partner or your standing in her eyes, go ahead and broach the subject.

"If you've had a standing fantasy where you like a certain kind of behavior or you're wearing certain outfits, or it's in a certain location, I'm in favor of talking to your partner about it," Dr. Pranzarone says. "You may be pleasantly surprised to find out she's had the same idea all along."

Just remember: Take it slow. Make gradual changes. And be willing to go first. If you want to try a little bondage, don't pressure her to be roped to the bedposts—maybe you should volunteer to be hog-tied. And remember to give and take. "Sex doesn't always have to be equal. Sometimes you can take turns. You play out the fantasy you want; next time, she plays out what she wants," says Dr. Arlene Goldman of the Jefferson Sexual Function Center. Don't expect her to go along with your fantasies when you're not willing to entertain her ideas.

In all of these situations, remember that the single most important tool in overcoming inhibitions is to talk about them. "Often, that's the biggest inhibition of all," Dr. Cassell says. "If you can get over your feelings of awkwardness and learn to discuss things openly, there's probably no inhibition you can't overcome."

Words of Love

Sexy Talk Adds Spice to Sex Life

The phone rings. You answer. It's a woman's voice; the throaty whisper sounds tantalizingly familiar. She starts talking. About what she's wearing—or not wearing. She describes her body in painstaking detail—the firmness of certain areas, the softness of others. She says she's hot. She wants you. She wants to tear your clothes off. She wants to lick you all over. She wants you to take her into a dark room and have your great, big, hard, sweaty, manly way with her. She wants this RIGHT NOW.

And right now, you hope to God this isn't a wrong number.

Having Social Intercourse

"Talking, rather than sex itself, is the aphrodisiac in seduction," says Barbara Keesling, Ph.D., a sex therapist in Orange, California, and author of *Talk Sexy to the One You Love.* "If you're a man or a woman who really knows how to verbally seduce your partner, that's a real turn-on."

Talking sexy with your partner is not just an aphrodisiac or a way to spice up sex play. It also can be an important tool in your relationship, a springboard that can launch you into the depths of greater intimacy and more satisfying sex for both of you.

"Talk gives you a chance to arouse your partner, but you can also use it as an opportunity to deal with some issues you might not otherwise discuss because one of you is uncomfortable," says Dr. Arlene Goldman

of the Jefferson Sexual Function Center. "For example, you can use talk as a way of letting your partner know what you would like her to do to you and, in turn, ask her what she wants you to do."

Having said that, sexy talk—even what some might consider dirty talk—serves another important purpose in your relationship. It can make sex a heck of a lot more fun—even if you didn't think such a thing was possible. "It fires the imagination, both when you're talking dirty to your partner and when you're on the receiving end of talk," Dr. Goldman says. She allows, however, that in the realm of sex, most men can walk the walk, but they can't always talk the talk.

"Women are much more verbal—they like to be talked to. But it's tough for men to verbalize their desires and fantasies. Dirty talk can help you bridge the gap, make you a more communicative lover, and a more playful one." Here are some ground rules to help make you a master of aural sex.

Talk first, act later. Use dirty talk as a form of foreplay. "My rule of thumb is 'Don't walk me to bed, talk me to bed,' " says Dr. Keesling.

That talk could start at the breakfast table; you could create a daylong thread of conversation that ultimately leads you to the bedroom. "Don't just say 'Wanna have some sex tonight?' Talk me into it," Dr. Keesling says.

Engage in pillow talk. Talking doesn't have to end at the bedroom door. "A lot of women complain that their husbands never talk during sex. In fact, they don't make any noise at all," says Dr. William Hartman of the Center for Marital and Sexual Studies.

So talk. You don't have to give a running commentary of the game at hand. But don't be afraid to tell your partner what feels good, or ask what she'd like to do next, or announce what you're about to do to her.

Watch your tone. Of course, sexy talk involves more than words; it also involves your tone of voice. "Tone, pitch, rhythm—it all factors into the effect talk will have on someone," Dr. Keesling says. For example, saying something very basic—I want to kiss you right here—in a breathy whisper can be much more romantic and arousing than a matter-of-fact statement in a normal tone of voice about where your lips are going next.

Watch your language. It's hard to talk sexy without using a few racy words—they don't call it dirty talk for nothing. Nevertheless, be mindful of what you're saying.

"Avoid four-letter words that your partner might find offensive," Dr. Keesling says. Some women might get turned on by saying or hearing that venerable Anglo-Saxon term euphemistically referred to as the f-word. "But to me, that doesn't say you're much of a silver-tongued devil," Dr. Keesling says. Instead of focusing on the salacious or the profane, communicate with words that you think will be particular turn-ons for your partner—and they might or might not be in the four-letter category.

Reach out and touch her. Using the phone for suggestive talk has been around since Alexander Graham Bell first shouted, "Come here, I want you." If you want to ring her bell during the day, Dr. Keesling says, call her up and give her a sexy earful.

Break the silence. At the opera, in a gallery, at the library—these are common places where silence is thought to be golden, where any talk is forbidden.

What better place for talking dirty to one another?

"It's the forbidden aspect," Dr. Keesling says. "You're not supposed to talk at all in

---

Phone Sex: Why Pay to Play?

You've seen them in the back of magazines, in the fine print of the classified ads, on late-night TV: a saucy wench with a sultry voice, guaranteeing you her undivided attention and talk that will burn the ears right off your head.

And then, you hear a monotone voice uttering the least sexy words in history: "Only $3.99 a minute. Must be 18 years or older." Welcome to the world of 1-900 phone sex.

"Have you ever listened to these? The women on the other end of the line are trained to talk so slowly, you'll have to spend a mint before you get any satisfaction," says sex therapist Dr. Carol Cassell. "That kind of dirty talk just isn't worth it, especially if you can get it for free with your partner."

And what if you have no partner or still want that thrill of racy stimuli from outside your happy union? "Buy a magazine—it's a lot cheaper, and you'll probably get more out of it," says Dr. Cassell.

---

the library or during 'Pomp and Circumstance.' So for some people, hearing sexy talk in so-called forbidden environments is especially arousing."

Speak your mind. If you're new to sexy talk, start slowly. You don't have to be overly creative—heck, you don't even have to be overly dirty. Just say what's on your mind. Make it like word association, Dr. Goldman advises. "Think about sex and then say the first thing that comes to your mind—unless you're absolutely sure it's not going to be a turn-on." Don't push yourself to come up with the naughtiest thing you can imagine the first time you try—chances are you'll just talk yourself into a corner, instead of into bed.

Sex Toys

Two Can Play That Game

Before sex, life's great pleasure was playing with toys. You probably had a favorite—the Super Bowl Limited Edition football, the G.I. Joe with the kung-fu grip, the die-cast metal cars that could race down an orange racetrack at the scale equivalent of 200 mph.

But then something happened. In the great Erector Set of your body, mechanisms started turning, glands began firing like hormone-squirting water pistols—and you had to grow up and put your toys away. Luckily, this was also around the time you started discovering girls, so it's not as if you've been totally deprived of fun. Yet since puberty, toys and sex have been separate entities in the minds of most men, two spheres of pleasure separated by some unnamed chasm.

Well, break out the Lincoln Logs: It's time to build a bridge.

Learning to Play Nice

Sex toys may not be for everyone. And that's fine. But if you're interested or just curious, talk with your partner about it. "Look through a catalog, go to a store together, pick out a toy for each of you," suggests Dr. Arlene Goldman of the Jefferson Sexual Function Center.

Here's a primer on the most common toys you'll find out there, how to use them and how much they're likely to cost.

Vibrators

Easily the most common—and popular—of sex toys, vibrators are just what you think they are: vibrating devices that, when applied to the right spots, produce mind-numbing pleasure. "They're popular because they provide consistent, reliable stimulation, and they're easy to use by yourself or with a partner," says Anne Semans, co-owner of the adult store Good Vibrations.

For women, predictably, many vibrators are phallus-shaped; some have ridges or bumps for better stimulation. Other vibrators are flatter and more pad-shaped, providing broader stimulation to skin surfaces and erogenous areas such as the labia. For men there are vibrating rings that you can slide onto the penis, as well as vibrating sleeves which you can slide over your penis like a big, trembling condom. Vibrators can cost as little as $8 for a cheap, battery-operated novelty item to $50 or $60 for an electric vibrating wand with multiple attachments.

Dildos

Like vibrators, most dildos mimic the look and feel of an erect penis, which can be a threatening object to men and women. "Not everyone is aroused by the idea of holding a big, amputated penis in their hands," Semans admits.

Consequently, many dildos these days are only vaguely phallic—some are even miniature sculptures of such smooth-looking animals as whales and dolphins. Other dildos  have an extra, smaller protrusion for clitoral or anal stimulation. Some vibrate as well. A basic rubber model runs $10 to $12, while premium silicone dildos can easily set you back $50.

"Many of the ones we offer are handmade," Semans says. "And silicone is a premium material to use—it's easy to clean, and it retains body heat well."

Anal Plugs

A smaller class of dildos are designed chiefly for anal stimulation. "Many men and women find anal stimulation as enjoyable as genital stimulation—there are a lot of nerve endings down there," says Semans.

For safety's sake, the toy should have a smooth surface and a flared base to keep it from getting caught in the rectum. Always be sure to use plenty of lubrication with an anal toy because anal and rectal tissue tears easily. You can buy a basic anal plug for $10 to $20.

Constrictor Rings

Also known as cock rings, these devices aren't just toys—they're tools to help men get and keep firmer erections. By placing one on the base of your penis, you'll trap blood in the erectile chamber, thus making you harder longer. Rings are made to accommodate all widths and are made with a variety of materials.

"Metal, leather, elastic—some have two rings or a harness to fit around the scrotum," Semans says. For safety's sake, don't wear one for longer than 20 minutes at a time—rings cut off blood flow to the penis. If fresh blood doesn't get pumped in there, you could be looking at serious tissue damage. Stick with elastic or latex rings, or else a leather ring with snaps or a Velcro release. "That way, if the pressure is uncomfortable or painful, you can quickly get out of it," says Semans.

Latex constrictor rings cost less than five bucks; a deluxe leather harness for all of your equipment can run $20.

Lotions and Ointments

While not toys in the strictest sense, lubricating yourself or your partner with scented or flavored lotions and oils can make

---

Do-It-Yourself Sex Toys

Here are commercial, household items you and your partner can convert to your own pleasurable devices.

• **Electric massager.** Don't tell us you've been using that handheld massager only for sore muscles. If so, let us give you permission to convert it to a sex toy. Trust us, everyone else has. "Our best-selling sex toy of all time isn't really a sex toy—it's the Hitachi Magic Wand, a handheld massager," says Anne Semans, co-owner of the adult store Good Vibrations.

Hint: If you or your partner have never used one before, try the massager on a low setting first—starting right out with a high setting could actually feel painful to your more sensitive areas.

• **Produce.** If you and your partner have been considering using a sex toy like a dildo but don't want to shell out $30 or more until you have some idea what it would feel like, check your produce bin for a nice, smooth, well-hung cucumber, or whatever other fruit or vegetable strikes your fancy. Of course, always wash all foods thoroughly before using them in sex play, warns sex educator, author and radio talk-show host Dr. Judy Kuriansky.

• **Shower head.** Maybe this is why so many couples have sex in the shower. "The pulsating, steady pressure of the water can be very arousing for both men and women," Semans says. Just make sure you don't use up all the hot water.

---

for some slick fun. If you and your sweetie are novice users of insertable toys, then lubricants such as K-Y Jelly or Astroglide should be an essential part of your toy box.

"Meanwhile, flavored massage oils and body gels really spice things up and help create a playful sexual atmosphere where you will both feel more at ease," says Renee Rand, founder of Party Girls, a sex-toy distributor in Las Vegas.

Note: If your skin should start to burn, itch or break out—especially around your genitals—stop using the lubricant.

Cybersex

The Virtues of Virtual Sex

When you bought that home computer, you probably figured the most fun you would have with it was playing a quick round of Solitaire in between balancing the family checkbook or working late on that spreadsheet. Terms like hard drive, software or log off had no sexual connotations for you.

It's time for some new programming.

If you've been watching the news, you already know there's sex in cyberspace—the vast electronic frontier of computer networks and services that you can tap into using a home computer and a modem. Cybersex takes many forms, including photos, drawings, lurid storytelling, marketplaces and, yes, venues where you can "meet" other sexual cybernauts and conduct "virtual" sexual encounters, all at the click of a mouse. Leave it to mankind to turn the most powerful tool of the Information Age into a toy for cheap thrills.

And leave it to lawyers and lawmakers to wrangle with the question of whether it's immoral and illegal. For years, the government has tried to rein in the amount of sexually explicit material on the Internet. The main reason—and it's a good one—is that they don't want children being exposed to the sort of truly graphic material that's available for any computer-savvy eight-year-old to discover. But because the Internet is so hard to regulate, many of the laws under debate are of the sweeping variety, making it illegal for anyone to upload, distribute or download most sexually explicit material.

"This could go on for a while. Laws will be proposed, enacted, then watered down or

shot down as unconstitutional," says Nancy Tamosaitis, author of *net.talk* and *The Penthouse Guide to Cybersex*. But from one day to the next, it's hard to know which way the wind blows. What could be perfectly legal titillation one day may be a crime the next. "Anyone who is interested in pursuing sex on the Net should keep up-to-date on the current climate and cybersex laws being discussed. It's for your own protection," says Tamosaitis. Think of it as electronic safe sex, and this chapter is your guide to practicing it.

How to Be Cybernaughty

It seems many people are quick to condemn sex via computer as "bad." Merely consider this image—a lonely, unsocial guy alone in his basement at 3:00 A.M., breathing heavily over a dirty conversation he's monitoring between two other strangers. Strikes you as pathetic, no?

Well, we suggest you be less judgmental about the whole thing. A compelling argument can be made for the many *advantages* to tapping into the vast online compendium of cybersex options.

"You could argue that cybersex is the ultimate form of safe sex. Whether you're downloading data for yourself or participating in an online encounter, you're in a very anonymous situation; there are fewer inhibitions. And it's not like you can catch a disease," Tamosaitis says.

More important, by taking advantage of the information online and interacting with some of the denizens there, you can come away with knowledge that can help your relationships off-line.

"It can be healthy if you're using your experiences online to expand your knowledge and understanding of women and what they want," says Phyllis Phlegar, a computer journalist in Colorado Springs and author of *Love Online*.

"Some men say they get frank information online that they'd never get from women face-to-face. The barriers can come down online because you can be anonymous—you're usually using an online handle, not your real name."

We won't judge whether online sex is healthy. If it's for you, fine—journey well, be careful out there and be respectful to yourself and others. Here's some advice on the different approaches available to you.

Look up the law. Before you go trolling for cybersex, stop in at the Internet site of the Electronic Frontier Foundation (EFF). EFF is a public interest organization that posts up-to-the-minute news and information about current and pending Internet laws. "It's the safest way to determine what's legal and what's not," says Tamosaitis. You can find EFF at http://www.eff.org or by doing an Internet search using the keywords "EFF" or "Electronic Frontier."

Take pictures. One of the most basic and passive forms of cyber-sexual activity is to download racy image files from any one of a number of resources—computer bulletin boards; commercial online services, like Compuserve, Prodigy or America Online; and the Internet, the vast international network of computer systems. On the Internet you can find these image banks in a place called Usenet or in sites on the World Wide Web, an image-based version of the Internet. If you're on the Web, you can do a simple search using terms such as "sex" or "photos." You'll find a real smorgasbord, too, from sexy shots of supermodels in swimsuits to serious porn. These days, the racier photo banks may be available only on a subscriber basis. Read the terms of service for each site carefully before deciding to subscribe.

Get advice. The Internet and most online services have discussion areas devoted to

---

Eavesdropping on the Internet

By now you've probably heard that the Internet—that global information network where the high-minded and computer-literate meet to discuss the big ideas in life—also just happens to have the biggest database of sex information and digital dirty talk this side of the Masters and Johnson database. With a computer and modem, you, too, can access any of the dozens of sexually related newsgroups—computer sites where people from around the world upload and download information. Here's a sampling of what you'll find in such places as the main sex newsgroup, alt.sex:

- Over a dozen different methods for a hand job, with such names as the Love Tug, the Double Whammy, Best Fist Forward, the Milker and the Doorknob ("turn the head of the penis like you're trying to open a doorknob coated with grease—it won't turn, but he may flip").
- What is the Venus Butterfly? Fans of the TV show *L.A. Law* may remember this alleged "ultimate sex technique," which was, of course, never explained. The Internet answer: "Put your palms together, finger to finger, spread your fingers, insert one pair into the vagina, another into the anus, plus another pair stimulating the clitoris."

---

sex and relationships. On the Internet look for "newsgroups" in the Usenet area. Tamosaitis says you can read questions and answers from hundreds of other people around the world at these newsgroup sites. And if you have a particular query, you can post your own question and get answers from around the world.

"Be sure to read the Frequently Asked Questions or FAQ file for any group first," Tamosaitis says. "If you have a question, chances are someone else has already asked it, and you'll find it there." Posting a question that's readily available in a FAQ is a serious breach of netiquette, and you could incur the wrath of veteran Netsurfers.

Tamosaitis recommends reading a newsgroup for a few weeks before you chip in your own two cents. When you think you've figured it out—and don't feel stupid, it can take people months—then you can start interacting.

Don't catch a virus. Even though you can't catch a disease from online sex, there's a chance your partner—the computer—could catch a virus. If you don't already own a virus detection program for your home computer, go out and buy one right now. Although many online services routinely check files for viruses, some can slip by. That sweet-looking snapshot of the supermodel you downloaded last night? She could be crawling with software bugs that will make your hard drive sag faster than you can say, "Byte me."

When downloading images, software or other computer files, always run a virus check on them before you open them. If your program clears them, you're probably okay. But be aware that virus programs can only detect viruses they know about, and new viruses are being created all the time. Always pay attention to any glitches your computer exhibits—slowing down, crashing, odd characters popping up in files. If you suspect you've downloaded an infected computer file, contact the online service or Internet site administrator you got the image from.

Having Cybersex

Yes, you can have sex from the comfort of your own keyboard. Using an online service and a computer bulletin board or Internet Relay Chat on the Internet, you can communicate with other online folks from around the world by typing messages back and forth to one another. If you find a willing partner, the two of you can go off to a private chat area and have

---

Online Adultery?

She's asleep in the next room. You're not tired—in fact, you're horny as hell. You fire up the computer, make your way to the "singles" chat room and pretty soon find yourself engaged in heated conversation with "Bunny44D" or "DonnaMatrix" or some other sultry online babe.

Before you step into that computerized parlor, ask yourself one question: Are you being unfaithful?

Online affairs are a kind of gray area—you could make the argument that comparing online sex to adultery is like comparing the "killing" of an opponent in a computer game to murder. After all, it's not like you're actually meeting anyone; it's not like you're exchanging bodily fluids—heck, you're not doing anything wrong. You're just typing, right?

Well . . . that depends.

"It's a question of mind-set," says Dr. Arlene Goldman of the Jefferson Sexual Function Center. "If you're doing something that you are deliberately concealing from your partner, then you need to rethink what you're doing."

---

your virtual way with one another.

Here's where you'll need a vital piece of equipment that's hardwired into any human computer—your imagination. Currently, cybersex is pretty low-tech; you simply exchange carnal knowledge with one another until one or both of you is satisfied. Some tech experts say that in the future you'll be able to use "teledildonics," devices that you hook to your erogenous zones and plug into the computer. An online lover would have a similar plug-and-play interface. Instead of typing back and forth, you'd actually be able to "touch" one another by sending signals through the ether that the computer systems and the dildonic devices would convert to tiny electric impulses that would simulate a touch or caress. This would be the safest sex of all—unless, say, a lightning bolt hits your

An online affair can be just as damaging as flesh-and-blood infidelity, argues Phyllis Phlegar, author of *Love Online*. "What's so injurious about an affair is not that you're having sex with someone else, it's the deception, it's the understanding that you are carrying on something secret and illicit outside of the marriage or relationship."

If you're single, of course, you're a free digital agent; go forth and sow your electronic oats, if that's your choice. But if you're in a relationship and want to perform some single-minded experiments in cyberspace, talk to your partner about it—see what her attitude is.

"If she has no problem with it, then explore away," says Nancy Tamosaitis, author of *net.talk* and *The Penthouse Guide to Cybersex*. "But consider that you're taking the first step down a slippery slope. Online affairs are a form of acting out. There's always the possibility that what starts out as a virtual relationship could lead to a real face-to-face meeting. And then you're really over the line."

power line while you're hooked up.

Meanwhile, it's all up to your creative verbal skills and your busy little fingers. Heed the following caveats—they'll help keep your adventures online from becoming too frustrating or dangerous.

Take it slow. As with any real relationship, if you find someone online who floats your electronic boat and you'd like to pursue her, don't push too hard to get personal too soon.

"Don't ask for or give out phone numbers too soon—and certainly take your time with F2Fs—face-to-face meetings," cautions Phlegar. Remember, you're total strangers—you've never even seen one another. "Take it slow. If you've spent several weeks messaging back and forth, then you might want to move to phone conver-

sations or exchanging pictures. Once you've done that, you may want to meet face-to-face. If you take your time and use common sense, it can really be worth it, though." Phlegar ought to know—she met her husband online.

Be a voyeur. If you're a newbie—an online virgin who still doesn't quite understand what he's doing—then don't do anything. Watch and learn.

"Be a lurker," Tamosaitis says. If you're in a chat room, see how other people interact with one another, and figure out the rules of engagement before you start typing.

Be mysterious. Some of us get so carried away with the wonder of technology, we forget ourselves.

"It's easy in the heat of discussion to give away bits and pieces of information that people can use against you if they really want to," warns Phlegar. Like a serial killer in a crowded bar, there are nefarious sorts in cyberspace, looking for their next victim. "Before you know it, they can find out where you hide the key to your house, what's in your house or when you're going on vacation. And you've told them because your defenses are down. Be coy," Phlegar says.

Be a skeptic. Take everything you see online with a grain of salt. "There's a classic *New Yorker* cartoon of a dog sitting at a computer terminal. The caption reads: 'On the Internet no one knows you're a dog.' When someone's telling you something online, you have no way of knowing whether it's true," Tamosaitis says.

That can be an asset for you if, for example, you want people to think you're tall, dark and handsome when you're actually not. But it can be a major downer when you consider that the person you've been chatting to for days could be, despite a feminine online handle, another horny guy like you. "It happens all the time," says Tamosaitis.

Sex on the Silver Screen

*Pillow Talk Isn't
Gone with the Wind*

Hollywood and sex. They go together like Bogey and Bacall. Burton and Taylor. And, sometimes, Abbott and Costello.

Generations of American men have learned a lot of what they know about sex in dark movie theaters. Some of that carnal knowledge even came from what was going on up on the screen.

But what are the *best* movies ever made about sex, love and romance? Which should you run out and rent *this weekend* to gain a deeper understanding of the magic of sex? For the answer, we asked four men who make a living watching movies and telling the rest of us what they think. On the following pages are their picks, in chronological order, for the best classical and comtemporary movies with memorable or cutting-edge sex themes.

Their lists offer a number of surprises. *Casablanca* (1942) is universally revered as a Hollywood classic, but what's sex got to do with it, you might ask?

Everything, our reviewers say. "*Casablanca* set the atmosphere and tone for sex and romance that's often been copied but never equaled. The sex was obvious but never seen," says Louis B. Parks, film writer for the *Houston Chronicle*.

Movie critic Bruce Williamson of *Playboy* agrees. Humphrey Bogart, playing the role of Rick, a cynical nightclub owner in the devastated World

War II town of Casablanca, has to choose between his desire for old flame Ingrid Bergman and the struggle against Nazi terror.

The film won three Oscars and is considered "the best movie of all time," by *Entertainment Tonight*'s movie critic, Leonard Maltin. "But the quintessential appeal of *Casablanca*," Williamson says, "is that it's exceedingly romantic."

They Coulda Been Contenders

Along with *Casablanca, North by Northwest* (1959) and *Last Tango in Paris* (1973) pop up again and again in our reviewers' lists of favorites. Other less obvious but intriguing picks include *Belle du Jour* (1967), *Body Heat* (1981) and *The Last Seduction* (1994).

North by Northwest features one of the late director Alfred Hitchcock's most memorable endings. "It has one of the all-time classic sex scenes when it shows the train plunging into the tunnel," says Malcolm Johnson, the longtime film and theater critic for Connecticut's *Hartford Courant*. "It was understatement at its best."

That was sex, Hollywood-style, in the 1950s. It was all in the imagination.

Last Tango in Paris left nothing to the imagination. The controversial, X-rated film—also available in an R-rating—features Marlon Brando as an American expatriate in Paris trying to purge memories of his dead wife through a tragic sexual encounter.

It was "highly erotic through and through," says Steve Persall, film critic for Florida's *St. Petersburg Times*. "It brought a level of sexual intensity and realism to the screen like no other film had in its time. Even by today's standards, it's fairly explicit."

Two other movies that

made repeat performances in our reviewers' lists include *Carnal Knowledge* (1971) and *The Bridges of Madison County* (1995).

Carnal Knowledge, which gives us a look at the insightful, if not morose, erotic obsessions of two college buddies, shows Jack Nicholson and his sex-kitten mistress, Ann-Margret, at their most sexually voracious. Persall says this movie appeals to him because it shows women in a more sexually liberated light. "Women were first starting to break out of their prescribed gender stereotypes. This movie helped define our sexual roles," he says.

And *The Bridges of Madison County* "was sexy in content," Williamson says. "You don't have to see someone's buns to be sexy. The romance and the love were through and through."

Each of the films on our critics' lists can shed fresh insights on the mysteries of love and sex. The 1967 classic French-Italian film *Belle du Jour* typifies the sexually liberated woman in its wry tale of a virginal Parisian newlywed by day who works affluent brothels by night. William Hurt and Kathleen Turner needed ice to cool off sex scenes that were hotter than the film's Florida backdrop in *Body Heat*. And *The Last Seduction*, with its animalistic sex in an alley and in a car by femme fatale Linda Fiorentino and Bill Pullman, absolutely sizzled.

"*The Last Seduction* had very little subtlety, but it made up for it with sheer, rolling passion," Williamson says.

Cinema Sex

When Lee de Forest premiered the first motion picture featuring sound at the Rivoli Theater in New York City in April 1923, he

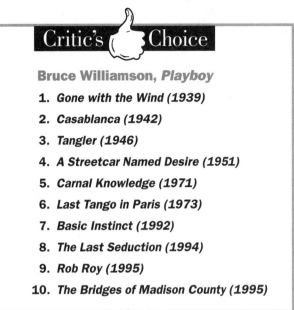

Critic's Choice

Bruce Williamson, *Playboy*

1. ***Gone with the Wind (1939)***
2. ***Casablanca (1942)***
3. ***Tangier (1946)***
4. ***A Streetcar Named Desire (1951)***
5. ***Carnal Knowledge (1971)***
6. ***Last Tango in Paris (1973)***
7. ***Basic Instinct (1992)***
8. ***The Last Seduction (1994)***
9. ***Rob Roy (1995)***
10. ***The Bridges of Madison County (1995)***

probably never foresaw the future changes about to unfold in his industry. At the time, his was an amazing breakthrough: The Silent Era had come to a close, and America welcomed the "talkies." Since then, moviegoers have been treated to a variety of multimedia bells and whistles, from surround-sound stereo to 3-D movies on 60-foot-high screens.

Yet not all the changes in movieland have been off-screen. The most dramatic changes have been on-screen, through a never-ending parade of stars, storylines and special effects. And nowhere have those changes been more pronounced than in the way Hollywood has handled—and defined—the roles of sex, love and romance.

"There have always been changes, decade by decade, period by period, in American films, reflected in large part by what's going on in our own lives," *Playboy*'s Williamson says. And back when de Forest was bandying about his latest big-screen breakthrough, guys like Rudolph Valentino and John Gilbert were defining the silver-screen man.

"While Valentino certainly wasn't the first sexual male on the screen, he certainly was the

Critic's Choice

Louis B. Parks, *Houston Chronicle*

1. *The May Irwin-John C. Rice Kiss* (1896)
2. *The Sheik* (1921)
3. *She Done Him Wrong* (1933)
4. *Casablanca* (1942)
5. *Pillow Talk* (1959)
6. *Dr. No* (1962)
7. *Last Tango in Paris* (1973)
8. *Deep Throat* (1973)
9. *Body Heat* (1981)
10. *Showgirls* (1995)

most famous specifically for that trait in that era," says the *Houston Chronicle*'s Parks.

As the years passed, stars like Cary Grant, Charles Boyer and Greta Garbo gave way to Marlon Brando, Richard Burton and Elizabeth Taylor. And Hollywood left behind in its wake such archetypal love stories as *Gone with the Wind* (1939), *Casablanca* (1942) and *Pillow Talk* (1959).

"The era had a certain style that left you with a lasting impression," says Johnson. "Cary Grant was the epitome of cool in *To Catch a Thief* in 1955. He had a cool car, cool wardrobe. I was pretty young when I saw that movie, but I remember thinking I would have liked to be like that."

Around 1970, Hollywood—and moviegoers everywhere—saw huge changes in sex on the silver screen. It was the beginning of lost innocence, Williamson says. Actors who exuded sex—like Jack Nicholson in *Carnal Knowledge* and John Travolta in *Saturday Night Fever* (1977)—helped redefine love, sex and machismo. The sexual symbolism of fireworks and

trains plunging into tunnels gave way to a far less subtle eroticism.

Overt sex continued into the 1980s with Richard Gere making his debut playing a male prostitute opposite Lauren Hutton in the sleazy story of *American Gigolo* (1980). That movie also marked the first time American audiences saw that much sex and nudity in a mainstream American film. "That just wasn't done much before this era—not in mainstream America," Williamson says.

Many lament the subtlety, smarts and lost innocence of Hollywood's past as they sit through mainstream films that—only decades ago—would have been considered blue movies. "If you see a train plunging into a tunnel, it's in a satirical manner," Persall says.

This leave-nothing-to-the-imagination portrayal of sex persists today to a much larger degree. Gone, for the most part, are love stories. In their stead, lament many reviewers, are sex stories.

Critic's Choice

Steve Persall, *St. Petersburg Times*

1. *North by Northwest* (1959)
2. *Belle du Jour* (1967)
3. *Barbarella* (1968)
4. *Carnal Knowledge* (1971)
5. *Last Tango in Paris* (1973)
6. *Looking for Mr. Goodbar* (1977)
7. *Fatal Attraction* (1987)
8. *Disclosure* (1994)
9. *While You Were Sleeping* (1995)
10. *The Bridges of Madison County* (1995)

Critic's Choice

Malcolm Johnson, *The Hartford Courant*

1. *Casablanca* (1942)
2. *Viva Zapata!* (1952)
3. *On the Waterfront* (1954)
4. *To Catch a Thief* (1955)
5. *North by Northwest* (1959)
6. *Wuthering Heights* (1970)
7. *The Way We Were* (1973)
8. *Heaven Can Wait* (1978)
9. *Like Water for Chocolate* (1992)
10. *The American President* (1996)

"A lot of movies we see today have these prolonged shots of people writhing about in half-lit bedrooms," says Johnson. "These sex scenes are just abstract close-ups of bodies that, truly, are kind of boring because they're so hackneyed."

Of course, that's not always bad. Who can forget Meg Ryan's fake orgasm scene in *When Harry Met Sally* in 1989? Or Sharon Stone's classic, groundbreaking leg-crossing shot in *Basic Instinct* in 1992? Or Demi Moore's portrayal of a wanton dragon-lady boss who sexually harasses Michael Douglas in *Disclosure* (1994)?

On the flip side—or, perhaps, the flop side—we've also seen our fair share of sexual bombs, as typified in the box office anchor *Showgirls*, which Parks says is "so dreadful it threatens to put sex in movies back 20 years."

What Does It All Mean?

The debate continues to rage over whether Hollywood is a decadent influence corrupting our morals or merely an unwelcome mirror reflecting what's happening in this country. The truth, says Robert T. Michael,

Ph.D., one of the lead researchers for the comprehensive 1994 *Sex in America* survey, probably lies somewhere in the middle.

"Because it's nearly impossible to get funds for sex studies, many scientists have looked to the media and entertainment industry as a reflection of our sexual norms," says Dr. Michael, dean of the Graduate School of Public Policy Studies at the University of Chicago.

The problem with movies, Dr. Michael says, comes when people confuse the fantasy in them with the reality of our culture's more traditional sex life. "Because there's so little accurate information out there about sex from scientifically sound studies, sex in movies might be interpreted as reality for people who don't know better."

Parks, however, believes there is a connection between the silver screen and the bedroom. "I think there's a reflection of sex in the movies and sex in our own lives," he says. "I think it's a circular connection: Our sex lives affect Hollywood, and Hollywood affects our sex lives."

Persall says this only goes so far: "By and large we get our images of what's considered sexy from movies, but I seriously doubt many people went home and tried everything they saw in *9½ Weeks*," he says. "It's probably good to have some kinks in our lives, but for every one person who takes home that kind of inspiration, there are five who are snickering about it during the car ride home."

Williamson feels that knowing what positive things to draw from movies and what *not* to draw from them makes for their greatest utility, next to entertainment. "I think some movies just teach us how to mistreat women," he says. "But what we can learn from most of them, especially many of the romantic classics, is that as far as approaches to sex go, kindness and subtlety usually are more effective."

Books and Tapes

Multimedia Sex

Ever since we discovered Dad's cache of *Playboy* in the toolshed, we've all been diligent students of the media that surrounds sex—magazines, books and, of course, videos.

Some part of us just can't help it. As men, we're hard-wired to respond to visual stimuli—nothing arouses us faster. In one study on this very subject, men were sexually stimulated two ways: first with direct stimulations from a vibrating sex toy, then by watching a pornographic film. Of the two, guys were more aroused by the film.

"It's an interesting gender difference: Men tend to be more visual; they respond quickly to the way a partner looks; they're stimulated by watching a woman undressing," says Dr. Arlene Goldman of the Jefferson Sexual Function Center. "Women, on the other hand, are more verbal and more auditory—they like to be talked to, and they respond to a certain type of erotic literature where the scene or the story line is what arouses, not pictures."

Let's Go to the Videotape!

Porn movies are a well-established trapping of manhood, the centerpiece of countless bachelor parties. But erotic movies and videos can serve a higher function in life than as a mere lurid backdrop in a male rite of passage. Instead, start thinking of them as a tool, a visual database of ideas, scenarios and, yes, even positions for you and your partner to explore.

That's right, include her, too. Just because women tend to be less visual than men, that doesn't mean they *never* respond to visual cues. "Many women do find erotic images arousing—it depends on how the image is presented and why they're looking at it," says Anne Semans, co-author of *The Good Vibrations Guide to Sex* and co-owner of Good Vibrations in San Francisco, a retail and mail-order adult store that carries an impressive selection of toys, erotic publications and videos. Statistics would seem to bear Semans out: According to the Adult Video Association, more than half of all skin flicks rented are checked out by women.

But don't automatically assume your woman harbors a secret passion for skin flicks.

"Commercial videos are often very threatening to women because they feel they can't compare to what they see on-screen," says sex educator, author and radio talk-show host Dr. Judy Kuriansky. Bearing this in mind, a pre-screening discussion is in order. First, make sure she's open to the idea of watching a video. And if she is, then give a little thought to what you want to watch. Odds are the extreme-close-up-of-every-orifice approach that makes for a rousing stag party may not make for an arousing evening for a party of two. But with a little patience and prudence, you can ensure your intimate night at the movies will be a blockbuster, not a flop. Here's how.

Start with the tame stuff. As always, the best way to test uncharted waters is to wade into them slowly. If you want to share your desire to be turned on by erotic images, start your partner out at the shallow end.

"If you think she's not going to be at all interested in some hard-core film, I'd definitely start off with something tame, such as a steamy R-rated or NC-17 film," Dr. Goldman says. Our staff favorites include *9½ Weeks*, *Last Tango in Paris*, *Body Heat* and

Sirens. From the R-rated, you can then progress to soft porn or instructional videos, both of which provide a good middle ground between tamer mainstream films and hard-core porn.

If you're looking for a clue to how explicit the movie is, don't pay much attention to how many Xs are on the box. Instead, read the box cover before you rent or buy—these days most adult videos will tell you on the slipcover what you can expect on the tape. As a general rule of thumb, anything described as "soft" means lots of dim lighting, few if any explicit close-ups and no male genitalia. "Hard-core" means anything goes: lots of close-ups, full frontal nudity all around and numerous "money shots"—ejaculation on tape, up close and personal.

Pick porn with plots. When you do move into porn, be it the stuff of late-night cable stations or adult video stores, you'll find plenty of skin to satisfy you. But women will enjoy sexually explicit movies more if those films boast a unique feature you don't often see in a porn flick—a plot.

"We find that women tend to like a movie that creates a certain romantic or sensual atmosphere, or at least has some plot—not just endless footage of screwing," says Semans. Some good examples of X-rated films long on atmosphere or plot include the long-running *Emmanuelle* series on Showtime. On the video racks, our trusted critics recommend *Devil in Miss Jones*, *Behind the Green Door* and *The Story of O* series.

Shop together. Whether you rent from your local adult store or buy from a catalog, don't let your video shopping be one-sided. "Make your selections together. If you go to a store, you both have a chance to read the box. And most good catalogs will have some

---

America's Sexiest Home Videos

If you're having sex and you own a video camera, the thought of combining the two may have crossed your mind.

Actually, making a sex movie starring you and your partner . . . well, that's for a chosen few. But they're out there; in fact, there are entire catalogs and video distributors devoted to steamy movies shot by amateurs at home.

But if you want to play this game, remember that you're making love to each other, not the camera. Because that's the case, there are a few unbreakable rules, notes sex educator, radio talk-show host and author Dr. Judy Kurianksy. First, both of you must agree to it. Second, both must know exactly when the camera is on or off. Third, both of you should agree on what happens to the tape afterward—where to store it, when to erase it and who gets to view it.

If you can settle on all that, there is the final issue of quality. Chances are your movie will be badly lit, poorly acted, a laugh riot—*America's Funniest Home Videos* meets *Debbie Does Dallas*. But it can also be more interesting than a mirrored ceiling and may bring out the exhibitionist in both of you. If this sounds like your idea of fun, then we say, "Lights, camera . . . action!"

---

description of what you can expect in a video," says Semans, whose Good Vibrations catalog has not only descriptions but a series of symbols denoting the content of each film— you can tell at a glance whether a video is hard- or soft-core, if it has any kind of plot or if it features any interesting or unusual sex scenes.

Take it off-screen. Ultimately, treat videos like any other sex toy—a side order to your sex life, not the main course. "What's best is when a couple starts watching a video and then lets it become part of the background," Dr. Kuriansky says. Let it serve to spark your interest or give you permission to experiment. "You may want to look over at it once in a while, but the two of you should be into your own thing by then," she advises.

Reading for Sex

Any man who has ever read the *Penthouse* Forum letters has some inkling that the written word—with or without illustrative support—can be as good a turn-on as video. From erotic stories that fire the imagination to explicit sex manuals that explain the finer points of oral sex, reading can be fundamental to enriching your sex life—and a novel addition to your usual pattern of foreplay.

And no doubt about it: When it comes to women, experts swear by the arousing power of the written word. "It doesn't have to be all that graphic, either," says Dr. Goldman, pointing to the success of romance novels, which tend to gloss over sexual acts but spend a long time setting up a scene, creating an atmosphere of seduction. "Because women tend to be much more verbal than visual, reading these stories—or having you read the stories to them—can be extremely arousing," she adds.

Not to mention educational. Stories and manuals, like videos, offer a glimpse of what else you can be doing in your sex life, providing you and your lover with volumes of new ideas to try out on one another. Here are a few quick tips for becoming a literate lover.

Seek out steamy stories. If your tastes turn to porn lit, try to find books that tell a story—avoid ones that read like the mere reporting of an event. "As with movies, the setting of a scene or the creation of a certain mood or atmosphere is what women respond to more than the description of actual intercourse," Semans says. Some great erotic literature that's

high on atmosphere includes *Emmanuelle*, the French classic about a woman's sexual coming-of-age; Pauline Reage's *Story of O*; or any works by Anais Nin (so you don't sound like a dope, it's pronounced Ana-ees Neen).

Skip over the centerfold. Should you bring those issues of *Playboy* in from the toolshed, bear in mind that if your sweetie's going to be interested in anything, it will probably be the articles (but then, that's the only reason you buy them, right?). Chances are she's not going to be very stimulated by the pictures, "but most of these magazines have letter columns and forums where readers tell racy stories or ask interesting sex questions. Reading those together can be fun and arousing—plus it may give you a chance to discuss similar issues in your own sex life," Dr. Goldman says.

Buy a manual. One way to turn your partner on to words and pictures may be through a sex guide or manual. "This is a tricky area because you don't want to send the message that you need an instruction book to have good sex. But many books are very helpful at giving you new ideas for positions or sex play," Dr. Goldman says. Our favorites include *Sex: A Man's Guide* by Stefan Bechtel and Laurence Roy Stains (everything a man needs to know about sex—and then some); *The Good Vibrations Guide to Sex* by Anne Semans and Cathy Winks (great in-depth discussions of all manner of sex play, plus a huge resource list); *The Magic of Sex* by Miriam Stoppard (great photos); and that perennial classic, *The Joy of Sex*, by Dr. Alex Comfort.

Make your own. Finally, if you're finding that the erotic literary choices in your area are woefully inadequate to the task of interesting either of you, then take up a pen and do it yourself. Write a letter to your partner describing what it is about her that arouses you. If you really want to impress her, write a poem. Don't think about it—just do it. You may find yourself forging a bond with her that will not only make you closer but could also lead to the kind of sex that's worth writing home about.

Part Five

Real Sex

Quest for the Best

For these highly successful men, sex is a way of life. But don't get the idea it's all work and no play. Here they share the insights they have gained into the mystical ways of love.

You Can Do It!

Real men. Real life. Real sex. These guys have lived and loved. And, just as important, they've learned. You can, too.

Sex Menus

The main ingredients couldn't be simpler—you and your lover. The secret is in the spices. Here are recipes for gourmet lovemaking, from the ultimate quickie to a weekend of great sex. *Bon appétit.*

Quest for the Best
For these highly successful men, sex is a way of life. But don't get the idea it's all work and no play. Here they share the insights they have gained into the mystical ways of love.

John Gray, Ph.D., Best-Selling Author

The Man from Mars

Most of us, when we get divorced, leave a little sadder and (hopefully, but not necessarily) a little wiser than we were before, glad perhaps that our skin is intact and we can walk away from the scene of the accident.

That wasn't enough for John Gray.

When his two-year-old marriage fell apart in 1984, John Gray, Ph.D., could not rest until he came to an understanding of what went wrong in that relationship and what he could do right in the next one.

"When my marriage failed, it really caused me to re-evaluate everything I ever thought would work," Dr. Gray says. "The divorce was a pivotal time in my life to say, 'Hey, John, you don't have all the answers. You need to start studying and finding out a different way of looking at it. Your basic way of dealing with things is faulty, and you need to correct it.'"

The fruits of that quest are evident today: His second marriage, to Bonnie Josephson, is in its second decade, and he is the father/stepfather of three children ranging in age from 9 to 21. Dr. Gray also is the author of two of the hottest-selling books ever written about how men and women can better get along, *Men Are from Mars, Women Are from Venus* and *Mars and Venus in the Bedroom: A Guide to Lasting Romance and Passion.*

Since it's clear that millions of men and women are turning to Dr. Gray for advice about their sex lives, it's only natural to wonder whether he practices what he preaches. How, you might ask, do *you* get on in *your* sex life, doctor?

His answer: Very well indeed, thank you.

"Most of *Men Are from Mars* is about my experience or related to my experience in some way," he says. "And lots of the examples in *Mars and Venus in the Bedroom* are straight from my marriage."

A Long Journey

Not that the line between Gray, the young man wondering what he was going to be when he grew up, and Dr. Gray, the sex-meister of our time, is a straight one.

Born in 1952, Gray was a child of the 1960s. He took a healthy interest in sex and took a few tokes of the most popular pharmaceutical of the day. He also took a page from The Beatles, becoming a follower of Transcendental Meditation guru Maharishi Mahesh Yogi.

Gray traveled a little farther down that road than The Beatles did, however. He earned a B.A. and an M.A. in "Creative Intelligence" from Maharishi European Research University in Vlodrop, the Netherlands, and was a celibate monk for nine years.

In 1979, he headed out to California, where he met and dated both his first and second wives. He married Bonnie the same year he got divorced from his first wife. And he learned a very valuable lesson about men and women and sex.

"The interesting thing that I've found is that when men get divorced from women, when the women leave them, I ask the man, 'Well, what was your sex life like?' " Dr. Gray says. "And they always say, 'Great.' They *always* say, 'Great.' Now you talk to any one of those women, and they're going to tell you it was *not* great. A woman doesn't leave a man if she has a great sex life with him.

"Now why does he think sex is working? Because she's faking it. A guy can be all turned on sexually and think, 'She has to be enjoying this. I mean, I am so much, so she must really be going wild,' " Dr. Gray says.

Keys to a Happy Marriage

Gray became Dr. Gray in 1982 when he got his Ph.D. in psychology and human sexuality from Columbia Pacific University in San Rafael, California. Since then, he has published five books, including the *Mars and Venus* books, and he has become a speaker in high demand on the national lecture/TV/radio circuit.

His success, he says, has put extraordinary pressures on his marriage.

"The more successful you are in life, the more demands are made on you, which kills relationships. There are business opportunities here, opportunities there, and suddenly it looks to your wife like your work is more important than her," says Dr. Gray.

The solution?

"You have to make your partner more important than your work, and you have to do things that say she's more important."

And one of the most important things, he says, is that you must never stop dating.

"We have date nights booked up a year in advance," he says. "And once a month we do an overnight outside of the house away from the kids. And during that time I make her the most important thing in the world. I take charge of the day. If we go shopping, it's primarily for her. If we go to a restaurant, we're going to go to the kind of restaurant she likes. If we go to a play or entertainment, it will be the kind of entertainment she really likes. We're not going to go to see my favorite basketball team on that romantic night."

Dr. Gray calls these overnighters gourmet sex. And the regular sex that most couples have he calls healthy, home-cooked sex.

"Then we have quickie sex," he says. "Which is very, very important. It keeps men turned on to their wives."

This menu of gourmet, home-cooked and, if you will, microwave sex, is guaranteed to satisfy the both of you, Dr. Gray says.

New Expectations

Women, Dr. Gray adds, are looking for different traits in men than they did in our mothers' day.

"We're expected to be more romantic now, we're expected to be better communicators and we're expected to be passionately in love with our partners," Dr. Gray says. "Men were never expected to be those things."

No, the man women dream of isn't the laconic Clint Eastwood character of *The Bridges of Madison County*. Well, okay, maybe they dream of him, but the guys they settle down with are "gentle and strong and sensitive, caring and considerate, good listeners, romantic, willing to do things for women and not willing to take abuse."

Though, Gray admits, there's a lot to learn about romance from Eastwood's screen character.

"He didn't slam the door. That was romance for her. When he went out the door, he kept it from slamming. Men have to realize that little things make a huge difference with a woman."

Samuel S. Janus, Ph.D., Sex Researcher

He Wrote the Book on Sex

As far as millions of Americans are concerned, when they want reliable information on sex, there's only one man to turn to: Samuel S. Janus, Ph.D.

Together with his wife, Cynthia, a physician, Dr. Janus wrote the landmark study *Janus Report on Sexual Behavior*, and in so doing became a household—make that bedroom—name as one of the foremost authorities on sex and the way people have it. Throughout the 1980s, Janus's scientific surveys of sexual behavior threw back the covers on the habits, desires and libidinous leanings of a nation. Thanks to Dr. Janus we learned valuable and fascinating information such as the fact that:

- Twenty percent of all men surveyed reported having had sex for money.
- Thirty-four percent of married men said sex was better in marriage than anywhere else. Ten percent said it was worse.
- Seventeen percent of men surveyed thought group sex was all right or very normal.
- Seven percent of men admitted to masturbating daily; 18 percent do it several times a week.

And that's just a fraction of the information packed into the *Janus Report*'s 400-plus pages. "Obviously, it was very rewarding work, but it was also certainly very challenging," Dr. Janus says.

In more ways than one. Picture it: Your day job is researching and tabulating sex data. With your wife. At worst, you'd think they'd become sick of each other or of hearing about sex. At best, working day in and day out on sex research with your wife might make it tough to concentrate on the job at hand. For the most part, though, Dr. Janus says their work together was a positive experience—a labor of love.

"It brought us closer together," he says. "Cynthia and I love sharing ideas—we really enjoy every minute with each other. Work-wise, we were able to divide and conquer different aspects of the study, spending long nights at the computer without competing or getting in each other's way. But being terrific partners working on the book just reflected the partnership we have in every other aspect of our lives."

Including the bedroom? Sam Janus has a one-word answer, accompanied by a smile that speaks volumes: "Yes."

But Dr. Janus does allow that there were times when they suffered from sex information overkill. "When that happened, we'd take a night off, go out to the movies, get away from it for a little bit. After all, you don't want sex to become the only way you interact as a couple," he says.

Family Affairs

That said, Dr. Janus is the first to admit that writing his famous report had a profound effect on both his life and his family's.

"There are a tremendous number of differences in how men and women express themselves sexually—our study made that very clear. It can't help but broaden my own perspective, not only about the way my wife and I relate to each other but the ways my kids have learned to deal with sex," he says. "It's also made me much more accepting about the different ways we come to terms with sexuality and express it."

And Dr. Janus has good basis for comparison. He has been married twice. He has a 35-year-old son and a 40-year-old daughter from his first marriage. "My daughter is very conservative and doesn't approve of my work at all. My son is the opposite—completely tolerant and supportive. I guess you can't do a study like this and not expect it to be controversial—even in your own family," he adds.

Meanwhile, Dr. Janus also has a five-year-old son from his marriage to Cynthia. "I find that Cynthia and I are much less restrained with our five-year-old than I was with my other kids," he admits. "We'll talk about different body parts with our little boy in a way that I never would have felt free to do in the 1950s and early 1960s. And as far as how my own parents told me about sex, or more specifically premarital sex—well, it amounted to three words: Don't do it."

The Future of Sex in America

Thanks in large part to works like the *Janus Report*, future generations won't have to grow up in such a restrictive educational environment when it comes to sex.

"There's an ongoing debate about whether our society will shift back to conservatism or toward further sexual freedom. I think we're continuing to move toward more sexual freedom," Dr. Janus says. There are dangers to this freedom, and Dr. Janus has over the years been something of an activist against them—he is an outspoken crusader against child exploitation in advertising and the media, for example.

"But as far as adults are concerned, a more liberal attitude is all to the good. We need to broaden our ideas about what's sexually permissible or normal, and overall, that's what's happening."

Of course, that only begs the question every man asks himself at one time or another: What *is* sexually normal? Simple, says Dr. Janus. "I'd say it's sex that gratifies both you and your

partner and that carries no physical violence or threat."

Other than that, anything goes.

Entering the Golden Age of Sex

With so many baby boomers hitting middle and late-middle age, the issue of sex and the older man has never been hotter. As a man in his sixties, Dr. Janus can well appreciate the interest in sex and aging, and he's here to report that the two are not mutually exclusive.

"Our study reported that there was very little diminution of sexual desire or frequency of sex between people in their forties and people in their twenties and thirties," Dr. Janus reports. "By the fifties and sixties, desire and frequency may slow down, but there's no reason you can't have a good, active sex life into your eighties—or beyond."

But the famed sex researcher does suggest that men remember to keep one tool ever ready in their sexual repertoire—no, not that tool. He's talking about your sense of humor.

"One man I know in his midseventies prides himself on his sexual prowess and regularly goes to dances to pick up women. Once, he zeroed in on a beautiful woman and remarked seductively that she appeared to be 'looking for something.' The woman looked him in the eye and said, 'Yes, a younger man.' Now, most men would have been devastated by that remark, but this guy just laughed and kept up his search. His attitude was—so what? Enjoy what you can, no matter how old you are."

Dr. Janus certainly is enjoying life to the fullest these days. But he allows that even famous sex researchers may find themselves hard up for good sex information. And while millions of people are turning to Dr. Janus for sound sex advice, whom does he turn to?

"Hmmm, probably Masters and Johnson—they put out a pretty good report themselves," he says.

Hoyt Richards, Male Supermodel

Some Like It Hoyt

You may not have heard of Hoyt Richards yet, but chances are you're familiar with some of his co-workers: Cindy Crawford, Kathy Ireland and Christy Turlington, to name a fetching few.

In the fashion world, Richards is regarded as the first male supermodel. And why not? He's six feet one inch tall, blond-haired, blue-eyed, well-muscled and well-paid. In fact, he's the highest-paid male model in the world, earning as much as $15,000 a day.

Male models usually come and go after only one or two seasons, but Richards has demonstrated staying power, having modeled for more than a decade. In that time he's also developed an unparalleled portfolio. He has worked on ad campaigns with the likes of Ralph Lauren, Valentino and Versace. He's been photographed by the best: Richard Avedon, Bruce Weber and Herb Ritts, to name a few. In Italy, the leading men's fashion magazine, *Mondo Uomo*, devoted an entire issue to him. And in 1995 he won the Best Award, an honor bestowed by the French Fashion Federation to people considered the best in their fields in matters of elegance and style.

But Richards is more than just another pretty boy pouting for the camera. Beneath that finely chiseled exterior pulses the brain of an Ivy Leaguer and the heart of a Renaissance man.

From Football to Fantasy

Richards didn't set out to be a model. Growing up in a large family in the suburbs of Philadelphia, Richards started out as a scholar. He studied

chemistry and biology in England, then went to Princeton, where he would earn his degree in economics. In fact, it was luck—bad luck—that first landed him in front of the camera.

"When I was at Princeton, I also played football—I was a free safety," he says. His Princeton team sported one other guy with super good looks—actor Dean Cain, TV's Superman. Unlike his famous teammate, however, Richards was no man of steel. "I had continuing shoulder injuries that kept getting worse. I went to New York to see a shoulder specialist in hope of finding a way to keep playing," he recalls.

A friend first broached the idea of modeling to Richards while he was in New York. With his good looks and football-star physique, Richards had a certain physical quality that made him as much a natural in front of the camera as he was on the field. It also didn't hurt that, early in his new career, Richards got an introduction to fashion photographer Bruce Weber, who recognized supermodel potential in the ailing varsity player.

"I remember one of my first assignments was working with Kathy Ireland," he recalls. "Three weeks before, I was ogling her in the *Sports Illustrated* swimsuit issue like any college kid. Suddenly, I was kissing her in front of the camera. It was incredible!"

It sounds like the ultimate male fantasy—being a fit, great-looking guy who travels to exotic locales to have his picture taken with the world's most beautiful women. And getting paid staggering sums of money for it. But Richards has sacrificed plenty to get where he is.

"I know most guys will have a hard time generating any sympathy when they hear that, and I certainly don't expect any," he acknowledges. "I think that any sacrifice I've made in my career is only relative to what anyone does in an effort to get ahead in any business. I love what I do, but it is a kind of fantasy. Not to mention it can only last a short time—gravity takes its effect. The reality is that at the end of the day, I have my fair share of troubles and insecurities, just like anyone else. Believe me, when I wake up in the morning and look in the mirror, I certainly don't feel like a supermodel."

A Model Life

Richards says modeling allows him time for little else. "I'm on the road 300 days a year. I just got in from Africa. Next week I'm in the Caribbean; at the end of the month I'm in France. I live like a nomad. Any guy who travels for a living knows how tiresome that can get. But I also have the opportunity to see the world. Like anything else, there is always give and take. I have come to really treasure my downtime."

One thing Richards has had to abandon is the idea of having a long-term relationship. "I've never been married—I think I'd have been divorced by now if I had been, with the schedule I keep. About five years ago, I gave up the idea of having any kind of steady relationship with a woman. It's too hard on both of us. Believe me, I've tried it, and what I've realized is that it's not fair to either person. Any guy who has ever had a long-distance relationship knows what I mean. Things get misinterpreted on the phone; one or the other of you is grouchy because maybe you're at the beginning of your day and three time zones away, while she's at the end of her day. Relationships are already difficult. I don't need to make them more complicated."

But that's okay for the moment, says Richards. "At this point in my life, I just don't have any burning desire to get married anyway. I have another commitment: my work."

That said, the self-acknowledged nomad is hardly a self-avowed monk. "Well, come on now," he says. "I never said I was turning away the company of women. We all have to contend with the urges encoded in our primitive male DNA, you know what I mean?"

Going beyond Beauty

If his tenure in modeling has taught Richards anything about women, it's to look beyond the looks. "As men, we're all so tuned to the visual cues, the physical attractions of a woman. Well, I work in a world where all the women are beautiful—let's face it, they've won the genetic lottery. But I've been forced to try to see past it, but only by getting burned many times. I think we give people too much leniency when we find them physically attractive. It really is true that beauty is only skin-deep—I find when I focus on that, it always leads to trouble."

Richards has certainly found that to be true in his relationships; looks don't get him everywhere. "Sometimes it doesn't help one bit. But what always helps is being a great listener. And you have to make 'em laugh. That's practically a requirement."

It doesn't hurt if you have other interests, as well. Although Richards spends most of the year devoted to his work, he tries to keep himself busy by constantly exploring other projects and options beyond modeling. He is partner in a patient education company that specializes in nutritional analysis and supplementation. He's also working with some colleagues to develop an educational program to help Americans learn more about the Constitution. And when he's not doing that, he's branching into movie and television work. Currently, he hosts an entertainment show based in London, where he gets to interview rock stars, other supermodels and celebrities like his old football friend Dean Cain.

"As busy as I am, I try not to let my job control me," he says. "I want to keep exploring, pushing boundaries, trying new options. I think it is important not to rest on any laurels. Complacency is a killer. There is always room for improvement."

Mitchel Gray, Lingerie Photographer

Bringing His Life into Focus

Mitchel Gray gets paid handsomely to do what most of us can only dream about: taking pictures of the world's most beautiful women in sexy lingerie and other states of undress.

Among the stars Gray has photographed over the past 20 years are some of the brightest in the fashion constellation: Christie Brinkley, Kathy Ireland, Iman, Carol Alt and Jane Seymour, to name a few.

He's published two photographic volumes on lingerie. *The Lingerie Book*, published in the early 1980s, documents in pictures and prose the history of lingerie in the 1900s. His second work, *Lingerie Fantasies*, is a series of pictorial fantasies. Other high-profile assignments have included work for *Vogue*, *Harper's Bazaar*, *Cosmopolitan*, *Life* and countless cover shots for *Men's Health* magazine. He also photographed the cover of *Sex: A Man's Guide*.

More Than Meets the Eye

Now in his late forties, Gray has learned much about beautiful women during his years behind the camera lens. And one of the most important lessons was how little he really knew before.

"One of the things I've learned from the very get-go in this business is that women are entirely different from what you or I assumed growing up," he says. "You don't really learn this until you've had a lot of interaction with them. I grew up with an older sister, but what you learn as a kid is nothing compared to what women are really like.

"If you spend any time in the dressing room of a fashion studio, you'll never see women in the same light again," he says. "It's the most amazing psychological revelation you'll ever have. And not just on the superficial level of how they look."

Superficially is precisely the way most men deal with gorgeous women, Gray says. They are so blinded by beauty that they can't see the person behind the pretty face.

"Beautiful women have certain ways of dealing with things. They know how to get things through their looks, and they know how to manipulate people through their looks. They know how to use their looks as defense and offense. What happens to the average guy is he accepts a beautiful woman as a *beautiful woman*, not as an individual.

"After you've spent 90 percent of your time with beautiful women, you see them differently. A lot of times attractive women want to be treated as sex objects, just like we do. It pumps up their confidence," says Gray.

"We all like to know someone else considers us a potential bed partner—it's a primal thing that makes the species survive. But it is important to balance this with a rational approach. In other words, there's more to them than what meets your eye. You just don't drool."

The most important lesson Gray's learned in dealing with women is hardly new. The fact that it remotely resembles a revelation only underscores how men's minds turn to mush when faced with a beautiful woman in a revealing dress. It's simply that old golden rule: Treat people the way you want to be treated.

"Sure, there'll be some jerks in your life who need to be kicked around a bit in order to get the picture," he says. "But generally speaking, I think most people, especially women and particularly beautiful women, want to be treated with respect and dignity. Just like me and you."

Building a Career

Gray began his career serendipitously. He first took up photography seriously in his senior year of college, when he asked his professor at the University of Virginia if he could photograph a term paper instead of writing it. He was majoring in English at the time and had "really burnt out on writing.

"I thought this was a way I could do the paper and give my arm a break," he says. "My professor was a neat guy, and he said yes. So I went to Newark, New Jersey, and shot a bunch of inner-city stuff."

The photographic paper was a success. So much so that it sowed the seeds for Gray's career. He left college and took several jobs as a photographic assistant in New York City, starting at just $40 a week. He then plunged full-time into the world of freelance fashion photography.

"In the early years, I was always interested in photographing women because women are great subjects," he recalls. "The stimulation of seeing beautiful women in front of my face was really, really exciting. It combined my two greatest loves in life: women and taking pictures."

Finding Serenity

These days, Gray enjoys his job partly because of the challenge. There's lab work, traveling, studio time and, of course, the live shoot. "When you're behind the camera, looking through the lens, there's a lot of pressure. You're seeing a mini, focused, magnified version of what everyone sees, but you have to manipulate it the way you want to get the picture you want. Meanwhile, you're trying to exclude everything in the scene you don't want to show up."

Gray, however, has learned there's more to life than his work.

"Any career, particularly freelance photography, is fickle. Sometimes you're swamped; sometimes you're starving," Gray says. "But you always have to remember that whether the work is up or down, you're still the same guy. You can't attach your entire value system to your job. You can't peg your self-worth to your career, or you'll be bouncing up and down like a rubber ball."

When he's not behind the lens, Gray spends his time with Katie, his wife of more than a dozen years, and their son, Morgan Henry, born on November 26, 1995. He credits the lessons of a short-lived first marriage and his on-the-job training in interpersonal skills with helping him cultivate the right attitude for a lasting relationship.

"I'm very happy to be married. There was an earlier point in my life when I was very happy to be single, but things happen the way they're supposed to," he says. "This is a wonderful time in my life. Work is great. My relationship is great. I have a kid. I'm feeling serene—I'm no less ambitious, mind you, but I'm feeling a sense of serenity and peace that I don't recall having before."

Inquiring Minds

Before we fade to black, two burning questions remain. First, do famous photogs bed the beautiful women they photograph?

"I think people like to believe that, but that whole notion is fantasy. You have to be really naive to believe that, or you really want to believe it. Just because you see them doesn't mean you're in bed with them. Of course, your odds are better," he adds with a smile.

And, finally, does Katie get jealous after her husband's been out shooting half-naked women all day?

"That's something women ask Katie all the time—if it puts her off that I'm around beautiful women so much," Gray laughs. "I'll tell you what she says verbatim: 'No, not at all.' Because when I come home, she gets all the benefits."

You Can Do It! Real men. Real life. Real sex. These guys have lived and loved. And, just as important, they've learned. You can, too.

An Open Mind—And Heart

Kent Arnold, Beaverton, Oregon

Date of birth: June 16, 1958

Profession: Certified public accountant, specializing in training nonprofit organizations to use accounting software

Marital status: Married

I've always tried to stretch my horizons, to be more open-minded about everything, not just sex. But you know, sex is a big part of life, and I've always felt that if you can learn to be open in that arena, it makes you a more well-rounded person in other aspects of your life.

I have a son now, and one thing I want him to learn that I did not is to be safe in sex. I hit my experimentation phase in the 1970s—sex was free for the taking with *any* willing partner. If I were a teenager today with that attitude, I can only cringe at the risks I'd be taking.

But I got lucky. I didn't get into too much trouble and ended up meeting a wonderfully exciting and uninhibited woman. We had a very open relationship from the beginning. We spent hours teaching each other what we liked and talking about things we'd like to try. Of course, I ended up marrying that woman, and we constantly share the best sex we've ever had.

I have no doubt that the reason our sex life is so good is our ability to discuss what we want and push our boundaries. For example, we enjoy watching erotic movies and discussing our thoughts about the situations presented. And we love our sex toys. My advice to my fellow man: Don't be intimidated by using toys. We've found that they greatly enhance our

sexuality, and believe me, we've tried most of them—vibrators, dildos, butt plugs, nipple clamps, cock rings—you name it. It's ridiculous to think there's something wrong with these. I see them as fun and useful tools to help make sex better and more satisfying.

Now I'll admit that it has taken us a while to get to this point, and we did talk about what we wanted to try—it wasn't like I went out and bought something and surprised her with it. Spontaneity is great in sex, but when you're moving into an area where one of you might be uncomfortable, I say take it slow. If one of you is unsure about using this accessory or that, don't retreat from the idea with a shocked look on your face. Talk about it. If you're still uncomfortable with it, then table the idea for a few months and come back to it. Don't push it and don't be pushed into it.

But more important, don't be afraid of yourself, which I think a lot of men are, frankly. We're afraid to go out on a limb, to talk about the things we want to do or want to have done to us.

When it comes to communicating, we could learn a thing or two from women. They chat for hours, in great detail, about things we wouldn't admit even under threat of death. As men, there's this blockade we've built around certain sensitive issues. We feel if we try to break past them, we're somehow weakening ourselves, exposing some vulnerability.

Well, maybe we are. But look at the payoff—you can get closer to the woman you love, you stand a better chance of getting what you want out of a relationship and you open yourself up to a world of great sex. You don't need an accountant to tell you what this adds up to: a highly erotic, highly satisfying life. Kind of like the one I'm living right now.

Affairs of the Heart

Bob Dunn, Portland, Maine

Date of birth: May 10, 1944

Profession: Supermarket service clerk

Marital status: Divorced

I don't know what the hell you're going to think about me, but I'm not a bad guy. I lost a 19-year marriage because I had two affairs. I'm not proud of it. It hurt my wife very deeply, and I don't like to hurt people. I absolutely felt awful when she found out. I never thought about having an affair, let alone two. They just happened. But I learned a lot from them. About myself. About women. About relationships. About life.

The first affair started soon after my family and I moved to Portland from Yarmouth. I was coaching a Little League team in Yarmouth, but we moved so my son could play baseball in a Class A school. Right after we settled in, I received this letter at work from a mother of one of the girls on the Little League team. It said, "I miss you." It blew me away and things just took off from there. It lasted five years.

The second affair was with a girl I worked with when I was at a different job. Believe it or not, it went on at the same time the first affair was going on.

If I had to rate them, I'd rate the second affair a little higher. But only because she was more into cuddling and kissing. That's very important to me. Cuddling was one thing the other woman—and my wife—weren't into much. I like being held. I like cuddling. I like intimacy. I guess some guys are like wham, bam, thank you, ma'am, but I've never been like that. The second affair didn't last long. She knew about the other woman and my wife. Neither one knew about her.

The first affair, the one that lasted five years, was outrageous. Not to sound egotistical, but the sex was great. We just clicked. She was willing to try new things, and she liked everything—I mean everything. She liked to wear lingerie, and she knew I liked her wearing it. I didn't mind buying her lingerie, and I still get Victoria's Secrets catalogs in the mail, even though I haven't bought anything in years.

What worked best for me sex-wise in the first affair was fingers. Multiple fingers especially. I don't want to sound like an egomaniac, because I'm not, but I guess a lot of men don't have good technique. From a woman's viewpoint, I'm sure that's a real turn-off. I also really loved that we clicked so well.

In five years we never had a bad sexual experience. One day, I think it was a weekday, we had somehow gotten together and wound up at the Portland Headlight. Portland Headlight is a famous lighthouse in Maine that attracts thousands of people. So there we were on a cloudy day, walking literally in the shadow of the lighthouse when one thing led to another and, before I knew it, it became the most bizarre place I ever had sex.

Now that it's all over, I know I'll never get married again. I've been single for six years now, and I know inside I don't want to commit, even to a serious relationship. I come and go as I please. I do what I want, when I want, and I don't want to give that up.

The biggest fear I have is that my son will be against marriage because of what happened between his mother and me. I don't want him to be against marriage, but I *do* want him to know there's a lot of give-and-take in any relationship.

There has to be communication. That's one thing my wife and I never had. We never fought, mind you, but we never talked either. I will make sure my son knows that you have to work hard to make any relationship last. Sometimes they don't work. And even when they do, things aren't always going to be smooth. There's bound to be disagreements. You just have to work through them.

Online Lover

Hal Day, Colorado Springs, Colorado

Date of birth: November 4, 1947

Profession: Communications manager for a pay phone company

Marital status: Married

I know a lot of men see computers as something used by guys who can't get a date, but if it wasn't for the computer, I never would have met my wife.

I wasn't always interested in computers, though—I didn't really work with one until I was in my forties. Before that, the sort of crashes I had dealt with didn't involve a hard drive—they involved helicopters. I joined the Army in 1965, then went to Vietnam in 1966. I was in five crashes during my tour and walked away from them—well, ran away is more like it—every time. I had a good career in the Army, though. I was in for 25 years and had won the Purple Heart, the Air Medal, the Bronze Star and the Legion of Merit. But my very last assignment in the Army was with a signal battalion, and they had a lot of computers. That was a milestone. I started learning and reading more about them, and then I actually bought one. Before I knew it, I had become something of a computer guru where I lived in California.

When the online service Prodigy first started up, I was on it from day one, and I spent a good bit of time online, especially in the computer bulletin board area. That's where people would ask technical questions or discuss problems and those of us who knew anything would try to get an answer. That's where Phyllis and I met. I had answered several questions for her in the public area, then one day I got a private message from her and gradually our relationship became more social. Instead of computers, we started talking about ourselves.

She was in broadcasting in Colorado, and it turned out that the radio show she hosted was on in my area. I tuned in one night and heard her voice—it was kind of exciting to suddenly hear this person who I'd previously only known through words on a screen.

Eventually, we ended up talking on the phone, exchanging pictures. We were becoming closer, and what was great about the whole thing was that we weren't distracted by details like hormones or looks. We were operating on a level of sheer personality—it was a very deep and intimate experience.

Eventually, though, we did have our first F2F—face-to-face meeting—in January 1992. In August I moved to Colorado. I proposed to her on top of Pike's Peak, and we got married in January 1993. We became kind of notorious in online circles, and Phyllis even wrote an advice book about online relationships, called *Love Online*. Now, we have a daughter, Hallie. And all this came from one question thrown out there into the vastness of cyberspace.

I'd like to point out that Phyllis and I didn't go online looking for love; it was really just a happy accident. But I know that these days a lot of guys out there are prowling cyberspace, looking for a good time. And it can be a good time. But follow some guidelines to protect yourself—and to keep from looking like a jerk.

First and foremost: Always tell the truth. Remember to be yourself out there. Don't come on too strong and say stupid things. If it's inappropriate to say face-to-face, it's inappropriate to say online.

Second, take your time. Phyllis and I took our relationship very slowly, over the course of several months really, and we were very careful not to rush things.

Third, although it's important to be open and honest, be very guarded about giving out personal information—phone numbers, addresses and so forth—especially in a public place such as an online "chat room."

But don't let these factors deter you. It's a lot of fun, you can meet a lot of interesting people online and it can be very enriching. Trust me, I know.

Sex from the Neck Up

Wellington Pendell, Lansing, Michigan

Date of birth: September 19, 1967

Profession: Michigan manager (sales) for Bacardi Rum

Marital status: Engaged

I've spent a lot of time in bars in my life—because of the business I'm in, not because I'm a barfly—and the whole male/female contradiction is played out better in bars than anywhere else I've ever seen.

When you walk into one of these "pickup bars," you can almost feel the tension. The women have their guard up, and the men are on the charge. Now, if men and women knew what each other needed, you wouldn't have that.

With women, everything you do up until the actual act is foreplay, all the way from the time you said "Hello" to her when you first met.

Have you ever seen the erotic movies that are designed and directed by women for women? Sex movies for guys are just all sex from start to finish. But the women's movies, if they're an hour long, at least 55 minutes is everything that happens *before* the sex. They're like a Harlequin Romance novel on film.

Basically, women want to be made love to from the neck up, and men want to be made love to from the neck down. Women are emotional, and men are physical.

What women want in bed is a romance novel. They want their partner to look into their eyes, caress their face and pay attention to things that are from the neck up. Men are exactly the opposite. They want a pornographic movie.

If women pretended to be more interested in the man from the neck down (with most of the attention going to the mighty sword), and men acted like they were the perfect lover on the cover of the Harlequin Romance novels, I feel that both parties would get more out of it.

I say this now, but it's funny, because in the 2½ years that I've been with my fiancée, I've probably violated every rule that I know on how to make a successful relationship. If you asked me for advice, I would say, "Don't make the mistakes I made."

The problem that I've run into in my relationship is that while it's easy to understand how somebody else thinks, it's impossible to actually relate, because you've never been that person.

A lot of people, because the only life they've ever had is the one they're living, have a tendency to think, "Well, if I like this, then this other person must like this." That, in most cases, is dead wrong. It's like, "I like chocolate, so here, have some chocolate," and "I don't understand why you don't like chocolate."

To make a relationship successful, first off you have to understand that what your mate wants is very, very possibly completely different than what you want. And second, if that is the case, learn what she wants and then give her that.

If women knew what men want and men knew what women want, they would be able to give those things to each other and make each other happy, and everybody would be happy. It's a give-and-take thing. But usually the problem is that men and women don't know.

There's always this assumption that when it comes to sex, it's her giving it to him. Now, *that* I hate. Because that means she is giving something up that she doesn't want to give up. It should be a mutual exchange where both people get an equal amount of fulfillment.

But typically, because it's the act that ends up happening, the men talk about, "Hey, I got some last night." It's almost like they're stealing money. That's a wrong relationship. If you have to talk about it that way, then you're doing it wrong.

Sex Menus
The main ingredients couldn't be simpler—you and your lover. The secret is in the spices. Here are recipes for gourmet lovemaking, from the ultimate quickie to a weekend of great sex. *Bon appétit.*

The Ultimate Quickie

When Time Is Always on Your Side

In this take-your-time era of slow sex, it's nice to know that men and women alike can still enjoy a good down and dirty quickie.

"Because of the emphasis placed nowadays on taking your time in sex—so the woman has plenty of time to be aroused and brought to orgasm—I think there's a misconception that a quickie is something that only men will find appealing and enjoyable. Nothing could be further from the truth," says Carol Cassell, Ph.D., a sex therapist in private practice in Albuquerque, New Mexico, and author of *Tender Bargaining.*

"Women, too, find the idea of a stolen moment of carnal passion just as exciting and arousing," she says. "If the woman is turned on, she doesn't necessarily need all the time the sex manuals say." In fact, in one study Dr. Cassell conducted of couples in long-term relationships, an overwhelming majority were quick to point to quickies as among their most exciting sexual moments together.

Proper Etiquette

Sex therapists say the lure of the quickie harkens back to our early sexual life, when any carnal contact had to be done on the sly.

"These were experiences that were stolen moments. In many cases, couples had to make their couplings quickly, as soon as the opportunity arose," notes Arlene Goldman, Ph.D.,

coordinator for the Jefferson Sexual Function Center in Philadelphia. "A quickie can help recapture some of that excitement and passion—and even fear—that you had back when sex was brand new."

You don't have to be 18 years old, bursting with equal parts lust and anxiety, to enjoy the rush of a quickie. In fact, the quickie is one of those things that truly does get better with age. So here are a few fast-and-loose guiding principles to get you going. And even if you're the king and queen of the quickie because, say, the kids are always just on the other side of the bedroom door, we've provided some novel suggestions to help you make the most of your stolen moment.

Finish later. Don't feel you have to finish a quickie. There doesn't have to be total resolution, if you have enough self-control. Not only is a quick bout of *coitus interruptus* less messy (and therefore quicker), "it can be an extremely erotic and elaborate form of foreplay," says Dr. Goldman. "Basically, you're giving each other a taste of what's to come later."

Make a date. Although most of the fun of a quickie comes from the wonderful spontaneity of it, there's no reason you can't plan it in advance. "If you decide at breakfast to meet at a hotel at lunch, it can be just as exciting," says Dr. Goldman. "The buildup over the morning hours, the waiting, the anticipation—it can be a very powerful aphrodisiac."

Take a nooner. Although quickies can occur any time, any place, a commonly accepted form of quickie is the nooner. "Arranging a rendezvous over

Dress for Success

Since speed is, by definition, a key component of the ultimate quickie, you might want to dress for the occasion. Here are some sartorial suggestions for the ideal quickie outfits.

You

Top: The kind of shirt doesn't matter, unless you want to go for the Superman effect, in which case choose a button-down. Of course, you won't be able to wear it back to work.

Bottom: Wear loose-fitting slacks or pants—jeans are hard to slip on and off in a hurry. Buttonflies are easy to rip open quickly, but unless you practice, buttoning them can take twice as long as zipping.

Underneath: Boxer shorts seem constructed with quickies in mind, since most gap open the moment you put them on. Meanwhile, instead of the old, awkward, side-opening fly, some new briefs have flies that open on top, providing more convenient access. Of course, you could wear nothing at all.

Her

Top: Nothing that buttons up the back or that buttons, period. For speed's sake, loose pullovers or sweaters are probably the best bet.

Bottom: One of the great advantages women have over men is their ability to wear skirts and dresses in public. Anything that you can hike up easily makes for great quickie togs.

Underneath: Unless she has a run in a very strategic spot, panty hose are out. For that matter, undergarments are optional, too. Some good choices, however, include a sexy teddy or a leotard that unsnaps at the crotch—both provide discreet access for today's woman. She'll be ready for sex in a snap.

lunch makes the most sense for a lot of busy couples. You can actually meet and have a little fun without shirking work too much," Dr. Goldman suggests. So next time you make a lunch date with your sweetie, you might want to include dessert on the menu.

Keep your clothes on. If your quick exchange is so quick you have to confine it to the elevator or stairwell, learn the fine art of having sex with your clothes on, says Dr. Cassell. Train at home first and practice with the fervor of an Olympic team hoping to win the gold.

Once you have the technical aspects down—how to speedily remove or open strategic items of clothing with minimal confusion—you might want to fine-tune your artistic skills.

"There are some couples out there who are so good at it, they can have sex with their clothes on in broad daylight and no one's the wiser," Dr. Cassell says. To the rest of the world, they just see a woman sitting on a guy's lap on the subway or on a park bench. Hint: Practice your poker face, too.

Seize the moment. Unless you have some life- or job-threatening crisis to deal with and assuming it's not something you do every day, you should always take advantage of the occasional quickie. "There's a certain excitement and passion of the moment in a quickie that's really impossible to duplicate," Dr. Cassell says. "If your partner calls and suggests a quickie, don't try to put it off until you get home. Go for it." *Carpe diem*!

A Night of Passion

Rekindling the Flames of Love

It's the kind of night you live for. Both of your children are sleeping over at friends' houses. All is quiet. No pitter-patter of feet. No shouting. No arguing. It's just you and the woman you love. Alone—at last.

What could be more refreshing, more energizing, more desperately, critically, profoundly needed than a long-overdue night of passion? Not just a few hugs and kisses, but an all-out conflagration of romance, sweet talk and making love. We talked to some of the nation's leading sex experts and asked them to help us plan an all-night strategy for making love. We think you'll like their advice, but feel free to ad-lib. After all, it's your night.

In the Mood

6:00 P.M.: Just remember: This is also her night. So take the initiative. Prepare a sumptuous dinner for two. Order take-out. Or simply take her out.

Are you noticing a common theme here? *You're* taking care of *her.* Such simple gestures are the first, critical step in stoking the sexual fires. Even if your mind is focused on other things—like the king-size mattress in the bedroom—taking time to create a romantic, caring mood leads to better love later on. The best foreplay is what you do all day, not just what you do 15 minutes before jumping in the sack.

You don't have to be extravagant for effective wining and dining (although a good wine and Chateaubriand for two is a sure way to make a heart grow fonder). And sometimes the simple pleasures are the best.

• Wok this way. Take-out Chinese is fast and convenient. Plus, it's easy to clean up, which means you can focus on each other instead of on a sinkful of dirty dishes.

• Have an indoor picnic. Spread a blanket on the floor, light some candles and serve cheese and luscious fruit slices. Throw in a loaf of French bread, a bottle of wine and a basket and you have a romantic, personal picnic—without the ants.

• Boy meets grill. Weather permitting, grill some vegetables and skewer some meat chunks for a home-cooked barbecue. There's something primal and intimate about eating with your hands. Plus, it's easy, so you can spend more time together and less on the messy details.

• Let the food match the mood. In a survey of 1,000 Americans, the Revlon company found that the most sensual foods—individually, not all at once—are strawberries, chocolate, whipped cream, ice cream, honey and oysters.

6:03 P.M.: Enjoy a drink. You certainly don't need alcohol to have a romantic evening, but as Dorothy Parker pointed out, "Candy is dandy, but liquor is quicker." In one survey 45 percent of men and 68 percent of women said alcohol somewhat or greatly enhanced their sexual enjoyment. But don't overdo it. Too much alcohol makes you numb, not romantic. It also interferes with the signals that send blood to the penis, with predictable—and disappointing—results.

6:15 P.M.: Add atmosphere. Give your private dining room some ambiance. According to the Revlon survey, more than three-quarters of respondents believe candlelight provides a sensual complement to any setting. Music is also good, particularly classical music. Don't forget to turn on the answering machine, turn off the ringer and, above all, lock the door.

6:30 P.M.: Loosen up. Get out of your work clothes and slip into something a little more comfortable. Have her do the same. While she's relaxing and you're taking care of the chores (remember, foreplay!), talk to her. Ask how things are going. And really listen. Let her know she has your undivided attention—unless, of course, you're burning something on the stove, in which case you should extinguish the flames, then resume the conversation.

While you're listening, gently massage her shoulders for 10 or 15 minutes. Give her an invigorating foot massage. "These little touches help you and her open up and be intimate," says Erica M. Goodstone, Ph.D., a sex therapist in private practice in New York City. "Almost any kind of touching makes a woman feel better."

Dinner, Dance and Romance

7:00 P.M.: Sit down to a sensual feast. Take your time. Enjoy each other's company, as well as the food. And make sure you don't dominate the conversation. Spend more time listening than talking. *Bon appétit*!

8:00 P.M.: Leave the dishes and ask her to dance. Sixty-four percent of respondents in the Revlon survey ranked dancing as highly sensual. So hold each other close and move to the music.

8:30 P.M.: Light a few candles and take a long, hot bath together. Lather her up, then rinse her off slowly, spending extra time on her breasts, buttocks, neck, legs and stomach. Gently massage her scalp as you wash her hair. These are erogenous zones, and bathtime will naturally progress into playtime.

Ecstacy Awaits

9:00 P.M.: No matter how hot and eager you both are, you want to keep the passion boiling, not boiling over. For the next hour or so, avoid the "act" and concentrate instead on exploring each others' bodies. Enjoy:

• A leisurely full-body massage with warm baby oil. "I just want a big bed, some baby oil, dim lights and naked bodies," says Barbara Keesling, Ph.D., a sex therapist in Orange, California, and author of the best-selling *How to Make Love All Night (And Drive a Woman Wild)* and *Sexual Pleasure*. For detailed massage tips, see Becoming a Handy Man on page 86.

• A lot of sensual kissing and licking.

• A romantic look in the mirror. If you and your partner are reflective types, you may enjoy kissing or touching in front of the mirror.

10:30 P.M.: By now you're both chomping at the bit, so we'll let you take it from here. Feel free to experiment with one or more new positions. For ideas, see Positioning Yourself for Great Sex on page 98.

11:30 P.M.: While a man winds down rather quickly after sex, for a woman the process is much more gradual. That is why women still have a strong desire for intimacy after sex, while men are more likely to withdraw somewhat.

When you're finished, stay close. Keep yourself inside her, even if you're no longer erect. Cuddling, spooning and other forms of afterplay give the evening closure. Another advantage is that some men find their arousal regenerates quickly when they cuddle after sex, allowing them to head into round two instead of turning over and falling sleep.

8:00 A.M.: Get up early and make her breakfast in bed, even if it's just coffee and English muffins.

8:20 A.M.: Provide room service she couldn't enjoy in even the finest hotels. Making love in the morning is a great way to renew the magic of the night before. Unless . . .

8:21 A.M.: "Mom? Dad? We're home!" Okay, the kids just walked in, so maybe you'll have to put the morning exercise on hold. But, hey, we only promised you a night of passion.

A Weekend of Great Sex

The Pause That Refreshes

Game shows hawk them as coveted prizes; travel agencies package and sell them in droves; countless couples throughout history have tried to plan the perfect one—the romantic weekend, the weekend getaway, the weekend for two.

No matter how you slice it, weekends and sex seem made for each other. Sex during the week is all very good, but weekend sex is something else again.

During the week there are bills to be paid and chores to be done, and even when you can muster the time and energy for a quick roll in the hay, the basic housekeeping of your life always lies just on the other side of the bedroom door, waiting for your brief interlude to end.

No wonder, then, that so many busy couples look to the weekend for sexual salvation, a time when they can take all the time they want. Weekends are also a ready-made opportunity for planning a quick getaway, a minivacation that will put more spring in your step and glow in your cheeks.

Getting Away from It All

A weekend away with that special someone not only revitalizes mind and body, but weekending can also put an extra spark in your sex life.

"Getting away for a romantic weekend combines a number of basics you need to keep your sex life healthy and robust," says Dr. Arlene Goldman of the Jefferson Sexual

Function Center. "You have the element of surprise, and you have the variety of going to someplace different instead of the same old bedroom."

It's a chance to pamper yourselves and remove yourselves from the everyday grind. You can be more relaxed, so you're more likely to take your time and enjoy yourself and your partner more, Dr. Goldman adds.

There's no universal weekend planner for couples—often all you need is a quiet place to be alone together for a couple of days. But if you're looking for some ground rules to the perfect weekend, bear the following in mind when the whistle blows on Friday afternoon.

Avoid overplanning. Remember what was said about best-laid plans? Well, that goes double when your plans revolve around romance.

"Don't put too much emphasis on making this the perfect weekend. These days a couple might have only a few opportunities in the year to get away from it all. It's understandable that you might want to plan something down to the last detail so it's perfect, but that may end up being counterproductive to what you really want to do," says sex therapist Dr. Carol Cassell.

Down-to-the-minute planning will make you feel more like a cruise director than an idle passenger, Dr. Cassell warns. You run the risk of completely missing the point of enjoying yourself because you're spending so much time making sure everything's perfect.

So keep your plans to a basic sketch, a bare minimum—don't go too far beyond making a reservation at a nice place and bringing along a bottle of wine.

Follow your nose. Sometimes, the best plan is to have no plan.

"There's a certain excitement and adventure to having

no set plan. I know a couple who spent a weekend where the plan was to have no plan. They just hit the road, stopped where it suited them, ate where they wanted, stopped at interesting sites—and had a great time along the way," says Dr. Cassell.

There's something very hedonistic about following your impulses. And that, of course, is going to translate into good sex, Dr. Cassell adds. So make your weekend a total surprise for the both of you. Open up a map, close your eyes and point. Where your finger lands is your destination. Or, don't even plan that far ahead. Just pack a bag, get in the car and go.

Don't be selfish. Let's say your idea of the perfect weekend puts the two of you in a tent in the middle of the forest primeval, a trout-stuffed stream bubbling nearby. Now you know from experience that she's game for this sort of weekend but bummed by the lack of, say, indoor plumbing.

Meanwhile, she'd rather spend the weekend in that simply precious bed-and-breakfast—the one with potpourri on the nightstand, brass fixtures in the bathroom and a cute old couple who makes fresh bread and muffins every morning and fusses over you all weekend. This is why you left home as soon as you were old enough—it's certainly not your idea of a sexy getaway-from-it-all weekend.

So which do you choose?

If you've spent any time as a couple, you probably can guess the answer: you compromise.

"Think about it for a minute. If the idea here is to create a romantic situation where you'll both be at ease, then don't go to a place that one of you hates," says Dr. Cassell.

A Touch of Magic

The American Animal Hospital Association reported last year that 79 percent of pet owners give their pets birthday and Christmas gifts. And, by the way, each year we spend about $20 billion on pets and pet supplies.

What, you ask, does this have to do with a weekend of great sex?

"Millions of people are buying presents and spending all this money on pets because it's where you get the touch and the affection," says Patricia Love, Ed.D., author of the book *Hot Monogamy*.

Touch. Many women complain that the only time their partners touch them is when they want to have sex.

"Touch is a human need," says Dr. Love. "When you're an infant, you have to have it to survive; when you're an adult, you have to have it to thrive. It literally lowers your heart rate. That's why couples that are happy together live longer. It's healthy for you."

So as you go away for your romantic weekend together, take this advice: Touch her. Often. For no particular reason. And you will feed her.

Dr. Love tells of one woman who told her: "'Do you know if we get up and go to the bathroom in the middle of the night, when my husband passes me in the hall, he touches me?' Now that's a couple who had been married for about 50 years. It's no surprise."

A weekend away from it all is a good time to put a touch of magic into your relationship. Just make sure you continue your loving touch once you're back home.

If you can't see eye-to-eye on your ideas about idyllic weekends, meet in the middle: Pick an old country inn with the quaintness and rustic charm she likes, but close to the great outdoors you crave. Or, if you're trying to get her more in the mood, why not consider caving in?

"Another viable alternative is to create a dream weekend for your partner—making reservations at the hotel or inn she always wanted to go to. You can let her show her appreciation later," suggests Dr. Cassell. Plus, this gives you the right to suggest that camping weekend next time.

Don't wait for the weekend. If you truly want to enjoy the thrill of a getaway, why wait for the weekend to roll around?

"Some of the most exciting sexual encounters can be had when you feel like you're sneaking away from other responsibilities," says Dr. Cassell. So you and your sweetie might want to try calling in sick or taking a vacation day in the middle of the week. Go bike riding or skiing; pack a picnic lunch; hole up in a hotel for the day. "It's the notion of playing hooky, of getting away with something. It loosens your inhibitions, which is certainly going to help you relax and enjoy sex more," says Dr. Cassell.

The Stay-at-Home Getaway

You wanted to shoot the works, to take her to that little mountain resort with the heart-shaped whirlpool, mirrors on the ceiling, in-room adult movies and vibrating bed with satin sheets. Or maybe it was the old bed-and-breakfast in the country with the Laura Ashley wallpaper and the big mahogany bedstead. Either way, it's a bust—the kid needs braces, the water heater's about to explode and Uncle Sam didn't give you the refund your were planning on. You just can't afford it.

Relax. If for whatever reason you can't swing the getaway part of a romantic weekend, you can still plan a romantic weekend for two—and in relative solitude—right in your own home. Here's how.

Rip the phone out of the wall. Okay, maybe not literally. But you know what we mean—be incommunicado. Put a message on the machine that says you are gone for the weekend and then turn the ringer off. "If you really went away for the weekend, you probably wouldn't be checking your calls. So don't do it when you're at home," says Dr. Cassell.

Pack up the kids. Though they may be the love of your lives, nothing dampens the libido like a little one bursting through the bedroom door just when Mommy and Daddy are about to get busy. So give the kids a weekend adventure: send them away. Put them up with Grandma and Grandpa or let them sleep over with friends.

Order out. If you want it to be a totally relaxing weekend, stay out of the kitchen. Take yourselves out to a nice restaurant. Or don't even leave the house: Be totally decadent and order in.

Play the chef. Having said that, you may want to dazzle your partner with your culinary expertise. If so, pick the meal you're best at and get cooking. If it's breakfast, serve it to her in bed. If it's dinner, make it from scratch and serve it by candlelight.

Watch her, not TV. Much as you might want to sneak a look at the game, consider unplugging the TV when you unplug the phone.

"The idea is to create a little isolation, to create something different in the confines of a familiar setting. If you always sit around and watch the game on the weekend, try not to do that this weekend. Make this weekend a time when you'll do things for yourself and each other that you wouldn't ordinarily do at home. Stay in bed until noon; take a bath together; go for a long walk. If you'd do it on vacation, try to figure out ways to do it at home," says Dr. Goldman.

Or make it easy on yourself—schedule your romantic weekend after football season ends. Then rent some erotic videos or put on romantic music and light some candles to set the mood.

Index

Note: <u>Underscored</u> page references indicate boxed text and illustrations. **Boldface** references indicate primary discussion of topic.

A

Abstinence, <u>38</u>
Adventure, romance and, 67
Aerobic conditioning for sex, 11
Affairs, online, <u>134–35</u>
Afterplay, **110–12**
Afterplay, 110, <u>111</u>
Age, sex and, **8–9**, 97
Aggression from steroids, 19
AIDS, 2, 3, 36, 37, 108
Alcohol, sex and, <u>13</u>
Amphetamines, sex and, <u>21</u>
Amygdala, conscience and, 23
Anabolic steroids, 19
Anafranil, <u>94–95</u>
Anal plugs, 131
Anal sex, **108–9**
Anatomy
    female, **75–77**, <u>81</u>
    male, **72–74**
Anatomy of Love, 22, 56
Anderson, Barbara L., 49, 50
The Angry Marriage, 46
Antidepressants, <u>94–95</u>
Aphrodisiac, <u>117</u>
Armelagos, George, 12
Arnold, Kent, **152**
Arousal
    alcohol and, <u>13</u>
    exercise and, 10–11
    in men, 88–89, 110
    testosterone and, <u>23</u>
    from visual cues, 89
    in women, 89
Astroglide, 131
Attraction, physical, **26–27**

Augmentation surgery, penile, 4, 7
Autoerotic asphyxiation, <u>126–27</u>

B

Barbach, Lonnie, <u>50</u>, 56, 58–59, 60, 67
Bathing before sex, 84–85
Be a Man!, 44, 64
Bechtel, Stefan, 142
Benokraitis, Nijole V., <u>47</u>, 48–49, 50, 51, 53
Bergland, Richard, 23
Birth control, 20
Body chemistry, sexual, **18–21**
Body/facial language, 56–57
Bondage sex fantasies, 124–25
Books about sex, <u>115</u>, **140–42**.
    See also specific titles
Brain, sex and, 13, **22–23**
Breathing during sex, 94
Brown, Lucy, <u>23</u>

C

Carroll, Richard A., 3, 8, 9, 14, 15, 19, 20, <u>93</u>, 112
Cassell, Carol, 62, 63, 115, 116, 118, 119, 120, 121, 124, 127, 129, 156, 157, 160–61, 162
Cassolette, 25
Cervix, <u>76</u>, 77
Chancre, as symptom of syphilis, 39
Chlamydia, 37
Chocolate, sex and, 12, 13
Circumcision, 73
Clap, the, 38
Cleland, John, 60
Cleveland, Grover, <u>117</u>
Climax. *See* Orgasm
Clitoris, 75–76, <u>76</u>, 80, 89, 111
Clomipramine, <u>94–95</u>
Closter, Reuven, 46, 47

Cocaine, sex and, <u>21</u>
Cock rings, 6–7, 131
Coitus interruptus, 156
Comfort, Alex, 25, 104, 142
Commitment, 49–50, <u>49</u>
Communication, **54–57**, 64
    afterplay and, 112
    about anal sex, 109
    difficulty of, for men, <u>55</u>
    dirty words and, 129
    of enlightened lover, 41
    erogenous zones and, 78
    first time for sex and, 64–65
    honesty in, 54–55, 65, <u>65</u>
    importance of, 52–53, 55
    inhibitions and, overcoming, **62–63**
    listening and, 56, <u>56–57</u>
    nonverbal, 56–57
    sex and, 54–57, 64
    sex talk, **128–29**
    small talk and, 56
    tone of voice and, 57, 129
    as turn-on, **58–59**
    women's desire for, 48–49, 52–53
Computers, sex and, 132–135
Condoms
    in anal sex, 108
    duration of sex and, 95
    female, <u>39</u>
    flavored, <u>63</u>
    lubrication and, <u>109</u>
    in prevention of sexually transmitted diseases, <u>39</u>
Constrictor rings, 6–7, 131
Coolidge Effect, 29
Cornog, Martha, <u>6–7</u>
Corona, 73
Corpus cavernosa, 91
Corpus spongiosum, 91
Cowper's gland, <u>73</u>, 74
Crabs (pubic lice), 37
Cunnilingus, **106–7**
Cybersex, **132–35**

D

Danoff, Dudley Seth, 21
Dating, as relationship booster, 67
Day, Hal, **154**
Delaney, Gayle, 41
Depilatory, 74
Diamond, Jared, 26–27
Dildos, 130
Dodson, Betty, vi, 2, 3, 17, 25, 82, 83, 84, 90, 92, 93, 94, 96
Dopamine, 21
Dreams, sex, 41
Dress for sex, 157
Drugs, sex and, 20–21, 94–95
Dunn, Bob, **153**
Dunn, Marian E., 96
Duration of sex, **90–95**

E

EFF, Internet laws and, 133
Effleurage massage technique, 87
Ejaculation, 96
    alcohol and, 13
    female, 30, 77, 81
    fluid in, 74
    premature, 91
    in process of male orgasm, 89
Ejaculatory duct, 74
Electronic Frontier Foundation (EFF), Internet laws and, 133
Elgin, Suzette Haden, 54, 56, 57
Endogenous morphines, 12, 22
Endorphins, feelings of love and, 12, 22
Endurance, sexual, **90–95**
Enlightenment about sex, 40–41
Epididymis, 73, 74
Erection, 23, 91
    aging and, 8
    duration of, 90–91

myths, 28
problems, 91, 92–93
Erogenous zones, **78–81**
    brain and, 22–23
    communication and, 78
    finding, 79–80
    G-spot, 74, 77, 80–81, 81, 99
    guidelines in touching, 78–79
    in masturbation, 83
    skin, 86
    top ten, 79
The Erotic Edge, 56
Erotic Interludes, 50–51
Estrogen, 20
Exercise
    effects of, 10–11, 11, 15
    Kegels, 94–95
    for pubococcygeal muscles, 94–95, 97
    self-esteem and, 10
    sensate focus, 16–17
    sex and, **10–11**
    sex drive and, 11
    in stress management, 16
    testosterone levels and, 11
Exhibitionism for the Shy, 62

F

The Fabric of Mind, 23
Fallopian tubes, 76, 77
Fanny Hill, 60
Fantasies, sexual, **122–27**
    acting out, 127
    autoerotic asphyxiation and, 126–27
    benefits of, 122, 123
    bondage, 124–25
    female domination, 125–26
    foreplay, 50–51
    group sex, 124
    home items used in, 124
    love map and, 122–23
    myths of, 31
    role-playing, 124, 125
    same-sex, 123
    spanking, 126

Fantasy model of sex, 60
FAQ file, 133–34
Fat injection, penile, 7
Fears about sex, overcoming, **62–63**
Feet, myth about big, 29
Female domination sex fantasies, 125–26
Fight-or-flight reaction from stress, 15
Films, sex and, 12, 65, **136–39**
First time for sex, **64–65**
Fisher, Helen, 22, 56, 57
Fitness, sex and, **10–11**
Fluoxetine, 94
Food
    for masking taste in love-making, 63
    mood for sex and, **12–13**
    sex drive and, 24–25
    as sex toy, 131
For Each Other, 56
Foreplay, **84–85**
    aging and longer, 9
    fantasy, 50–51
    in setting mood for sex, 84
    techniques, 84–85
    women's view of, 48
Foreskin of penis, 73
Fox, Robin, 23
Frenulum, 73, 83
Frequently Asked Questions (FAQ) file, 133–34
Freud, Sigmund, 21, 24
Friedman, Sheila, 55

G

Gangestad, Steven, 26
Gender roles, 2, 3, **44–47**, 46–47
Genderspeak, 54
Generation Sex, vi, 2, 98, 109, 116
Genital warts, 38
Gifts, as turn-on, 59
Glans of penis, 73, 91

Goldman, Arlene, 63, 114, 115, 118, 119, 121, 127, 128, 129, 130, 134–35, 140, 142, 156, 157, 160, 162
Gonorrhea, 38
Goodstone, Erica M., 78, 79, 87, 159
Good Vibrations, 79, 86, 141
The Good Vibrations Guide to Sex, vi, 36, 42, 79, 86, 93, 108, 140, 142
Grafenberg, Ernst, 80
Grant, Hugh, 117
Gray, John, vi, 48, 49, 51–52, 53, 60–61, 61, 67, 69, **144–45**
Gray, Michael, **150–51**
Group sex fantasies, 124
G-spot, 74, 77, 80–81, 81, 99

H

Halpern, James, 110, 111
Hart, Gary, 117
Hartman, William, 62–63, 114, 128
Hawkins, Robert O., 123, 127
Headaches, sex, 16–17
Head of penis, 73, 91
Henkin, William A., 123, 125, 126–27
Herpes, 38–39
Hirsch, Alan R., 24–25
HIV virus, 37, 39, 108
Homosexual fantasies, 123
Honesty in communication, 54–55, 65, 65
Hooper, Anne, 78–79
Hormones and sex, **18–21**. *See also specific hormones*
Horton, Charles, 7
Hot Monogamy, 49, 56, 66, 161
How to Love a Nice Guy, vi, 2, 98, 109
How to Make Love All Night (And Drive a Woman Wild), vi, 2, 17, 84, 88, 90, 97, 159
Hygiene, 25, 58, 84–85

Hypogonadism, 20
Hypothalamus, 13, 18, 23

I

If Only You Would Listen, 45, 46
Illicit drugs, sex and, 20–21
Impotence, 92–93
Inhibitions, overcoming, **62–63**
Injection therapy for erection problems, 93
Insights on sex
  from famous men, **144–51**
  from ordinary men, **152–55**
Intercourse
  coitus interruptus and, 156
  first time, **64–65**
  for G-spot stimulation, 81, 99
  myth about, 31
  after orgasm vs. before orgasm, 61
Internet, sex and, **132–35**
In the Mood, 12
Intimacy, 3, 17, 49, 112
The Intimate Touch, 85

J

Jacobson, Bonnie, 45, 46–47
Janus, Cynthia, vi, 146–47
Janus, Samuel S., vi, **146–47**
The Janus Report on Sexual Behavior, vi, 146
Johnson, Malcolm, 139
Johnson, Virginia E., 6, 18, 41, 90, 106
The Joy of Sex, 25, 104, 142

K

Kama Sutra, 98, 99
Kaplan, Helen Singer, 21
Keesling, Barbara, vi, 2, 3, 10, 13, 14–15, 16–17, 41, 84, 88, 90, 93–94, 97, 99, 128, 129, 159

Kinky sex, myth of, 29. *See also* Fantasies, sexual
Kinsey, Alfred C., 4, 80, 90, 96, 106
Kissing, 39, 85, 112
Klein, Marty, 94
Kolodny, Robert C., 6, 18, 106
Kriegel, Marilyn Harris, 50–51
Kuriansky, Judy, vi, 2, 3, 8, 9, 11, 98, 109, 116, 131, 140, 141, 142
K-Y Jelly, 83, 109, 131

L

Labia majora, 75, 76
Labia minora, 75, 76, 80
Leg cramps during male orgasm, 11
Lewdness, public, 120
Ligament transection, 7
Lights on during sex, 63, 118
Listening skills, 56, 56–57
Living with the Passive-Aggressive Man, 56
Locations for sex, **119–21**
Lotions for sex, 131. *See also* Lubrication
Love, Patricia, 49, 56–57, 66, 161
Love map, 122–23
Love Online, 132
Lover, unforgettable, 59
Love Triangles, 45, 46
Lubrication
  for anal sex, 109
  condoms and, 109
  for massage, 63, 87, 131
  for masturbation, 83
Lucretius, views of, on sex, 98
Lue, Tom, 4
Lust, 48–49

M

The Magic of Sex, 142
The Male, 18
Male Sexual Armor, 16

Manners as turn-on, 58–59
Manuals about sex, 142. *See also
specific titles*
Marijuana, sex and, 20–21
Marquis de Sade, 117
Marriages and Families, 48
Mars and Venus in the Bedroom,
vi, 48, 49, 51, 60, 144
Maslin, Bonnie, 46, 47
Massage, **86–87**
foot, 79–80
lubrication for, 63, 87, 131
skin's sensitivity and, 86
techniques, 86–87
touch's importance and, 78,
87
Massager, electric, 131
Masters, William H., 6, 18, 41, 90,
106
*Masters and Johnson on Sex and
Human Loving*, 6, 18,
106
Masturbation, **82–83**
aging and, 9
erogenous zones in, 83
euphemisms for, on Internet,
133
lubrication for, 83
myths, 29
statistics on, 82
in stress management, 17
techniques, 82–83
McIlvenna, Ted, 11, 18, 19, 20,
27, 36, 107
Medications, sex and, 9, 94–95
*Men Are from Mars, Women Are
from Venus*, vi, 48, 49,
60, 61, 144
Menstruation, 30, 77
Michael, Robert T., vi, 2–3, 32,
33, 139
Micropenis, 4
The Miracle Worker Organizing
Service, 68
Moller, Anders, 26
Mons pubis, 76
Montagu, Ashley, 78, 85

Mood (for sex)
attraction and, 27
food and, **12–13**
foreplay in setting, 84
stress and, 14
More Time for Sex, 56, 58
Mound of Venus, 76
Movies, sex and, 12, 65,**136–39**
Multimedia sex, **140–42**
Myths about sex, **28–31**

N

Natural sex, myth of, 29
Nero, Emperor, 117
Neuroscience, sex and, **22–23**,
23
The New Male Sexuality, vi, 47
Nicotine, sex and, 20
Night of passion, **158–59**
Nonoxynol-9, 39
"Nooner," 156–57

O

Ointments for sex, 131. *See also*
Lubrication
*On a Clear Day You Can See
Yourself*, 55
One-night stands, 3
Oral sex, 9, 39, **106–7**
Orgasm
attachment feelings and, 23
drugs causing, 94–95
female, **89**
aging and, 9
clitoris and, 80, 89, 111
fake, 30
process of, 89
signs of, 30
vagina after, 111
from G-spot stimulation, 81
intercourse after vs. before, 61
male, **88–89**
aging and, 97
leg cramps during, 11
"mini-orgasms," 96

multiple, **96–97**
process of, 88–89
myths, 28, 29–30, 31
pleasuring women first and,
60–61
power of, 88
refractory period after, 89, 96
relaxation in prolonging, 94
simultaneous, 29–30, 60
statistics on, 84
in stress management, 17, 83
talk during, 57
Osherson, Samuel, 45, 46, 47, 55
Ostergaard, John R., 16–17
Ovaries, 76, 77
The Overworked American, 68
Oxytocin, 21, 23

P

Parks, Louis B., 138, 139
Passion, 52, **158–59**
Passive aggressiveness, relationships and, 55–56
PC muscles, 94–95, 97
PEA, 21, 22
Pendell, Wellington, **155**
Penis
anatomy, 72–73, 73
augmentation surgery for, 4, 7
measuring, 5–6, 5
personification, 6–7
size, **4–7**
increasing, 4, 6–7
length, 4, 31, 72
micropenis, 4
myths about, 28, 29, 31
sex and, 6, 77
thickness, 4, 7, 28
weight loss and, 5–6
smells and blood flow to, 24
Penis pump, 6–7
Penis rings, 6–7, 131
Pennebaker, James W., 55
Penthouse Forum letters, 142
*The Penthouse Guide to
Cybersex*, 132

Performance anxiety, 5, 14–15, 31, 55
The Perfumed Garden, 99
Persall, Steve, 138, 139
Petrissage massage technique, 87
Phallic symbols, 24, 25
Phenylalanine in chocolate, mood-lifting effect of, 12, 13
Phenylethylamine (PEA), 21, 22
Pheromones, mood for sex and, 24–25
Phlegar, Phyllis, 132–33, 135
Phone sex, 129
Pituitary glands, 18, 23
Playacting, 67, 124, 125
Playfulness in sex, 42, 63, **114–15**
Pleasuring women first, **60–61**
Polanski, Roman, 117
Polarity sex, 61
Porn movies and tapes, 31, **140–41**
Positions for sex, **98–105**
    adventurous, 104–5, 104–5
        man on top, facing away, 104, 104
        seated wheelbarrow, 105, 105
        standing wheelbarrow, 105, 105
        woman on top, leaning back, 105, 105
    duration of sex and, 95
    exotic, 103–4, 103–4
        spoon, 103, 103
        spoon, facing, 103, 103
        squatted kneeling, 104, 104
        X position, 104, 104
    historical context of, 98
    man on top, **98–99**, 100–101, 100–101
        cross buttocks, 101, 101
        knees to chest, 100, 100
        missionary, 95, 98–99, 100, 100
        seated missionary, 100, 100

rear entry, **99**, 102–3, 102–3
    kneeling, 102, 102
    seated, 103, 103
    standing, 102, 102
    varying, for great sex and renewing love, 98
woman on top, **99**, 101–2, 101–2
    reverse missionary, 101, **101**
    woman astride, 101, 101
    woman astride, facing away, 102, 102
Pranzarone, Galdino, 122, 123, 124, 125, 126, 127
Pregnancy, 28, 30–31
Prepuce of penis, 73
Prostate gland, 73, 74, 74
Prosthetics for erection problems, 93
Prozac, 94
Psychology Today survey, 4
Psychopathia Sexualis, 96
Puberty, male, 18–19
Pubic hair, 73–74, 76
Pubic lice, 37
Pubococcygeal (PC) muscles, 94–95, 97

Q

Quality of sex, 33
Quantity of sex, **32–33**
Queen, Carol, 62
Quick sex, 30, 156–57

R

Race, quantity of sex and, 32–33
Rand, Renee, 131
Rectum, 74, 81
Refractory period, 9, 88, 96
Relaxation, 16, 94
Religion, quantity of sex and, 32–33
Renewing love, **66–67**

Renner, John, 12
Revlon survey on sensuality, 13, 112
Richards, Hoyt, **148–49**
Ridge of penis, 73, 83
Risky sex, **116–18**
Roberts, Tomi-Ann, 56
Rogovin, Sheila, 54–55
'Roid rages, 19
Role-playing, 67, 124, 125
Romance, 50, **66–67**, 159
Rosenstein, Melvyn, 4, 5, 6, 7
Roy, Laurence, 142
Rugas of vagina, 76–77
Runner's stretch for avoiding leg cramps, 11
Russell, Bertrand, 86

S

Sacks, Jen, 85
Safe sex, **36–39**
Same-sex fantasies, 123
Scent, sex and, **24–25**, 25
Schechter, Harriet, 56, 58, 68–69, 70
Schopenhauer, Arthur, 52
Schor, Juliet B., 68
Scrotum, 72, 73, 73
Secret Loves, 55
Self-centeredness, problem of, 66
Self-esteem, 10, 15
Semans, Anne, vi, 42, 86, 93, 130, 131, 131, 140, 141, 142
Semans, James, 95
Seminal vessel, 74
Sex, 142
Sex drive
    age and, 9
    alcohol and, 13
    exercise and, 11
    food and, 24–25
    headaches and, 16–17
    oxytocin and, 23
    smells and, 24–25
    testosterone and, 15, 18–20

Sex for One, vi, 2, 83, 96
Sex in America survey, 3, 8, 32, 38, 82, 91, 106, 108, 139
Sex in 1990s, **2–3**
Sex play, 42, 63, **114–15**
Sex problems, 30, 92–93
Sex roles, 2, 3, **44–47**
Sex talk, 57, 118, **128–29**
The Sexual Desire Disorders, 21
Sexual Dreams, 41
Sexually transmitted diseases (STDs), **36–39**
 AIDS, 2, 3, 36, 37, 108
 chlamydia, 37
 crabs (pubic lice), 37
 genital warts, 38
 gonorrhea, 38
 herpes, 38–39
 incidence of, 3, 36
 preventing, 38–39
 risk of, 2, 36
 syphilis, 3, 39
Sexual Pleasure, 2, 84
Sexual scene, 1–2, 34–35
Shaft of penis, 73
Sherman, Mark A., 110, 111
Shower head as sex toy, 131
Showering before sex, 84–85
Silber, Sherman J., 18
Skill in sex, 41–42
Skin as erogenous zone, 86
SM 101, 124
SM/DS, 126
Smell, sex and, **24–25**, 25
Smoking, sex and, 20
Spanish fly, 117
Spanking sex fantasies, 126
Sperm, 74
Spermicide, 39
STDs, **36–39**
Stearns, Peter N., 44, 46, 64
Stephens, Ralph R., 78, 79, 86
Stereotypes, sex and, 33, 48
Steroids, 19
Stoppard, Miriam, 142
Stress, sex and, **14–17**

Stress management, **15–17**, 83
Stretching before sex, 11
Striptease techniques, 85
Superpotency, 21
Suraci, Patrick, 16
Surprises, romance and, 66–67
Survey on sex, private, 34–35
Symmetry, attraction to physical, 26–27, 27
Syphilis, 3, 39

T

Talk Sexy to the One You Love, 128
Tamosaitis, Nancy, 132, 133–34, 135
Tannen, Deborah, 52–53
Tender Bargaining, 62, 115, 116, 119, 156
Testicles, 72, 73, 74
Testosterone
 arousal and, 23
 bioavailable, 19, 20
 deficiency, 4, 20
 effects of
  negative, 19–20
  positive, 19
 exercise and, 10, 11
 function of, 18
 gender differences in, 18
 production, 9, 11
 sex drive and, 15, 18–20
 stress and, 15
The Third Chimpanzee, 26
Thornhill, Randy, 26, 27
Time for sex, making, 67, **68–70**, 156
Time-saving tips, 70
Tom Jones, 13
Touch, 59, 85, 87, 129, 161. *See also* Massage
Touching, 78, 85
Toys, sex, 107, 115, **130–31**
Tubing of penis, 74
Turn-ons and turn-offs for sex, **58–59**, 85

U

The Ultimate Sex Book, 78
Undressing, seductive, 85
Urethra, 74, 91
Uterus, 76, 77

V

Vagina
 aging effects on, 9
 anatomy, 76–77, 76, 81
 after orgasm, 111
 sensitivity of, 4
Vas deferens, 73, 74
Vasopressin, 21
Venette, Nicolas, 4
Venus Butterfly, 133
Vibrators, 89, 107, 130–31
Videotapes, sex and, 115, **140–42**
Virtue, Doreen, 12
Volker, Marilyn K., 5, 13, 14, 16, 17, 42, 84, 85, 92, 110, 112
von Krafft-Ebing, R., 96
Vulva, 75

W

Warm-up before sex, 11
Weekend of great sex, **160–62**
Wetzler, Scott, 55–56
Williamson, Bruce, 136, 137, 139
Wilson, Glenn, 85
Winks, Cathy, vi, 36, 42, 79, 108, 142
Wiseman, Jay, 124
Women's desires, **48–53**
Wrestling with Love, 45, 55

Z

Zilbergeld, Bernie, vi, 47, 60, 64, 65